Elizabeth I, Queen of England

Edited and with an
introduction by
Richard L. Greaves

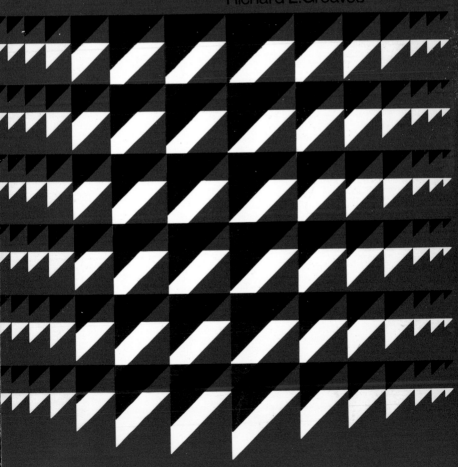

THE PROBLEMS IN EUROPEAN CIVILIZATION SERIES
(Arranged in approximate chronological order)

(continued inside back cover)

Elizabeth I,
Queen of England

PROBLEMS IN
EUROPEAN CIVILIZATION

Under the editorial direction of
John Ratté
Amherst College

Elizabeth I, Queen of England

WITHDRAWN

Edited and with an introduction by

Richard L. Greaves
The Florida State University

D. C. HEATH AND COMPANY
Lexington, Massachusetts Toronto London

For my parents

CONTENTS

IV AFFAIRS OF STATE

The Early Years

The Exercise of Royal Authority

V EPILOGUE

INTRODUCTION

Despite the fact that "few rulers have impressed themselves so forcibly on the memory and imagination of the English race as Queen Elizabeth I,"[1] much about the magisterial queen remains enigmatic and controversial. The rapid growth of critical scholarship in the twentieth century has not dissipated either the often fervid response to her or the range of historical problems associated with her reign. It is the purpose of this volume to introduce the reader to a sampling of the varying analyses of Elizabeth and to some of the controversy surrounding such key problems as Elizabeth's religious views, her treatment of the Roman Catholics, the enigma of Mary Stewart, her relationship to her government, and the question of marriage and succession to the throne. Each problem both illumines and complicates the fascinating question of Elizabeth's character. The markedly different ways in which writers have depicted her character provide a reminder that Elizabeth's impression on the memory and imagination of the English is a multifaceted one, devoid of harmony and unity.

As in the case of Elizabeth's father, Henry VIII, there are several discernible traditions of historical writing about her reign.[2] There is an avowedly Protestant tradition represented here by William Camden, Robert Naunton, and Bishop Mandell Creighton. James Froude also wrote from the Protestant standpoint, but unlike the others his study of Elizabeth led him from a position of admiration to one of marked criticism. The Catholic tradition is represented by William Allen and Edward Rishton, both hostile contemporaries of Elizabeth.

[1] J. B. Black, *The Reign of Elizabeth, 1558–1603*, 2nd ed. (Oxford, 1959), p. 1.
[2] Arthur J. Slavin's Introduction to *Henry VIII and the English Reformation* (Lexington, Mass., 1968).

FIGURE 1. Elizabeth I, *c.* 1575. This anonymous portrait, believed to have come from Cobham Hall, was perhaps the last to depict Elizabeth realistically. Subsequent portraits are increasingly stylized. The whiteness of her face reflects

Two Catholic historians, both of whom sought vainly to be objective, are included—John Lingard and Philip Hughes. The growing inclination to approach historical figures from a psychological perspective is perhaps best illustrated in Elizabethan studies by the work of Elizabeth Jenkins. Bishop Creighton earlier sought to explain the influence of heredity and a traumatic emotional experience on Elizabeth's character. Generally, however, modern historians have avoided the speculative pitfalls of a psychological approach to Elizabeth. The best biography in most respects continues to be that of J. E. Neale; his work is characterized by sound scholarship, a conservative approach, and a sympathetic portrayal of the queen. Neale is also an outstanding representative of those modern historians who have intensively studied Elizabeth's relationships with her government. Others who have dug deeply in this vein include Wallace MacCaffrey and Conyers Read. R. B. Wernham has applied the critical tools of the modern historian to Elizabeth's foreign policy, correcting older misconceptions about Elizabeth and incidentally providing new insight into her character. In the aftermath of such major studies new biographies of the queen have been written, notably those of Neville Williams and Joel Hurstfield. As in the case of her father's historians, there is a growing inclination among most modern scholars to skirt the fires of religious passion and to concentrate more on other aspects of Elizabeth's reign. The result has not been less controversy but more, as disagreement over interpretation and significance spreads to a broader spectrum.

Elizabeth's contemporaries reacted in markedly different ways to her rule. The enthusiasm which generally greeted her accession is described by William Camden, a teacher and headmaster at Westminster School and subsequently a member of the College of Heralds. Although he did not commence *The Annals or History of Queen Elizabeth* until 1608, he was actively engaged in historical writing during Elizabeth's reign as he composed his *Britannia,* a survey of English history. He was first encouraged to write *The Annals* about Elizabeth by Lord Burghley, who put his own papers and those of the royal archives at Camden's disposal in 1597. *The Annals* were intended to celebrate "the Memory of that Princess (which amongst

current fashion, providing a vivid contrast with her brilliantly-colored costume. A crown and scepter rest behind the queen's left arm. (*National Portrait Gallery, London*)

English-men ought ever to be gratefull and sacred)," yet Camden also sought to write as an unprejudiced, critical historian. His models were Polybius and Tacitus. He was convinced that a factual rendering of Elizabeth's reign would serve as a self-evident record of her greatness.

Camden provides an early estimate of Elizabeth's religious views —one of the more vexing questions surrounding her. For him Elizabeth was genuinely concerned to promote Protestantism, though he was also careful to note both the positive and the negative political implications of the adoption of a Protestant policy. Froude's assessment of Elizabeth's religious views is very different from Camden's. Froude, an avowed admirer of the English Reformation who saw its history as great drama, was convinced of Elizabeth's open contempt for Protestantism. She is likened by Froude to the Bourbon monarch Henry IV; both sovereigns, he believes, were impatient with the differences in outward expression between Protestants and Catholics. Both believed "in certain elementary truths lying at the base of all religions." Elizabeth adopted a Protestant policy, but only because of political exigencies involving England's relationship with the Continent. Froude's judgment has been essentially reiterated in this century by Wallace MacCaffrey. His Elizabeth is coolly indifferent to religion, possessing the politician's flexibility and moral neutrality. Yet her political acumen was such that she used members of her Council (e.g., Bedford and Knollys) to mediate between her religious indifference and the Protestant passions of many of her subjects. The views of Froude and MacCaffrey have not, however, proved totally compelling. Some scholars continue to find deep religious convictions in Elizabeth. Joseph Hodges (who is not included in this volume) has argued in *The Nature of the Lion: Elizabeth I and Our Anglican Heritage* (London, 1962) that Elizabeth was an Anglo-Catholic in her religious views.

Closely related to the problem of Elizabeth's religious position is the question of her treatment of Catholic subjects. Catholic authors from the sixteenth to the twentieth centuries have been strong in their indictments of her. Yet one of the earliest tracts is surprisingly sober and reasoned, if critical. *A True, Sincere, and Modest Defense of English Catholics* was written by the influential William Allen. Allen, principal of St. Mary's Hall, Oxford, was forced into exile at Elizabeth's accession. In 1568 he founded a college at Douay in the

Netherlands to train missionary priests. His efforts were largely responsible for his condemnation to death in 1581 (in absentia). Allen's work was written in response to a tract by Burghley entitled *The Execution of Justice in England* (1583). Burghley's purpose was to defend the penal action of the Elizabethan government against Catholics on the ground that Catholics were seditious. Burghley cited the foreign seminaries (including Allen's college at Douay) as centers to train men to sneak into England and persuade Elizabeth's subjects to adhere to the papal bull of 1570 excommunicating her. Catholics were not, Burghley insisted, being persecuted for religious reasons. Allen's reply, published the following year, insists that the persecution is religious in nature, and ties the government's action to Elizabeth's position as supreme governor of the Church of England. Edward Rishton, a product of Allen's college at Douay, writes on a lower level, accusing Elizabeth of hypocrisy and cunning cruelty. The brunt of his charges echo those of Allen: the Catholics are the victims of religious persecution.

The white-hot emotion of Rishton has since cooled, but Catholic historians have not deviated from the essential charge of Allen and Rishton. John Lingard sought to write only the truth, regardless of its impact on Catholics. The notes to his work, however, were to be laden with evidence in favor of the Catholic cause. Moreover, he admitted that "whatever I have said or purposely omitted has been through a motive of serving religion."[3] His assessment of Elizabeth is unfavorable, in marked contrast to that of Camden. The immoral, irresolute sovereign is guilty of the persecution of Catholics for religious reasons. This too is the considered judgment of the premier Catholic historian of the English Reformation in modern times— Philip Hughes. A judicial review of Elizabethan penal legislation leads him to a ringing defense of the views expressed by William Allen in opposition to the "slanderous tract" of Burghley. Against the reaffirmation of the traditional Catholic charges, summed up in Hughes's accusation that "Queen Elizabeth put to death, solely because of their religion, between the years 1577 and 1603, 183 of her Catholic subjects," the student of history must weigh J. E. Neale's account of Elizabeth's relationship with her parliaments, especially

---

[3] Cited in C. H. Williams, "In Search of the Queen," *Elizabethan Government and Society: Essays Presented to Sir John Neale,* ed. S. T. Bindoff, J. Hurstfield, C. H. Williams (London, 1961), p. 9.

that of 1581. Neale credits Elizabeth with restraining and modifying the desire of Parliament to enact sweeping anti-Catholic legislation. Neale accepts Francis Bacon's observation that in matters of religion Elizabeth did not want consciences "to be forced," though she would not tolerate conscientious actions which became matters of faction. Neale's careful study of source documents has laid to rest the mistaken notion that Elizabethan parliaments were servile tools of the sovereign, but the student is still faced with the problem of assessing the nature of Catholic subjugation and Elizabeth's role in it.

Closely involved with the Catholic question is the enigma of Mary Stewart, whose very existence posed a threat (in whatever degree) to Elizabeth. The nature of the problem at the outset of the reign is discussed by Camden. Because of Elizabeth's illegitimacy in the eyes of the Catholic church, the appropriate claimant of the throne was Mary, granddaughter of Henry VIII's sister, Margaret Tudor. Once again the Catholic writers are highly critical of Elizabeth for her treatment of her Scottish cousin. In Rishton's partisan judgment the treatment accorded to Mary, a queen not subject to English law and also Elizabeth's "invited guest," was barbaric. With considerably more care, Lingard examined the events surrounding Mary's execution and pronounced Elizabeth guilty of dissimulation. Her major concern, having been responsible for the execution, was to avoid blame by pretending ignorance. Froude, on the other hand, credits Elizabeth with genuine feelings of mercy and kindness towards Mary. It is the Queen of Scots, not Elizabeth, who manifested fierce animosity as revealed in the historical record. Of the many historians who have discussed the problem, perhaps the best in his rendering of the tortuous period preceding and immediately following Mary's execution is Conyers Read. A careful examination of the events which transpired between Elizabeth's signing of the warrant for Mary's death and her actual execution led him to conclude that Elizabeth was indeed genuinely indignant over Mary's execution. However Elizabeth's role is viewed in this Marian "tragedy" determines to a significant degree the overall analysis of her character and ability as a ruler.

Elizabeth's role in the government of the state has also been an area of broad controversy. One of the earliest assessments of value was written by Robert Naunton about 1630. Regarding the queen with marked admiration, Naunton was an astute writer when he discussed her political involvement. Here the essential characteristic in his estimation was her rule by factions, a theme explored more fully in the modern works of Neale and MacCaffrey. He correctly recognized that Robert Dudley, Earl of Leicester, was not as powerful as had been assumed. Elizabeth's supremacy is emphasized. Even in her relationship with Parliament, Naunton comments on the mutual loyalty underlying their differences. Neale's classic study of the relationship between Elizabeth and her parliaments, however, necessitates some modification of Naunton's rather rosy picture, for in more than one parliament there was "pertinatious dispute" over such questions as religion, the succession, the fate of Mary Stewart, and monopolies. Still Neale's studies confirm the ultimate goodwill between sovereign and parliaments that Naunton observed. Naunton also handles the question of Elizabeth's notorious parsimony with acumen, noting her underlying financial troubles and the Irish "malady."

Lingard is more critical of Elizabeth as a sovereign. A zealous adherent of absolute monarchy, she presided over a judicial system characterized by arbitrary tyranny. She did not spare the blood of her subjects. Despite her parsimony, she imposed heavy financial obligations on her people. The blame, however, is placed by Lingard on "the foreign policy of the cabinet . . . [which] plunged the queen into a gulf of unfathomable expense."[4] Her relationship to Parliament is described in terms that emphasize its servile status—a view that must now be modified in light of Neale's research. One of the most striking facts about Elizabeth's rule is her habitual irresolution. To Lingard this was not a sign of cautious statesmanship but essentially resulted from a defect "in the constitution of her mind," due in part to an excessively suspicious nature. Froude, on the contrary, argues that Elizabeth's vacillations in governing were caused by the fact that she was forced to adopt policies favorable to Protestants but distasteful to a ruler who regarded religious controversy as useless speculation. MacCaffrey offers another explanation: her reluctance and suspicion were the result of the insecurity she felt as a *female* sovereign.

Any assessment of Elizabeth's role as a sovereign must, of course, take into account her relationship to her key advisers. Froude's

---

[4] Lingard, *A History of England from the First Invasion by the Romans to the Accession of William and Mary in 1688,* new ed. (Boston, 1855), vol. 8, p. 419.

provocative view (which later scholars have rejected) is that the sound decisions of the reign were made by William Cecil, Lord Burghley, and that whenever Elizabeth altered his recommendations the results were injurious. Still Froude recognized that the ultimate power and responsibility of decision making were the queen's. While MacCaffrey would not disagree on this point and would cite Elizabeth's belief in divine-right monarchy, he would also insist that by 1572 Cecil and Dudley become sharers in the supreme power of government, forming a "secular trinity." But the trinity, if there was one, did not last. Read, who has made the most intensive study of the relationship between Elizabeth and Cecil, describes the development of a partnership between the two, though a partnership in which the queen was the dominant member. Whatever personal attachments Elizabeth may have had for Dudley, it was Cecil who was her junior partner in government. Neale too confirms the ability of Elizabeth to handle her advisers as well as her parliaments.

A different portrait of Elizabeth the sovereign emerges in the work of R. B. Wernham, a leading expert in Elizabethan foreign and military affairs. In a closely argued study of Elizabethan war aims and strategy, Wernham demonstrates that there were important occasions when the queen was not hesitant. Moreover, against the prevailing view of Elizabeth's ability to exercise her ultimate sovereignty, Wernham depicts her lack of control over her men of war on more than one occasion. The latter are the target of some sharp criticism by Wernham, for though Elizabeth is recognized to lack the genius for war, she nevertheless had a better grasp of the problems than her military men. Wernham thus provides a dimension to understanding Elizabeth that is traditionally lacking.

One of the most pressing problems facing Elizabeth as a monarch was that of succession to the throne. Entwined with this was the political and personal question of marriage. Although the crown ultimately went to Mary Stewart's son, James VI of Scotland, the issue of the succession was in doubt much of the reign. Froude actually accuses Elizabeth of lacking interest in the question, and Mac-Caffrey concludes that she must not have had any dynastic ambitions. Beyond such superficial judgments is a complex problem requiring a thorough examination of domestic and foreign affairs as well as Elizabeth's personal desires. Camden discusses the question of (avoiding) marriage to Philip II of Spain, husband of Elizabeth's deceased sister Mary. Bishop Creighton, reflecting the Victorian sense of the importance of heredity on character, finds the key to Elizabeth's relations with men in her experience as a young girl with Lord Admiral Thomas Seymour, husband of her stepmother and brother of Lord Protector Somerset. The sensual Seymour, whom Creighton believes was typical of Elizabethan men, provided her with a lesson that "did more than anything else to form her character," especially teaching her how dangerous it was to give rein to her affections. Elizabeth Jenkins analyzes the same episode, concluding that the Seymour affair and her mother's execution left Elizabeth with permanent damage to her nervous system and sexual development. This is borne out, Jenkins believes, in her subsequent relationship with Dudley ("a sexual one which stopped short only of the sexual act") and her other suitors. Elizabeth had learned, in the subrational recesses of her mind, that sexual intercourse meant capitulation, terror, and (through the impact of her mother's experience) death. Lingard, on the other hand, true to his promise to print any evidence in his footnotes which might favor the Catholic cause, ransacked the sources for heresay evidence to prove that Elizabeth, far from being reluctant to consummate a sexual relationship, was licentious. The student of history, recognizing the partisanship of Lingard and perhaps wary of the speculative element in Creighton and Jenkins, may find Neale's explanation of Elizabeth's relationship with Dudley a key to the broader problems of marriage and succession. Although Elizabeth wanted to marry Dudley, the suspicious death of his wife, Amy Robsart, and the ensuing uproar provoked strong opposition from the Council. Elizabeth, placing her obligations as a ruler above her personal desires, yielded to the wishes of her councillors. Henceforth Elizabeth determined that, as queen, she would marry only if necessity required it. Yet neither would she name a successor, bearing in mind how the "inconstant" English people "preferred the rising to the setting sun."[5] Had satisfactory arrangements been worked out with Mary Stewart, she would have been designated Elizabeth's heir, despite the inconstancy of the English, but this was never to be.

Was Elizabeth a great ruler? Again the historians have not agreed. There is a sharp difference of judgment between MacCaffrey and

[5] Neale, *Queen Elizabeth* (New York, 1934), p. 108.

Neville Williams over the results of Elizabeth's rule to 1572. Mac-Caffrey's thesis is that by 1572 the queen had created a solid monarchy, restoring a political stability that had been lacking in England since the late 1520s. A key factor in that stability was Elizabeth's acquisition of two "surrogate husbands," Cecil and Dudley, who provided the political world with an air of permanence and predictability. Another important factor was the queen's use of prominent subjects to mediate between herself and her people. Royal control and stability were more basic, to MacCaffrey, than the uncertainties of the succession, the enigma of Mary Stewart, and the general problems of Europe. The judgment of Williams is gloomy in contrast. If the reign of Elizabeth had ended in 1572, it would have been a failure; she would have broken faith with those who placed their trust in her at her accession. The problem of succession was not settled; there was no unity in religion; she was in disagreement with her Council, with Parliament, and with Convocation; and England was isolated, lacking an ally. In short, by 1572 Elizabeth was "an unremarkable failure."

She reigned, of course, until 1603, but the assessments of her reign remain divided. It was a great *age,* but both the Protestant Naunton and the Catholic Lingard attribute the greatness fundamentally to favorable conditions, not to Elizabeth. Creighton, on the other hand, gives credit to the queen, and specifically to the instinctive sympathy she had for her people—a sympathy reflected in the article by Camden. She has been credited with much, including the early stability of the Bourbon monarchy and the salvation of the Dutch from Spanish domination (by Wernham), and a major contribution to the growth of the English liberal tradition through her efforts on behalf of Catholics (by Neale). The latter view, however, differs sharply from those of Lingard and Hughes. Ultimately each reader must decide the issues for himself. The difficulty is recognized in the final selection by Joel Hurstfield, one of the queen's most recent biographers. Here, to complement the controversial issues already raised, are fresh questions requiring further research by historians. The answers will vary, creating yet more controversy about one of England's most intriguing monarchs.

Note: All footnotes to these articles, except footnote 9 to R. B. Wernham's article, are those of the editor of this volume, not of the authors of the articles.

I CONTEMPORARY PERSPECTIVES

William Camden
BELOVED DEFENDER OF PROTESTANTISM

William Camden, born in London in 1551, attended St. Paul's School, founded by Dean Colet to emphasize humanistic studies. Camden continued his education at Oxford, studying at Magdalen, Pembroke, and Christ Church. For the next four years (1571–1575) he traveled throughout England, gathering historical and geographical data for his survey of English history, Britannia. *Published in 1586, it established his reputation as a major European scholar. In 1575 he was appointed second master at Westminster School, and in 1593 headmaster.* The Annals or History of Queen Elizabeth *is the earliest authoritative history of her reign, and manifests the transition from the English chronicles to modern historical writing. The first half (to 1588) was published in 1615. Camden completed the remainder by 1617, but refused to allow publication in his lifetime. The latter first appeared at Leyden in 1625, two years after his death. The present text, translated by R. N[orton] from the original Latin, was published in 1635.*

The first yeere of her Raigne, beginning the 17. of November, Anno 1558. and ending in November, Anno 1559.

The Death of Queene *Mary* having beene certaine houres concealed; the first newes thereof was brought to the Bishops and Nobility in the Parliament Chamber, (for the Estates of the Realme were assembled a little before in Parliament.) They, out of singular griefe for a time stand mute: yet comforting one another, they sooner gather heart againe; and mingling mirth with mourning; lest they should seeme either to sorrow for her which was to succeed, or to joy for her which was dead, they turne themselves to the publicke cares of the State, and with general consent decree the Lady Elizabeth to be proclaimed true and lawfull Heire to the Crowne, according to the Act of succession, of the 35. yeere of *Henry* the eighth. Soone after, those of the Lower-house being assembled, *Heath,* Archbishop of *Yorke,* Lord Chancellor of the Realme, with sighs and sobs, signifieth unto them, that their most excellent Queene is by untimely death taken away both from Religion and Commonwealth, that every of

From William Camden, *Annales or, the History of the Most Renowned and Victorious Princesse Elizabeth, Late Queen of England,* trans. R. N[orton] (3rd ed., London, 1635), pp. 1–7.

them tooke such inward griefe thereat, as did exceede all consolation, were it not that Almighty God had of his mercy towards the English Nation, preserved the Lady Elizabeth, the other daughter of King *Henry* alive. Of whose most undoubted Title to the succession, seeing there is none that can, none that ought to doubt, the Prelates and Peeres had with one voyce and mind decreed, (in case they would assent,) presently to proclaime her Queene. Scarce had he spoken the word, when all from all sides cryed, and recryed, *God save Queene* Elizabeth, *Raigne shee most long, Raigne shee most happily.* And forthwith the Parliament breaking up, they with sound of Trumpets proclaimed her in the greater Palace of *Westminster,* and immediately after in Cheapside, the chiefe streete of the City of *London, Queene of England, France* and *Ireland, Defendresse of the Faith,* and that with happy acclamations, and most ioyfull applause of the people, and certainely with a most prosperous and auspicious beginning: neither did the people ever embrace any other Prince with more willing and constant mind and affection, with greater observance, more joyfull applause, and prayers reiterated, whensoever she went abroad during the whole course of her life, then they did her.

Shee being now five and twenty yeers of age, and taught by experience and aduersity, (two most effectuall and powerfull masters) had gathered wisedome above her age: the first proofe whereof, shee gave in choosing her Counsellours. . . . Whom as others substituted ever after in their roomes, she tempered, and restrained in such sort, that they were to her most devoted, and she was alwaies her owne free woman, and obnoxious to none.

In the first beginning of her Raigne, she applyed her first care (howbeit with but a few and those her inwardest Counsailors,) to the restoring of the Protestants Religion, which both by her instruction from her tender yeers, and by her owne judgement, shee verily perswaded her selfe to be the truest, and most consonant to the sacred Scriptures, and the sincerity of the primitive Church; and to restore the same she had with a settled and constant resolution determined in her mind. Then, with the rest of Her Councell she adviseth, That the Ports should be shut up; that the Tower of *London* should be committed to some man of approved fidelity; that a new Commission should be sent over to *Thomas* Earle of *Sussex* Lord Deputy of *Ireland*, (who kept *Ireland* in awfull duty, and never more quiet and peaceable, with three hundred and twenty horse, and eight

FIGURE 2. The "Coronation" Portrait, c. 1559. The mantle and dress match the description of Elizabeth's coronation robes as recorded in the wardrobe list of 1600. (*Warwick Castle, by kind permission of Lord Brooke, Earl of Warwick*)

hundred and sixty foote lying there in Garrison;) that the Commissions also to the Iuridicall Magistrates should be renewed, (lest the Terme or Iuridicall Assembly which was then holden, should be broken up,) with a clause added, *That they should not bestow any Office;* that new Iusticers and Sheriffes should be appointed in every Country; that money should not be transported in exchange, into Countries beyond the Seas; and that Preachers should abstaine from questions controverted in Religion. And for forraine matters, that Embassadours should be sent to the Princes of Christendome, to signifie unto them the death of Queene *Mary.* To the Emperour *Ferdinand* therefore is forthwith sent Sir *Thomas Chaloner* with letters, wherein the Queene with her owne hand gave him to understand, *That her Sister was dead, that she by Gods goodnesse did by right of inheritance and consent of her subiects, succeede her in her Kingdomes; and desired nothing more, then that the ancient amity betwixt the houses of* England *and* Austria *might not onely be kept, but also increased.* To the Spaniard in the *Netherlands* is sent the Lord Cobham, with instructions to the same purpose; and also with a Commission, whereby the Earle of *Arundell, Thurlbey* Bishop of *Ely,* and Doctor *Wotton,* Commissioners lately sent by Queene *Mary,* to treate a peace at *Cambray,*[1] are made Commissioners anew in the Queens name: And with them is joyned in Commission *William* Lord *Howard* of *Effingham.* Master *Henry Killegrew* also is privily sent to winne the minds of the German Princes, out of their affection to the purer Religion; *D.B.* to the K. of *Denmarke,* and *Armigill Waad* to the Duke of *Holstein.*

King *Philip* understanding of the death of Queene *Mary* his wife, fearing lest he should lose the strength and Title of the Kingdome of *England,* which were to him of speciall use, and that the Kingdomes of *England, Ireland,* and *Scotland,* would by *Mary* Queene of Scots, bee annexed unto *France,* dealt seriously with Queene *Elizabeth* by meanes of the Count of *Feria,* (whom he had sent to visit both his sicke wife, and her,) about a marriage to be contracted with her, promising to procure a speciall dispensation from the Bishop of *Rome.* This troubled her much, that the most potent Prince of *Europe,* and one that had very well deserved of her, should be rejected by her, when of his owne voluntary motion he sought to her

---

[1] The Treaty of Cateau-Cambrésis was concluded in April 1559, establishing peace between England, France, and Spain.

for marriage: which to her seemed the part both of an unwise and an unthankfull woman. This also troubled the *French* King, who could not but misdoubt *France,* if by this new marriage *England* should fall againe to the Spaniard, his Enemy. He laboured therefore all he could at *Rome* by the Bishop of *Angolesme,* that no such dispensation might be obtained, forasmuch as Queene Elizabeth was thought to favour the Protestants Doctrine, yea, was pronounced as illegitimate. But these things he did very closely, lest he might seeme to incense the English, matters being not yet fully compounded betwixt them. The Count of *Feria,* to effect this marriage, beateth into the Papists heads every where in *England,* that they have no other meanes to uphold the Catholike Religion, and maintaine their ancient honour; and this marriage being neglected, he cannot but pitty *England,* as being exhausted of her wealth, needy of military men, ill strengthened with Fortresses and holds, as ill provided of warlike munition, and as if the Counsellors of the Land were voyd of counsell. And certainely the State of *England* lay now most afflicted, imbroyled on the one side with the Scottish, on the other side with the French warre, overcharged with debt incurred by *Henry* the eighth, and *Edward* the sixth, the treasure exhausted, *Calice*[2] . . . lost, to the great dishonour of the English Nation, the people distracted with different opinions in Religion, the Queene bare of potent friends, and strengthened with no alliance of forraine Princes.

The Queene when she had in her mind more advisedly considered of this marriage, soone found that the marriage of a woman with her deceased Sisters husband, is *ex rationis paritate,* that is, by the like reason prohibited by sacred authority, as is the marriage of a man with his brothers widow, and therefore unlawfull, notwithstanding the Popes dispensation: And she perceived that by contracting such a marriage by dispensation, she could not but acknowledge her selfe to be borne in unlawfull wedlocke, whom her Father King *Henry* had begotten, after he had put away Queene *Katharine* of *Spaine,* for that she was his Brothers widdow. Which wedlocke notwithstanding, the Vniversities of Christendome, and a Synode at *London,* had approoved to be most just by the Law of God, as that with Queene *Katharine* to be unjust, and altogether undispens-

[2] Calais, captured by the French in January 1558.

able. Her suitor therefore King *Philip,* she putteth off by little and little, with a most modest answer, and honest and maidenly shame-fastnesse, but in very deed out of scruple of conscience. But when he instantly pressed her by many letters, and shee admired and re-joyced to imitate the manners and behaviour of so great a King joyned with most modest gravity and grace, most beseeming his Royall Majesty, ever and anon extolling the same; forth stepped certaine Courtiours, which declaimed against the Spaniards, as a people puffed up with pride: and some of her inwardest Counsel-lours, fearing lest her mind being in doubt, might easily be perswaded, whispered daily into her eares, being a Virgin of a most milde disposition, that she and her friends were undone, and *England* overthrowne, if she once acknowledged the Popes authority in dispensing, or in any other matter whatsoever; that two Popes had pronounced her Mother to have been unlawfully marryed to *Henry* the eighth, and thereupon, by their sentence already pronounced, the Queene of Scots did lay claime to the Kingdome of *England;* that the Pope would never revoke his sentence, neither was any indif-ferent dealing to be expected from those of *Rome,* who had beene most unjust, both towards her Mother and her. Moreover, that the French King did now labour tooth and nayle at *Rome,* that *Mary* Queene of Scots might be pronounced lawfull Queene of *England.*

Queene Elizabeth being most averse from this marriage, and most desirous to promote the Protestants Religion; thought nothing more pleasing to God, nothing more effectuall to put off her im-portunate suitor, then that Religion should forthwith be altered. For, Religion being once changed, she doubted not but his mind in suing for marriage, would change also. She commanded therefore the consultation to be hastned amongst her most inwardest Counsailors, how the Protestants Religion might be re-established, and the Popish abolished, all perills being weighed which might grow thereby, and by what meanes they might be put by. These perils they foresaw would be either inward or outward: Outward, either from the Bishop of *Rome,* who would send his fulmination of excōmunica-tion, and expose the Kingdome as a prey to such as would invade the same; or from the French King, who taking occasion thereby, would delay the businesse of peace begun at *Cambray,* or rather move warre against the English, in the Queene of Scots behalfe, as against not onely enemies, but hereticks also, and would excite

Scotland to doe the like, which was now at his devotion; or from the Irish, a people most addicted to the Romish Religion, and most forward to Rebellion; or else from the Spaniard, a Prince most potent in the *Netherlands* hard by. They resolved that for the Popes excommunication it was not to be feared, but slighted as a sencelesse lightning: that peace, if it were offered by the French, was to be embraced, if not, then to be sued for, forasmuch as the same peace would comprehend *Scotland* also: neverthelesse, that the Protestants of *France* and *Scotland* were in no wise to be forsaken: that *Barwicke,* the Marches towards *Scotland,* as also *Ireland,* should be manned with stronger Garrisons; and especially that amity was to be holden with the Spaniard by any means whatsoever, and the ancient League with the house of *Burgundy* to be confirmed: The dangers inward they foresaw would be, from the Noblemen removed from the Queenes Councell, from the Bishops and Churchmen that were to be displaced, from the Iudges which sate in the Courts of Iustice, from the Iusticers of Peace in every County, and from such of the Common sort of People, as in the Raigne of Queene *Mary* were both in deed and estimation great men, because devoted to the Romish Religion. These they held were to be thrust out of their places, and restrained by rigor of Law, (as Queene *Mary* had done against the Protestants,) and that none were to be employed in any place of Government, nor chosen into any Colledges of both the Vniversities, but Protestants: and withall, that the Popish Presidents, Heads, and Masters were to be removed out of the Vniversities, and the Popish Schoole-masters out of *Winchester, Eaton,* and other Schooles: that those Protestants which then began to frame a new Ecclesiasticall Policy, being transported with a humour of innovation, should be repressed betimes: and that but one onely Religion was to be tolerated, lest diversity of Religions amongst the English (a stout and warlike Nation,) might minister continuall fire to seditions. The care of correcting the Liturgie, which under King *Edward* the sixth was set forth in the vulgar tongue, was committed to *Parker, Bill, May, Coxe, Grindall, Whitehead,* and *Pilkinton,* learned and moderate Divines, and to Sir *Thomas Smith* Knight, a most learned Gentleman. . . .

But some Ministers of the Word, impatient of delay, whilest they chose rather to fore-run than expect Lawes, began to sowe abroad the Doctrine of the Gospell more freely, first in private houses, and then in Churches; and the people greedy of novelties, began to flocke unto them in great number, and to wrangle amongst themselves, and with the Papists about questions controverted in Religion; in such sort, that to cut off occasions of contentions, the Queene set forth a straight Proclamation, that they should not handle any such questions. But the Epistles, Gospels, and ten Commandements shee permitted to be read unto the people in the English tongue, howbeit without any exposition: also the Lords Prayer, the Apostles Creed, and the Letany she suffered to be used in the vulgar tongue. But in all other things, they were to use the Romish Rites and Ceremonies, till a perfect forme of Religion should be concluded on by authority of Parliament. In the meane time, she performed the Exsequies[3] of her Sister Queene *Mary,* with solemne and sumptuous preparations in the Church of *Westminster,* and shortly after of *Charles* the fifth also, who had two yeeres before, (a rare example amongst Emperours, but more glorious then all their victories,) overcome himselfe, renounced the Empire, and given over the world, that he might wholly live to God, and attend upon his Service onely.

The Second Yeere of her Raigne.
Anno Domini, 1559, and 1560.

. . . Now is she brought with Royall pompe from the Tower of *London,* thorow the middest of the City, to *Westminster,* with incredible applause, (which by her sweet countenance and gracious speech she increased above measure,) where the next day, after the Rites of her forefathers, she is inaugurate and anointed by *Oglethorp* Bishop of *Carlile,* for that the Archbishop of *Yorke,* and the rest of the Bishops, refused to performe that office, out of a suspicious and jealous feare of the Romish Religion, which both her first breeding up in the Protestants Religion had stricken them into, and also for that shee had very lately forbidden the Bishop in saying Masse, to lift up the Host to be adored, and permitted the Letany, with the Epistle and Gospell to be read in the vulgar tongue, which they held for most hainous sinnes. Yet was shee truely religious, who every day as soone as shee arose, spent some time in prayers to God, and afterwards, also at set houres in her private Chappell: every Sunday

[3] Obsequies.

and Holy-day shee went unto her Chappell; neither was there ever any other Prince present at Gods service with greater devotion. At the Sermons in Lent shee was alwayes present, being apparrelled in blacke after the manner of old; although she many times said (as she had read of *Henry* the 3. her predecessor,) that she had rather talke with God devoutly by prayer, then heare others speake eloquently of God. Concerning the Crosse, the blessed Virgin, and the Saints she had no contemptuous opinion, nor ever spake of them but with reverence, nor suffered others patiently to speake unreverently of them.

Sir Robert Naunton
AN ASTUTE POLITICIAN

Born in 1563 at Alderton, Suffolk, Robert Naunton was educated at Trinity College, Cambridge. In 1592 he was made a Fellow of Trinity Hall, Cambridge. He was sent to the Continent by the Earl of Essex, nominally as a tutor, but with the real purpose of providing Essex with political intelligence. The dual role was not to Naunton's liking, and about 1600 he returned to Cambridge to resume his earlier post of public orator. He was a member of the Parliaments of 1606, 1614, 1621, 1624, and 1625. Knighted in 1614, he became master of requests and surveyor of the Court of Wards two years later. From 1618 to 1623 he was secretary of state, following which he became master of the Court of Wards. The Fragmenta Regalia *was first published in 1641, six years after his death. The present text is based on the revised edition of 1653.*

I come to her Person; and as she came to the Crown by the decease of her Brother and Sister. Under *Edward* She was his, and one of the darlings of Fortune: for besides the consideration of Bloud, there was between these two Princes a concurrency and sympathy in their natures and affections, together with the Celestiall (conformity in Religion) which made them one, and friends; for the King ever called her his sweetest and dearest Sister, and was scarce his own man,

From Sir Robert Naunton, *Fragmenta Regalia,* ed. Edward Arber (London, 1870), pp. 14–22.

She being absent, which was not so between him and the Lady *Mary*. Under his Sister She found her condition much altered: For it was resolved, and her destiny had decreed to set her an Apprentice in the School of Affliction, and to draw her through the Ordeall fire of tryall, the better to mould and fashion her to rule and Soveraignty; which finished, and Fortune calling to mind, that the time of her servitude was expired, gave up her Indentures, and therewith delivered up into her custody a Scepter, as a reward for her patience, which was about the twenty sixth year of her Age; a time in which (as for externals) she was full blown, so was she for her internals grown ripe, and seasoned with adversity, and in the exercise of her Vertue; for it seems Fortune meant no more, than to shew her a piece of her variety, and changeablenesse of her Nature, and so to conduct her to her destined Felicity. She was of personage tall, of hair and complexion fair, and therewith well favoured, but high nosed, of limbs and feature neat, and which added to the lustre of those exteriour Graces, of Stately and Majestick comportment; participating in this more of her Father than Mother, who was of inferiour allay, plausible, or as the French hath it, more *debonaire* and affable, vertues which might well suit with Majesty; and which descending, as Hereditary to the daughter, did render of a more sweeter temper, and endeared her more to the love and liking of the people; who gave her the name and fame of a most gracious and popular Prince; the atrocity of her Fathers nature, being rebated in hers, by the Mothers sweeter inclinations. For to take, and that no more than the Character out of his own mouth; He never spared man in his anger, nor woman in his lust.

If we search further into her intellectuals and abilities, the whole course of Government deciphers them to the admiration of posterity; for it was full of magnanimity, tempered with Justice, and Piety; and to speak truly, noted but with one act or taint; all her deprivations either of life or liberty, being legall, and necessitated: She was learned (her sex, and the time considered) beyond common belief; for letters about this time, and somewhat before, began to be of esteem and in fashion, the former ages being overcast with the mists and fogs of the Romane ignorance; and it was the maxime that overruled the foregoing times, that ignorance was the mother of devotion. Her warres were a long time more in the auxiliary part, in assistance of forraign Princes and States, than by invasion of any, till common policie advised it for a safer way, to strike first abroad, than at home to expect the warre, in all which she was felicious and victorious. The change and alteration of Religion upon the instant of her accession (the smoak and fire of her Sisters Martyrdomes scarcely quenched) was none of her least remarkable accounts: But the support and establishment thereof, with the meanes of her subsistence, amidst so powerfull enemies abroad, and those many domestique practises, were (me thinks) works of inspiration, and of no humane providence, which on her Sisters departure she most religiously acknowledged, ascribing the glory of her deliverance to God alone. . . . Her Ministers and Instruments of State . . . were many, and those memorable, but they were onely Favourites, not Minions; such as acted more by her own Princely rules and judgements, than by their own wills and appetites, which she observed to the last: . . . for it valued her the more, it awed the most secure, and it took best with the people, and it starved all emulations, which are apt to rise and vent in obloquious acrimony (even against the Prince) where there is onely *Amator Palatii*.[1]

The principall note of her Reign will be, that she ruled much by faction and parties, which her self both made, upheld, and weakened, as her own great judgement advised. For I disassent from the common received opinion, that my Lord of *Leicester* was absolute and above all in her Grace: and though I come somewhat short of the knowledge of those times, yet (that I might not rove, and shoot at randome) I know it from assured intelligence, that it was not so. For proof whereof (among many that I could present) I will both relate a short, and therein a known truth, And it was thus. *Bowyer,* a Gentleman of the Black rod, being charged by her expresse command to look precisely to all admissions into the Privy-Chamber, one day stayed a very gay Captain, and a follower of my Lord of *Leicesters,* from entrance; For that he was neither well known, nor a sworn servant to the Queen: at which repulse, the Gentleman bearing high on my Lords favor, told him, he might perchance procure him a discharge: *Leicester* coming into the contestation, said publikely . . . that he was a Knave, and should not continue long in his office; and so turning about to go in to the Queen, *Bowyer* (who was a bold Gentleman, and well beloved) stept before him, and fell at her

---

[1] A lover of the palace.

Majesties feet, related the story, and humbly craves her Graces pleasure; and whether my Lord of *Leicester* was King, or her Majesty
Queen? Whereunto she replyed with her wonted oath (Gods death)
my Lord, I have wisht you well, but my favour is not so lockt up for
you, that others shall not partake thereof; for I have many servants,
unto whom I have, and will at my pleasure bequeath my favour, and
likewise resume the same; and if you think to rule here, I will take
a course to see you forth-coming: I will have here but one Mistress,
and no Master, and look that no ill happen to him, lest it be severely
required at your hands. Which so quelled my Lord of *Leicester,* that
his fained humility was long after one of his best vertues. Moreover
the Earl of *Sussex,* then Lord Chamberlain, was his profest Antagon-
ist to his dying day. . . . She was absolute and soveraign Mistress of
her Graces; and . . . all those, to whom she distributed her favours,
were never more than Tenants at will, and stood on no better ground
than her Princely pleasure, and their own good behaviour. And this
also I present as a known observation, that she was (though very
capable of Counsell) absolute enough in her own resolutions, which
was ever apparent even to her last, in that her aversation to grant
Tirone[2] the least drop of her mercy, though earnestly and frequently
advised, yea, wrought only by the whole Councell of State, with
very many pressing reasons, and as the state of her Kingdome then
stood, (I may speak it with assurance) necessitated Arguments. If
we look into her inclination, as it is disposed either to magnificence
or frugality, we shall find in them many notable considerations, for
all her dispensations were so poysed, as though discretion and
justice had both agreed to stand at the beam, and see them weighed
out in due proportion, the maturity of her years and judgement meeting in a concurrency, and at such an age as seldome lapseth to ex-
cesse. To consider them apart: We have not many presidents of her
liberality, or of any large donatives to particular men. . . . Her rewards consisted chiefly in grants of Leases of Offices, Places of
Judicature: but for ready money, and in any great summes, she was
very sparing; which we partly conceive was a vertue rather drawn
from necessity, than her nature, for she had many layings out, and
to her last period. And I am of opinion with S. *Walter Rawliegh,* that

2 Hugh O'Neill, Earl of Tyrone, led a major revolt against English rule in Ireland,
beginning in 1595.

those many brave men of our times, and of the *Militia,* tasted little more of her bounty than in her grace and good word, with their due entertainment, for she ever paid the Souldiers well, which was the honour of her times, and more than her great adversary of *Spain* could perform. So that when we come to the consideration of her frugality, the observation will be little more, than that her bounty and it were so inter-woven together, that the one was suited by an honourable way of spending, the other limited by a necessitated way of sparing. The Irish action we may call a malady, and a consumption of her times, for it accompanied her to her end; and it was of so profuse and vast an expence, that it drew neer a distemperature of State, and of passion in her self: For toward her last she grew hard to please; her Arms being accustomed to prosperity, and the Irish prosecution not answering her expectation and wonted successe for a good while, it was an unthrifty and inauspitious war, which did much disturb and mislead her judgement, and the more, for that it was a president which was taken out of her own pattern: For as the Queen (by way of diversion) had at the coming to the Crown supported the revolted States of *Holland,* so did the King of *Spain* turn the trick on her self towards her going out, by cherishing the Irish rebellion. Where it falls into consideration, what the State of the Kingdome and the Crown-Revenues were then able to embrace and endure; if we look into the establishment of those times, with the list of the Irish Army, considering the defeatments of *Blackwater,* with all precedent expences, as it stood from my Lord of *Essex* undertaking to the surrender of *Kingsale* under the Generall *Mountjoy,*[3] and somewhat after; we shall find the Horse and Foot Troops were for three or four yeares together, much about 20000. Which besides the Navall charge, which was a dependant of the same Warre, in that the Queen was then forced to keep in continuall pay a strong Fleet at Sea, to attend the Spanish Coasts and Ports, both to allarum the *Spaniard,* and to intercept his Forces designed for the Irish assistance: so that the charge of that Warre alone did cost the Queen 300000l. *per annum* at least, which was not the moity of her disbursments, an expence which (without the publique ayd) the

---

[3] Tyrone captured the fort at Blackwater in 1598 and annihilated an English army coming to its relief. Elizabeth dispatched Robert Devereux, Earl of Essex, in 1599, but had to replace him with Charles Blount, Lord Mountjoy. The latter defeated both Spanish forces and Tyrone's Irish troops at Kinsale in 1601–1602.

State and the Royall receipts could not have much longer endured. . . .

We are naturally prone to applaud the times behind us, and to vilifie the present: for the current of her fame carries it to this day, how Royally and victoriously she lived and dyed, without the grievance and grudge of the people; yet that truth may appear without retraction from the Honour of so great a Princesse, it is manifest she left more debts unpaid, taken upon the credit of her Privy Seales, then her Progenitors did, or could have taken up that way, in a hundred yeares before her; which was an enforced piece of State, to lay the burthen on that horse, that was best able to bear it, at the dead lift, when neither her receipts could yield her relief at the pinch, nor the urgency of her affaires endure the delays of a Parliamentary assistance: And for such ayds it is likewise apparent, That she received more, and with the love of the people, than any two of her Predecessors, that took most; which was a Fortune strained out of the Subject, through the plausibility of her Comportment, and, as I would say without offence, the prodigall distribution of her Graces to all sorts of Subjects: For I believe, no Prince living, that was so tender of Honour, and so exactly stood for the preservation of Soveraignty, that was so great a Courtier of her people, yea, of the Commons, and that stoopt and descended lower in presenting her person to the publique view, as she past in her Progresses and Perambulations; and in the ejaculation of her prayers on her people. And truly, though much may be given in praise of her magnanimity, and therewith comply with her Parliaments, and for all that come off at last with honour and profit; yet must we ascribe some part of the commendation to the wisdomes of the times, and the choice of Parliament men: for I find not that they were at any time given to any violent or pertinatious dispute, elections being made of grave and discreet persons, not factious and ambitious of fame; such as came not to the House with a malevolent spirit of contention, but with a preparation to consult on the publique good, rather to comply than contest with her Majesty: Neither doe I find, that the House was at any time weakned and pestered with the admission of too many young heads, as it hath been of later times. . . . Sure we are, the House alwayes took the common cause into their consideration, and they saw the Queen had just occasion, and need enough to use their assistance; neither doe I remember that the House did ever capitulate or preferre their private to the publique, the Queens necessities, etc. but waited their times, and in the first place gave their supply, and according to the exigency of her affaires; yet failed not at last to obtain what they desired, so that the Queen and her Parliaments had ever the good Fortune to depart in love, and on reciprocall tearmes. . . .

William Allen

THE SUPREME GOVERNOR AS PERSECUTOR

William Allen, born at Rossall, Lancashire, in 1532, was educated at Oriel College, Oxford. In 1556 he was chosen principal of St. Mary's Hall, Oxford. Sometime after Elizabeth's accession he resigned, and was at the University of Louvain in 1561. Reasons of health necessitated a secret return to England the following year, but in 1565 he was back on the Continent, where he was ordained. Following a pilgrimage to Rome he founded an English college at Douay in 1568 in order to provide young Englishmen with a Catholic education and train missionary priests. In 1575 Gregory XIII summoned him to Rome to give his advice on founding a new college. On a return visit in 1579 he persuaded the Jesuits to become involved in the task of reconverting England. He returned to Rome for the last time in 1585, staying there until his death in 1594. Sixtus V made Allen a cardinal in 1587, with the intention that he would be appointed as a legate to England if the Great Enterprise of Philip II succeeded.

The truth is, that in the first yeare and Parliament of the Q[ueen's] reigne, when they abolished the Popes authoritie, and wolde haue yeelded the same authoritie with the title of *Supreame head* to the Q[ueen] as it was giuen before to her Father and Brother: diuers speciallie moued by Minister Caluin's writing (who had cōdemned in the same Princes that calling) liked not the tearme, and therfore procured that some other equiualent but lesse offensiue, might be vsed. Vpon which formalitie, it was enacted that she was *the Cheef*

From William Allen, *A Trve, Sincere, and Modest Defence of English Catholiques* ([1584]), pp. 7–11.

gouernour aswell in causes ecclesiastical or spiritual, as civil and temporal: And an othe of the same was conceiued accordinglie, to be tendred at their pleasures to al the spiritual and tēporal officers in the Realme, by which euerie one must sweare that in conscience he taketh and beleeueth her so to be: and that no Priest or other borne owt of the realme, can haue or ought to haue anie maner of power in spiritual matters ouer her subiectes. Which othe is compted the verie torment of al English consciences, not the protestantes them selues beleeuing it to be trew: & of al trew catholiques, as before it was deemed in her Father a lay man, and in her Brother a childe very ridiculous: so now in her self, being a woman, is it accompted a thing most monstruous and vnnatural, and the verie gappe to bring anie Realme to the thraldome of al sectes, Heresie, Paganisme, Turcisme or Atheisme, that the prīce for the time by humane frailtie may be subiect vnto: al our religion, faith, worship, seruice, and prayers, depending vpon his soueraine determination: a thing that al nations haue to take heede of by our example, for the redresse of which pernicious absurditie, so manie of our said brethren so willinglie haue shed ther blood.

In the first Parliamet of her Maiesties reigne, it was indeed in a maner thrust vpon her against her wil: because otherwise ther could haue bene no colour to make new lawes for change of Religiō: and this title, of Cheefe gouernesse, was thought to be a qualification of the former tearme of Headship. But in truth it is al one with thother, or rather worse: for in some kinde of improper speach, the king may be called the Head or cheef of the Church of his countrie, for that he is soueraigne lorde and ruler of bothe persons spiritual and temporal: al sortes bound to obey his lawful ciuil lawes and commandementes, and so in that sense is he Head of the cleargie and of al others.

But when in the new forme of our statute it is expreslie and distinctlie added, that she is the onelie Supreame gouernour euen in al causes, *as well Spiritual and Ecclesiastical as temporal & Ciuil:* and furthermore enacted that al iurisdictions, priuiledges, superiorities, and preeminences ecclesiastical, as by anie power spiritual haue bene or may be exercised, are taken frō the Pope, (to whom Christ gaue them in most ample maner,) and are vnited, or rather (as they say) restored by an old decree to the crowne of England: this can haue no excuse, nether trew or likelie sense in the world, making indeed a King and a Priest al one: no differēce betwixt the state of the Church and a temporal common wealth: giuing no lesse right to heathen Princes to be gouernours of the Church in causes spiritual, then to a christian king: it maketh one parte of the Church in different teritoires to be independent and seueral[1] from an other, according to the distinction of realmes and kingdomes in the world. And finallie it maketh euerie man that is not borne in the kingdome to be a forreiner also in respect of the Church: thes and a thowsand absurdities and impossibilities more doe ensue, which for breuitie we omitt: onlie this which is in most mens memories we may not ouerpasse, that the verie same yeare that this new preeminence was giuen by lawe to the Q[ueen] and th' othe accordinglie ministred to many, some hauing remorse of the matter, for to auoide daunger, pretended for their refusal, that it seemed to them by the wordes of th' othe and acte, that the Q[ueen] might minister also the Sacramētes, wherunto they wolde not sweare by anie meanes.

Wherupon in her next visitation of the cleargie, a special iniunction was printed and published by her commaundement, declaring that in truth she had no such intent, and that no suche thing was implied in her title or claime of spiritual regimēt,[2] nor no other thing, nor more then was before graunted to her father by the tearme of Supreame head: requiring al her louing subiectes to receiue th' othe at least in that sense, and so it should suffice her highnesse. By which it is now cleare, by ther owne authentical declaratiō, that we speake no vntrewth (as this libeller sayth) nor abuse not the world when we say she is called and taken for the Supreame head of the Church of England: albeit (the thing it self being far more absurde and of more pernicious sequele, then the makers of the law, which were mere laymē and most of them vnlearned, could then perceiue) their folowers now, would disauow the same. For this article therfore as the famous bishoppe of Rochester,[3] Sir Thomas More, and a great number more in king Henrie the 8. his dayes: so did thos twoo last named martyrs, and diuers others

[1] i.e., separate.
[2] i.e., government.
[3] John Fisher, who was executed in 1535 for refusing to take the Oath of Succession, which included a clause acknowledging the King as head on earth of the Church of England.

before them most gladlie and constantlie yeld vp their lyues, and so consequentlie dyed for mere matter of religion onelie.

And to end this point, we lastlie referre the aduersarie[4] to the late Martyrdome of Cartar a poore innocent artisan: who was made away onelie for printing a catholique booke *De schismate:*[5] in which no worde was found against the state, the quarel onelie most vniustlie being made, vpon a certaine clause, which by no likelie honest construction could apperteine to the Q[ueen's] person: viz. that the Catholike religion should once haue the vpper hand of heresie, and Iudith cutt of the head of *Holophernes:*[6] which they in their extreame ielousie and feare of all thinges wold needes wreast against her Maiestie.

And the place serueth here to saye some-what of the cause also of their racking of Catholiques, which they wold haue strangers beleeue neuer to be done for anie point of religion. As for example, (say they . . .) none is asked by torture, *what he beleeueth of the Masse or Transubstantiation or suche like.* As though (forsooth) ther were no question perteining to faithe and religion, but touching our inward beleefe. Wheras in deed it concerneth religion no lesse to demaund and presse vs by torture, wher, in whos houses, what dayes and tymes we say or heare Masse, how manie we haue reconciled, what we haue h[e]ard in confession: who resorteth to our preachinges: who harboreth catholiques and Priestes: who susteineth, aideth, or comforteth them: who they be that haue their children or pupilles in the Societie or Seminaries beyond the seas: wher such a Iesuite or suche a Preist is to be found: wher catholique bookes ar[e] printed, and by whom, and to whom they be vttered in England? which thinges being demaunded of euil intēt and to the annoyance of the Catholique cause, Godes Priestes, and innocēt men: no man may by the lawe of God and nature disclose, though he be expreslie commaunded by anie Prince in the world, for that God must be obeyed, more then man.

---

4 William Cecil, Lord Burghley, whose tract, *The Execution of Justice in England* (1583), Allen is refuting. Cecil claims Catholics are persecuted only on grounds of sedition, not religion.
5 William Carter was executed in 1584 for printing an English translation of Gregory Martin's *A Treatise of Schism* (1578).
6 Judith 13:8.

Edward Rishton

THE CRUEL HYPOCRITE

Born in the diocese of Chester in 1550, Edward Rishton studied at Oxford before commencing theological studies at Allen's college at Douay. He was ordained at Cambray in 1577 and went to Rome. In 1580 he returned to Douay and was appointed to the English Mission. He and others were apprehended by the English authorities and tried in November 1581. Although convicted of high treason and condemned to death, he and twenty others were instead banished to the Continent. He completed a history of the English Reformation written by a fellow English Catholic, Nicholas Sanders (ca. 1530–1581); it was published at Cologne in 1585. The following year Rishton died of the plague.

Meanwhile the governor of the Church applies herself to the creation of new bishops and clergy of her sect. In the distribution of offices and ecclesiastical rank, and in the very form of government, the queen paid no heed to the Zuinglian or Calvinistic model, nor indeed did she accurately copy that of the Lutherans; but she wished to be regarded as one that was more of the Lutheran than of any other heresy, not only in ceremonial, but also in her way of believing. She pretended to a certain moderation; for as she had been considered a Catholic not long before, she was not willing at once to appear as a heretic of the worst kind. Accordingly that seditious assembly, which is called the Consistory, and those degrees or ministries of elders, ministers, and the rest, she put on one side. But whether it was her own act or the result of the advice of others, she resolved that it would be more for the honour of her spiritual prelates, more for the splendour of her temporal kingdom, and lastly, more for the security of the sect, that the clergy she was instituting should, according to the arrangements of the old Church, consist of archbishops, bishops, priests, and even deacons—for they allow no order lower than this.

In the same way the cathedral and collegiate churches were to

From Edward Rishton's Continuation of Nicolas Sanders, *Rise and Growth of the Anglican Schism,* trans. and ed. David Lewis (London, 1877), pp. 270–72, 293–95, 319–25. Originally published at Cologne in 1585 as *Doctissimi . . . N. Sanderi de origine ac progressu Schismatis Anglicani liber. Continens historiam maxime ecclesiasticam annorum circiter sexaginta . . . Editus et auctus per E. Rishtonum.*

have, as before, provosts, deans, archdeacons, chancellors, canons, and other officers, according to the custom of each place. All these men were to retain the titles of the ancient dignities and honours, the possessions of the old clergy, and almost all the privileges which they had both in Church and State. Moreover, the religious woman made an effort to have Religious of her belief, for she asked that illustrious confessor the abbot of Westminster[1] not to allow his monks to go away because of the change, and to assure them of her kindly feelings towards the monastery; that she wished them to remain there, and to pray for her, celebrating divine service according to the order of her laws. But those good men saw no reason why they should forsake the rule of St. Benedict to keep that of Calvin.

The queen is in the habit of boasting before strangers and the foreign ambassadors that the clergy of her sect are held in honour, and are not mere starvelings like those of Geneva, and other Churches of the kind, not so well ordered as hers; and that she had not gone so far from the faith of other princes and of her own ancestors as many think. The better to keep up this fraud, she retained for some years on the table, which she had set up in the place of the altar, in her chapel, two wax candles, which were never lighted, with a silver crucifix between them. And then in order to please the Catholics, and to impose the more easily upon foreigners, she used to say from time to time that she was forced, not by her own convictions, but by the clamours of her subjects, to make a change of religion, but that she had practised great moderation in making it.

*   *   *

It was discussed in the council whether Elizabeth, on account of her unendurable obstinacy, should not be publicly denounced as a heretic, seeing that she was according to law an excommunicated person. Nothing, however, was done, for the emperor,[2] whose son she had led to hope and expect to be her husband, obtained from the fathers a respite; for he told them that when she was married

---

[1] John Fecknam, who was made abbot of Westminster in November 1556.
[2] Ferdinand I, father of Archduke Charles of Austria, a leading candidate for marriage to Elizabeth.

to a Catholic husband, she must come to a better mind. But she deceived this suitor as she had deceived others, and was day by day more obstinate, and to the Catholics more cruel.

At this time Mary Queen of Scots resolved upon flight. She had been harassed by the treachery of English heretics, and the unutterable cruelty of her own subjects: she had been shut in a prison and compelled to resign. She lost her husband by a most iniquitous murder, and then was herself accused of the crime. She might easily have made her way into the territories of some Christian king, and there were among the Scotch nobles some who begged her to do so. But the letters, messengers, and presents of Elizabeth prevailed, she was invited to pass over the Border into England, and troops were promised her, by the help of which she was to recover her kingdom. But as she had not thoroughly learned that they are not to be trusted who have abandoned the faith of Christ, she went to England against the will of her people, to another prison, to be guarded there by other soldiers.

Not long after her arrival, Mary was placed in the custody of the earl of Shrewsbury, who treated her always with excessive harshness because of her unwavering profession of the Catholic faith; but afterwards, when she was placed in the charge of others, who were more merciless than the earl, her life was a death rather than life, for she was tormented in various and unseemly ways, and made the butt of false accusations wholly undeserved. She was herself a queen, not a subject of Elizabeth, nor bound by her laws, but, nevertheless, she could not obtain—what is not refused to foreign princes and their ambassadors—a priest to say Mass or to administer the sacraments, that she might serve God as her forefathers had done; and the privation was a heavier affliction than exile and a prison.

This treatment of the Queen of Scots was strange and barbarous, for she was of all people the nearest in blood to Elizabeth, and also her invited guest; nevertheless, for these seventeen years, notwithstanding the most earnest entreaties, she was never once allowed to speak to her, or even to see her.

*   *   *

In other parts of the kingdom also, especially in Lancaster, York, and on the Welsh borders, many Catholics were most grievously tortured; some even were put to a dishonourable death, which is the extreme punishment of traitors or thieves, as were James Bell, a priest, being then sixty years of age, and John Finch, a layman, at Lancaster, and Richard White, a schoolmaster, in Wales.

It would answer no purpose to recount, in this brief sketch, the offences for which these innocent persons were so inhumanly punished, for everybody knows that the true and only reason was their profession of the old religion, and their defence of the Apostolic See, and communion therewith, against the rebel children of the Church. For when they had shown without difficulty how false were the charges which were brought against them in court, they were forthwith required to reveal their more secret thoughts by means of crafty questions touching their future behaviour with regard to the declaratory Bull of Pius V.:[3] whether in their judgment the sentence of the Pope was a lawful sentence; whether they believed that the Pope could depose princes, and release subjects from their allegiance; what they would do themselves, or how would they direct the consciences of others, if any one began a war on account of religion. Many other questions of the same kind were put to them. If in their replies to these questions they behaved themselves with caution and prudence, or said anything in favour of the Papal jurisdiction, their offence was said to be not one of religion, but high treason.

The queen and her advisers now were not satisfied, in their cunning cruelty, with all they had done against priests, and people of moderate fortunes who kept the faith, so they began to treat with the grossest indignities persons of higher rank, especially the peers, for they saw that these hated more and more the falsehood, the meanness, and immeasurable cruelty of the new religion. But as it was impossible for them to destroy at once every noble person who held the faith, in order to gratify the hate or the greed of each upstart courtier, they assailed them, one after another, by lying accusations and falsehoods. Thus they shamefully put to death

---

[3] The bull *Regnans in Excelsis* (1570) deposed Elizabeth and absolved Catholic subjects from allegiance to her.
[4] The Catholic Throckmorton (also spelled Throgmorton) was executed in 1584 for plotting with the Spanish ambassador Mendoza to overthrow Elizabeth and replace her with Mary Stewart.

Francis Throgmorton[4] and Edward Arden,[5] and others, men of the old religion and of ancient descent. Thus the powerful Earl of Northumberland,[6] and the most devout and noble personage, William Shelley,[7] were thrown, on mere empty suspicion, into their miserable and fatal prisons. Lord Paget and Charles Arundel would have been dealt with in the same way, though most innocent, if they had not saved their lives and their consciences by timely flight.

I will not stop to describe the cruelty with which they have now for some time treated the most illustrious person in the whole kingdom, the Earl of Arundel,[8] the eldest son and heir of the duke of Norfolk,[9] who also has been put to death by their hands stained in blood. The earl had taken to flight solely to save his conscience, but they laid hands upon him and put him in prison. They dishonour his name by shameless lying, and harass his brothers, his sisters, and all his kindred, who are all perfectly innocent.

Beside these miseries already mentioned, and the manifold extortions and molestations which they are forced to endure at the hands of most worthless men, the lay nobility are in this more unhappy than the priests: they cannot run away for conscience-sake, nor sell their estates, nor give up their goods to their wives and children, nor take them with them for their support; everything must be left behind for the exchequer and for the use of heretics: nothing more slavish and miserable can be imagined or described.

It is said that this cruelty is inflicted on all ranks of men for the safety of the queen and the state, more and more endangered—so they say—by the Catholics every day becoming more numerous and attached to the Queen of Scotland, and not at all on account of their

---

[5] Arden, former sheriff of Warwickshire, was hanged in 1583 for plotting to assassinate Elizabeth.

[6] Henry Percy, eighth Earl of Northumberland, was sent to the Tower three times (1571, 1582, 1584) for plotting to aid Mary Stewart. He apparently committed suicide in his cell in 1585, though Catholics believed he was murdered.

[7] Shelley was attainted of treason in 1582, but was not executed. He was accused of plotting with Charles Paget, a Catholic double agent (attainted of treason in 1587) and brother of Lord Thomas Paget, who fled to Paris after the government discovered Throckmorton's plot in 1583.

[8] Philip Howard, Earl of Arundel, was converted to Catholicism in 1584. Attempting to flee England he was apprehended and committed to the Tower, where he died in 1595.

[9] Thomas Howard, fourth Duke of Norfolk, was executed in 1572 for his part in the Ridolfi plot.

religion. Certainly we all think so, and all sensible men think so too, who now for many years have observed that the people who now govern England are utterly regardless of religion, whatever they may pretend to be, and careful only of their own interests. This is the source of those new terrors which have laid hold of their minds, and of the suspicions which they entertain that there are people bent on the murder of Elizabeth. They are like children, afraid not only of men and things which have a real existence, but of unsubstantial ghosts and shadows. So much so that in order to ward off all dangers to the life of the queen, or to punish the authors thereof, if any such there be, they have banded themselves together, and bound themselves by oaths—a thing never heard of before, and contrary to the custom and law of the land—not only against those who may do the evil they dread, but against the very next heirs to the crown. At first this arose out of private zeal and fury, but afterwards an act of Parliament was obtained in favour of it in a certain modified form.[10]

But to return to our subject. In the midst of this cruelty exercised upon all Catholics of every rank, in order to conceal at times in some measure from foreign princes, and even the Pope himself, the severity of the persecution, and gain for themselves the reputation of being moderate and merciful, they show their mercy so fraudulently, that while they are harassing, torturing, and killing one, the royal indulgence is often extended to another. Thus when there is a lucid interval or rest from the slaughter of innocent people in London, the fury of the persecution breaks out in the country with greater violence, and while they seem to allow greater freedom to some, they at the same time harass others in the most cruel way. And in order that this their cunning may the better subserve their end, they keep certain persons in the courts of princes whose business it is to insist upon, set forth, and enhance this dishonest and delusive mercy in the presence of those who are unacquainted with our affairs, and at the same time to lessen or excuse the dreadful deeds of their unmeasurable cruelty, or to explain them in a sense contrary to the faith.

[10] The Bond of Association, devised by the Privy Council, bound adherents to obey and defend the Queen against any who would plot to place another person (implicitly Mary Stewart) on the throne, even to the point of executing the person for whom the plotting was undertaken. The Parliament of 1584–1585 enacted a modified version in its act for the queen's safety.

II REFLECTIONS FROM THE NINETEENTH CENTURY

John Lingard

IRRESOLUTE AND IMMORAL DESPOT

John Lingard was born at Winchester in 1771 and entered the English college at Douay in 1782. Eleven years later he returned to England and was ordained a Roman Catholic priest in 1795. He pursued an academic career at Crookhall College and at St. Cuthbert's College, Ushaw, before going to the mission at Hornby, near Lancaster, in 1811 to devote the remaining forty years of his life to research and writing. His History of England *was very popular. In recognition of his work Pius VII made him a Doctor of Divinity, Canon Law, and Civil Law, and he was subsequently honored by Leo XII.*

Before the execution of Mary, Elizabeth had balanced between the fear of infamy and the gratification of revenge. The blow had now been struck; her revenge was gratified; and it became her object to escape the infamy, under the shelter of pretended ignorance. The reader will recollect that Davison,[1] instead of despatching the warrant immediately after it had been signed, retained it till the following morning. Of this he had apprised the queen, but she was careful not to iterate the order: she even suffered six days to elapse without any mention of the warrant to Davison. Early on the next morning the Lord Talbot arrived with the official intelligence. Burghley communicated it to his colleagues of the privy council,—joyful tidings to men who during so many years had thirsted in vain for the death of the Queen of Scots; but he proposed that, instead of imparting the fact to Elizabeth then, time should be allowed to open it to her cautiously and by degrees. To this singular proposal—so singular that it provoked a suspicion of collusion between the hoary statesman and his mistress—the lords consented. Elizabeth took her usual airing, and after her return entertained herself in the company of Don Antonio, the pretender to the crown of Portugal. By noon the report was spread through the city; the bells announced the joyful intelligence, and numerous bonfires illuminated the darkness of the night. That evening one of the queen's ladies mentioned before her,

From John Lingard, *A History of England from the First Invasion by the Romans to the Accession of William and Mary in 1688* (Boston and New York, 1855), Vol. 8, pp. 266–71, 416–21, 424–29.

[1] William Davison, appointed second secretary to Elizabeth in 1586.

as it were casually, the death of Mary Stuart. Elizabeth maintained an air of perfect indifference, but in the morning sent for Hatton,[2] expressed the most violent indignation, and indulged in threats of the most fearful vengeance against men who had abused her confidence and usurped her authority, by putting the Queen of Scots to death without her knowledge or consent. Hatton acquainted his colleagues of the council with the queen's threats. They sent for Davison, and advised him to keep out of her sight till her wrath should have subsided. Had they not already conspired to make him their scapegoat? He repaired to his own house, under pretence of indisposition, but on the Tuesday he was committed to the Tower, and on Wednesday Elizabeth, sending for Roger, groom of the chamber to the French king, desired him to assure his sovereign of her regret for the death of the Scottish queen, of her ignorance of the dispatch of the warrant, and of her resolution to punish the presumption of her ministers. To account for so late a communication it was reported that the council had concealed the death of Mary from the queen, who first learned that event from a casual conversation with a lady of the court.

Elizabeth now attempted to prove the sincerity of her regret by the execution of her threats. She suspended the obnoxious ministers from their offices, and ordered them to answer in the Star Chamber for their contempt of her authority. But her anger was gradually appeased. In all humility they acknowledged their offense, pleaded the loyalty of their intentions, and submitted to her pleasure. One after another, all, with the exception of Davison, were restored to office and favor. He had earned this distinction by his constant reluctance to unite with his colleagues in their persecution of Mary. He had declined to subscribe "the association," even at the request of the queen; he had eluded the task of examining Babington[3] and his associates in the Tower; he was absent, though named in the commission, from the trial at Fotheringay;[4] nor did he afterwards, as the other absent commissioners had done, sign the condemnation of the Scottish queen. To add to his demerits, in answer to the questions put to him in prison, he did not imitate the humility of

---

2 Sir Christopher Hatton, Elizabeth's vice-chamberlain.

3 Anthony Babington, executed in 1586 for conspiracy to assassinate Elizabeth and enthrone Mary Stewart.

4 Mary was tried at Fotheringay in October 1586 and found guilty.

his colleagues, but in defending himself, charged the queen indirectly with falsehood, and alluded in obscure terms to her message to Paulet.[5] In court, however, he acted with more reserve than prudence. To the invectives of the crown lawyers he replied, that to acknowledge the offense would be to tarnish his own reputation, to contend with his sovereign would be to transgress the duty of a subject; that they did him injustice by reading garbled passages from his answer: let them read the whole, or rather let them read none, for it contained secrets not fit for the public ear: he would only say, that he had acted under the persuasion that he was obeying the queen's commands, and for the rest would throw himself on her mercy. He was condemned in a fine of 10,000 pounds or marks, and to be imprisoned during the royal pleasure. The treasury seized all his property; and the queen, though she lived seventeen years longer, would never restore him to favor. She was deaf to his repeated petitions to be admitted into her presence. Even the young Earl of Essex, in the zenith of his influence, prayed for Davison in vain. Perhaps she deemed him unworthy of pardon because he would not plead guilty; perhaps she thought by this severity to convince the world that she did not dissemble; certainly she effected one important object: she closed the mouth of her prisoner, whom the spirit of resentment or the hope of vindicating his innocence might have urged to the secret history of the proceedings against Mary, and reveal the unworthy artifices and guilty designs of his sovereign. He himself appears to have attributed the queen's severity to the unfriendly offices of Burghley, who looked upon him as a rival in the way of his own son Robert.[6]

It may appear surprising, but a full month elapsed before the King of Scotland received any certain intelligence of the execution of his mother. At the news he burst into tears; he talked of nothing but vengeance; the people shared the resentment of the king, and the estates offered to risk their lives and fortunes in the national quarrel. Robert Carey, son to Lord Hunsdon, who arrived with a letter from Elizabeth, would have fallen a victim to the fury of the Scots, had not James sent him a guard for his protection. The

---

[5] Elizabeth had a letter sent to Mary's keeper, Sir Amyas Paulet, to determine whether or not he might dispose of Mary in accord with the Bond of Association. Paulet refused.

[6] Robert Cecil ultimately became secretary in 1596.

queen in her letter assured the young monarch that the death of Mary was not owing to her; that the ministers, who ordered it without her knowledge, should be severely punished; that she would be to him in the place of his mother, whose condemnation should prove no prejudice to his rights and expectations.

*   *   *

In the judgment of her contemporaries, and that judgment has been ratified by the consent of posterity, Elizabeth was numbered among the greatest and the most fortunate of our princes. The tranquility which, during a reign of nearly half a century, she maintained within her dominions, while the neighboring nations were convulsed with intestine dissensions, was taken as a proof of the wisdom or the vigor of her government; and her successful resistance against the Spanish monarch, the severe injuries which she inflicted on that lord of so many kingdoms, and the spirit displayed by her fleets and armies, in expeditions to France and the Netherlands, to Spain, to the West, and even the East Indies, served to give to the world an exalted notion of her military and naval power. When she came to the throne England ranked only among the secondary kingdoms; before her death it had risen to a level with the first nations in Europe.

Of this rise two causes may be assigned. The one, though more remote, was that spirit of commercial enterprise which had revived in the reign of Mary, and was carefully fostered in that of Elizabeth by the patronage of the sovereign and the cooperation of the great. Its benefits were not confined to the trading and seafaring classes, the two interests more immediately concerned. It gave a new tone to the public mind, and diffused a new energy through all ranks of men. Their views became expanded; their powers were called into action; and the example of successful adventure furnished a powerful stimulus to the talent and industry of the nation. Men in every profession looked forward to wealth and independence; all were eager to start in the race of improvement.

The other cause may be discovered in the system of foreign policy adopted by the ministers; a policy, indeed, which it may be difficult to reconcile with honesty and good faith, but which, in the result, proved eminently successful. [They had been] . . . perpetually on the watch to sow the seeds of dissension, to foment the spirit of resistance, and to aid the efforts of rebellion in the neighboring nations. In Scotland the authority of the crown was almost annihilated; France was reduced to an unexampled state of anarchy, poverty, and distress; and Spain beheld with dismay her wealth continually absorbed, and her armies annually perishing among the dikes and sandbanks of the Low Countries. The depression of these powers, if not a positive, was a relative benefit. As other princes descended, the English queen appeared to rise on the scale of reputation and power.

In what proportion the merit or demerit of these and of other measures should be shared between Elizabeth and her counsellors, it is impossible to determine. On many subjects she could see only with their eyes, and hear with their ears; yet it is evident that her judgment or her conscience frequently disapproved of their advice. Sometimes, after a long struggle, they submitted to her wisdom or obstinacy; sometimes she was terrified or seduced into the surrender of her own opinion; generally a compromise was effected by mutual concessions. This appears to have happened on most debates of importance and particularly with respect to the treatment of the unfortunate Queen of Scots. Elizabeth may perhaps have dissembled; she may have been actuated by jealousy or hatred; but, if we condemn, we should also remember the arts and frauds of the men by whom she was surrounded, the false information which they supplied, the imaginary dangers which they created, and the despatches which they dictated in England to be forwarded to the queen through the ambassadors in foreign courts, as the result of their own judgment and observation.

It may be that the habitual irresolution of Elizabeth was partially owing to her discovery of such practices: but there is reason to believe that it was a weakness inherent in the constitution of her mind. To deliberate appears to have been her delight, to resolve her torment. She would receive advice from any, from foreigners as well as natives, from the ladies of her bedchamber no less than the lords of her council: but her distrust begot hesitation; and she always suspected that some interested motive lurked under the pretence of zeal for her service. Hence she often suffered months, sometimes years, to roll away before she came to a conclusion; and then it required the same industry and address to keep her steady to her purpose as it had already cost to bring her to it. The ministers, in their confidential correspondence, perpetually lamented this infirmity in the queen: in public they employed all their ingenuity to screen it from notice, and to give the semblance of wisdom to that which, in their own judgment, they characterized as folly.

*   *   *

An intelligent foreigner had described Elizabeth, while she was yet a subject, as haughty and overbearing: on the throne she was careful to display that notion of her own importance, that contempt of all beneath her, and that courage in the time of danger, which were characteristic of the Tudors. She seemed to have forgotten that she ever had a mother, but was proud to remind both herself and others that she was the daughter of a powerful monarch, of Henry VIII. On occasions of ceremony she appeared in all her splendor, accompanied by the great officers of state, and with a numerous retinue of lords and ladies, dressed in their most gorgeous apparel. In reading descriptions of her court we may sometimes fancy ourselves transported into the palace of an Eastern princess. . . .

Yet while she maintained this state in public and in the palace, while she taught the proudest of the nobility to feel the distance between themselves and their sovereign, she condescended to court the good will of the common people. In the country they had access to her at all times; neither their rudeness nor importunity appeared to offend her; she received their petitions with an air of pleasure, thanked them for their expressions of attachment, and sought the opportunity of entering into private conversation with individuals. Her progresses were undoubtedly undertaken for pleasure: but she made them subservient to policy, and increased her popularity by her affability and condescension to the private inhabitants of the counties in which she made her temporary abode.

*   *   *

To her first parliament she had expressed a wish that on her tomb might be inscribed the title of "the virgin queen." But the woman who despises the safeguards, must be content to forfeit the reputation, of chastity. It was not long before her familiarity with Dudley provoked dishonorable reports. At first they gave her pain: but her feelings were soon blunted by passion; in the face of the whole court she assigned to her supposed paramour an apartment contiguous to her own bedchamber; and by this indecent act proved that she was become regardless of her character, and callous to every sense of shame. But Dudley, though the most favored, was not considered as her only lover; among his rivals were numbered Hatton, and Raleigh, and Oxford, and Blount, and Simier, and Anjou;[7] and it was afterwards believed that her licentious habits survived, even when the fires of wantonness had been quenched by the chill of age. The court imitated the manners of the sovereign. It was a place in which . . . "all enormities reigned in the highest degree," or . . . "where there was no love, but that of the lusty god of gallantry, Asmodeus."

Elizabeth firmly believed, and zealously upheld the principles of government, established by her father, the exercise of absolute authority by the sovereign, and the duty of passive obedience in the subject. The doctrine, with which the lord keeper Bacon opened her first parliament, was indefatigably inculcated by all his successors during her reign, that, if the queen consulted the two houses it was through choice, not through necessity, to the end that her laws might be more satisfactory to her people, not that they might derive any force from their assent. She possessed by her prerogative whatever was requisite for the government of the realm. She could, at her pleasure, suspend the operation of existing statutes, or issue proclamations which should have the force of law. In her opinion the chief use of parliaments was to vote money, to regulate the minutiae of trade, and to legislate for individual and local interests. To the lower house she granted, indeed, freedom of debate: but it was to be a decent freedom, the liberty of "saying ay or no"; and those that transgressed that decency were liable . . . to feel the weight of the royal displeasure.

A foreigner, who had been ambassador in England, informs us, that under Elizabeth the administration of justice was more corrupt than under her predecessors. We have not the means of instituting the comparison. But we know that in her first year the policy of Cecil substituted men of inferior rank in the place of the former

---

[7] Edward de Vere, seventeenth Earl of Oxford; Charles Blount, the future Lord Mountjoy; Jehan de Simier, envoy and friend of Francis of Valois, Duke of Alençon; Henry, Duke of Anjou, who reigned in France as Henry III from 1574–1589.

magistrates; that numerous complaints were heard of their tyranny, peculation, and rapacity; and that a justice of the peace was defined in Parliament to be "an animal, who, for half a dozen chickens, would dispense with a dozen laws": nor shall we form a very exalted notion of the integrity of the higher courts, if we recollect that the judges were removable at the royal pleasure, and that the queen herself was in the habit of receiving, and permitting her favorites and ladies to receive, bribes as the price of her or their interference in the suits of private individuals.

Besides the judicial tribunals, . . . there were, in the age of Elizabeth, several other courts the arbitrary constitution of which was incompatible with the liberties of the subject; the Court of High Commission, for the cognizance of religious offenses; the Court of Star Chamber, which inflicted the severest punishments for that comprehensive and undefinable transgression, contempt of the royal authority; courts of commissioners appointed occasionally for the public or private trial of offenses, and the courts martial, for which the queen, from her hasty and imperious temper, manifested a strong predilection. Whatever could be supposed to have the remotest tendency to sedition, was held to subject the offender to martial law; the murder of a naval or military officer, the importation of disloyal or traitorous books, or the resort to one place of several persons who possessed not the visible means of subsistence. Thus, in 1595, under the pretense that the vagabonds in the neighborhood of London were not to be restrained by the usual punishments, she ordered Sir Thomas Wyllford to receive from the magistrates the most notorious and incorrigible of these offenders, and "to execute them upon the gallows, according to the justice of martial law."

Another, and intolerable grievance was the discretionary power assumed by the queen, of gratifying her caprice or resentment by the restraint or imprisonment of those who had given her offense. Such persons were ordered to present themselves daily before the Council till they should receive further notice, or to confine themselves within their own doors, or were given in custody to some other person, or were thrown into a public prison. In this state they remained, according to the royal pleasure, for weeks, or months, or years, till they could obtain their liberty by their submission, or through the intercession of their friends, or with the payment of a valuable composition.

The queen was not sparing of the blood of her subjects. The statutes inflicting death for religious opinion have been already noticed. In addition, many new felonies and new treasons were created during her reign; and the ingenuity of the judges gave to these enactments the most extensive application. In 1595 some apprentices in London conspired to release their companions, who had been condemned by the Star Chamber to suffer punishment for a riot; in 1597 a number of peasants in Oxfordshire assembled to break down enclosures, and restore tillage; each of these offenses, as it opposed the execution of the law, was pronounced treason by the judges; and both the apprentices in London, and the men of Oxfordshire, suffered the barbarous death of traitors.

We are told that her parsimony was a blessing to the subject, and that the pecuniary aids voted to her by Parliament were few and inconsiderable, in proportion to the length of her reign. They amounted to twenty subsidies, thirty tenths, and forty fifteenths. I know not how we are to arrive at the exact value of these grants: but they certainly exceed the average of the preceding reigns; and to them must be added the fines of recusants, the profits of monopolies, and the monies raised by forced loans: of which it is observed by Naunton, that "she left more debts unpaid, taken upon credit of her privy seals, than her progenitors did take, or could have taken up, that were a hundred years before her."

The historians, who celebrate the golden days of Elizabeth, have described with a glowing pencil the happiness of the people under her sway. To them might be opposed the dismal picture of national misery, drawn by the Catholic writers of the same period. But both have taken too contracted a view of the subject. Religious dissension had divided the nation into opposite parties, of almost equal numbers, the oppressors and the oppressed. Under the operation of the penal statutes, many ancient and opulent families had been ground to the dust; new families had sprung up in their place; and these, as they shared the plunder, naturally eulogized the system to which they owed their wealth and their ascendancy. But their prosperity was not the prosperity of the nation; it was that of one half obtained at the expense of the other.

It is evident that neither Elizabeth nor her ministers understood the benefits of civil and religious liberty. The prerogatives which she so highly prized, have long since withered away; the bloody code which she enacted against the rights of conscience, has ceased to stain the pages of the statute book; and the result has proved, that the abolition of despotism and intolerance adds no less to the stability of the throne, than to the happiness of the people.

James Anthony Froude
THE MEDIOCRE POLITIQUE

Thomas Carlyle's chief disciple, James Froude, was born in Devon in 1818, and educated at Oriel College, Oxford. His busy career included fourteen years as a magazine editor and travels to South Africa, Australia, and the West Indies. The last years of his life (1892–1894) were spent as Regius Professor of History at Oxford. He devoted nearly twenty years of study to the history of England in the sixteenth century. The result was a classic twelve-volume study, six volumes of which were devoted to Elizabeth's reign. His magnum opus reflects his conviction that the Reformation was the most significant event in English history. Although Elizabeth is treated harshly, she is credited with completing the break with Rome.

While Parliament was busy with the condition of the people, the concerns of the church were taken in hand by the queen herself. Jealous of what she considered her prerogative, and distrustful of the temper of the Commons, Elizabeth never, if she could help it, permitted a religious debate in the lower house. As head of the church, she claimed unrestricted jurisdiction in her own department, and the exclusive initiation of all proposed alterations.

The spiritual anarchy had hitherto been even more complete than the secular. The Act of Uniformity was on the statute book; but it had been obeyed or disobeyed according to the humor of each minister

From James A. Froude, *History of England from the Fall of Wolsey to the Defeat of the Spanish Armada* (London: Longmans, Green, n.d.), Vol. 12, pp. 487–91, 493–96, 505–511.

or congregation. Even Sir Amyas Paulet, with the charge of the second person of the realm, had a Puritan service in the chapel at Chartley. Anglican theology had as yet no recognized existence. The religion of the Protestants, according to the received formula, "was the Bible, and the Bible only." In the Bible they had found, not a body of creeds or confessions of faith, but a rule of life, to which they were passionately endeavoring to conform. The services in which they took interest were the expositions of Scripture, or the voluntary prayers of those among them who had the power of expressing the general sentiment in words. To such men as these, much of the liturgy was indifferent, much was unpalatable; while the schismatics, as they were called, the conforming Catholics who consented to come to church, cared little for a ritual which, till the defeat of the Armada put an end to their hopes, they had expected to exchange at no distant time for the ancient canon.

For Protestantism Elizabeth had never concealed her dislike and contempt. She hated to acknowledge any fellowship in religion either with Scots, Dutch, or Huguenots. She represented herself to foreign ambassadors as a Catholic in everything, except in allegiance to the papacy. Even for the Church of England, of which she was the supreme governor, she affected no particular respect. She left the Catholics in her household so unrestrained that they absented themselves at pleasure from the Royal Chapel, without a question being asked. She allowed the country gentlemen all possible latitude in their own houses. The danger in which she had lived for so many years, the severe measures to which she was driven against the seminary priests, and the consciousness that the Protestants were the only subjects that she had on whose loyalty she could rely, had prevented her hitherto from systematically repressing the Puritan irregularities; but the power to persecute had been wanting rather than the inclination. The bishops with whom she had filled the sees at her accession were chosen necessarily from the party who had suffered under her sister. They were Calvinists or Lutherans, with no special reverence for the office which they had undertaken; and she treated them in return with studied contempt. She called them Doctors, as the highest title to which she considered them to have any real right: if they disputed her pleasure she threatened to unfrock them; if they showed themselves officious in punishing Catholics, she brought them up with a sharp reprimand; and if their Protestantism was conspicuously earnest, they were deposed and imprisoned.

Thus, with their functions reduced to zero, the Anglican prelates, like the rest of England, had looked for "a change," and prepared for it. Either they became great farmers and graziers, like the Bishop of Ely; or, by evasions of the statutes, they enriched their families with the estates of their sees; or they sold their spiritual functions, sold licenses, sold dispensations, and made priests for money "of the lowest of the people." They made it impossible in return for the Protestants to respect or care for them. With their ineffectuality, their simony, and their worldliness, they brought themselves and their office into contempt; and men who were trying resolutely to have done with lies and dishonesty, and to use the Bible really and truly as a guide to walk by, could not recognize the imposition of episcopal hands as conveying the sole title to be a teacher in the church. The very method in which the bishops were appointed—the *congé d'élire,*[1] the deans and chapters meeting with a premunire[2] round their necks, and going through the farce of a religious service and a solemn election, appeared a horror and a blasphemy to every one who believed God to be really alive. The order, and the system depending upon it, was passing into disrepute, and the tendency of every sincere English Protestant was towards an organization like that of the Kirk of Scotland.

To permit the collapse of the bishops however would be to abandon the Anglican position. Presbytery as such was detestable to Elizabeth. She recognized no authority in any man as derived from a source distinct from herself, and she adhered resolutely to her own purpose. So long as her own crown was unsafe she did not venture on any general persecution of her Puritan subjects; but she checked all their efforts to make a change in the ecclesiastical system. She found a man after her own heart for the see of Canterbury in Whitgift; she filled the other sees as they fell vacant with men of a

---

[1] In the strict sense, the royal permission for a cathedral chapter to fill a vacant see by electing a new bishop. Henry VIII added Letters Missive, nominating the person to be chosen; it is these to which Froude actually refers.
[2] The Statutes of Praemunire, enacted in the fourteenth century, were originally intended to forbid appeals to Rome, but praemunire charges became a general weapon to control the clergy in the sixteenth century.

similar stamp, and she prepared to coerce their refractory "brethren in Christ" into obedience if ever the opportunity came.

On the reconciliation of the Catholic gentry, which followed on the destruction of the Spanish fleet, Elizabeth found herself in a position analogous to that of Henry IV of France. She was the sovereign of a nation with a divided creed, the two parties, notwithstanding, being at last for the most part loyal to herself.

Both she and Henry held at the bottom intrinsically the same views. They believed generally in certain elementary truths lying at the base of all religions; and the difference in the outward expressions of those truths, and the passionate animosities which those differences engendered, were only not contemptible to them from the practical mischief which they produced. On what terms Catholics and Protestants could be induced to live together peaceably was the political problem of the age. Neither of the two sovereigns shared the profound horror of falsehood, which was at the heart of the Protestant movement. They had the statesman's temperament, to which all specific religions are equally fictions of the imagination. . . .

*   *   *

Serious difficulty only arose with the genuine adhesion of the Catholics. So long as they went to church as a form, and under protest, the services to which they listened there were indifferent to them. As soon as they had consented sincerely to dispense with their old ritual, they desired naturally to make the best of the new. They could not, in justice, be expected to see the sacraments slighted, the liturgy mutilated or altered, and all that they believed denied and execrated by a Puritan enthusiast; and when they had abandoned the pope once for all, retaining all other points of their creed unchanged, they had a right to demand the full benefit of the Catholic complexion of the services.

With forbearance and judgment, the problem need not have been insoluble; unfortunately, the queen allowed herself to be influenced by her personal dislike of the Protestants. She was forced into a Protestant policy in her relations with the Continent. She was the more determined to mold the church at home after her own pleasure. Without the Puritans, she would long before have changed her palace for a prison, and her scepter for a distaff. Through all her trials they alone had been true as steel. In times of danger she had caressed them and acknowledged a common creed with them. But she believed probably that but for the peremptoriness of Calvinism the compromises for which she had toiled would have long since given quiet to Europe. She had accepted the help of it in Scotland and Holland, but she had accepted it with steady aversion, as an unpalatable necessity. Murray, Morton, Gowrie, and Angus,[3] had felt one after another the value of her friendship, and had Philip II consented to distinguish between the schismatic orthodoxy of England and the heresy of the rest of Europe, she would have seen the Prince of Orange perish unmoved, or have sent her own fleet to assist in coercing him into obedience.

The general submission of the country relieved her, so far as her own subjects were concerned, from the obligation of humoring further their spiritual unreasonableness. She wished to prove to the conforming Catholics that the Church of England was not the disorderly body which Jesuit calumniators affirmed it to be. She wished to make their conversion easy to them, and relieve their consciences by showing distinctly that it held Catholic doctrines, and as little sympathized with heresy as the parent stock of Rome. She was assured that the Puritans would be loyal to her. Their constancy had been tried, and there was no fear that ill-usage would alienate them. The bishops therefore were instructed to restore order. The spiritual courts, long in abeyance, were reopened, and the old tyrannical processes recommenced. . . . The bishops' assessors summoned ministers and laymen, *ex officio,*[4] to answer any charge that private accusation or public fame had brought against them. . . .

\

*   *   *

Elizabeth's parliaments had been uniformly unfavorable to the exercise by the bishops of any kind of secular jurisdiction whatever. The reviving quarrel had been exasperated by libels, neither wise nor wholly just, but at the bottom with a basis of truth in them. The queen made the bishops' cause her own. She held them up against

---

[3] All four were political leaders of the Protestant cause in Scotland: James Stewart, Earl of Moray and regent (d. 1570); James Douglas, fourth Earl of Morton and a later regent (d. 1581); William Ruthven, first Earl of Gowrie (d. 1584); and Archibald Douglas, eighth Earl of Angus (d. 1588).
[4] The oath *ex officio,* required of those summoned before the High Commission, obliged them to answer all questions, regardless of self-incrimination.

the Puritan House of Commons; the Puritan libelers were prosecuted before an Ecclesiastical Commission, and Penry, a Welsh minister, the supposed author of "Marprelate," was put on his trial for felony.[5] He had said what was no more than the truth—that the queen being established in her throne by the Gospel, had suffered the Gospel to reach no further than the end of her scepter. There was good reason why the extreme developments of the Gospel should in some degree be controlled by the scepter; but it was a hard measure to indict the writer of such words for exciting hatred against the crown. Yet Penry's trial was pressed to a conviction, and he was hanged. Udal, another minister, was condemned and died in prison.[6] Both these men were sacrificed, as completely as any victim of pagan superstition, to a mere idol. The plea of conscience had not availed the Catholics who were executed for treason. The plea of conscience was no more allowed to avail the Puritans. The theory of papist and Protestant was held alike incompatible with the queen's authority, and the same measure which was extended to one was extended to the others.

It was politic, so far as it affected Elizabeth's immediate interests. The part of the nation whose loyalty had been most ambiguous was undoubtedly conciliated by it. The High Church Anglican system being grafted upon the throne, began definitely to grow. Whitgift administered its laws, an excellent Hooker[7] was found to construct its theology, and the recusants and schismatics—as the conforming English who still believed in transubstantiation were scornfully called at Rome—transferred themselves and their sentiments to the new body, to become the church party of the next generation; while the pillory, the slit ears, the Bishop's prison, or, on continued obstinacy, the gallows, became the portion of the representatives of the Reformers. It was impossible to alienate them from a sovereign who had delivered them from popery. . . .

Elizabeth's situation was from the very first extremely trying. She had few relations, none of any weight in the state, and those whom

---

[5] Between 1587 and 1589, seven tracts by "Martin Marprelate" were published, satirically attacking episcopacy. The unknown author may have been John Penry or Job Throckmorton.

[6] The Puritan John Udall (Uvedale) was found guilty in 1590 of illegally attacking episcopacy in print, and died in prison two years later.

[7] Richard Hooker's chief work is *Of the Laws of Ecclesiastical Polity.*

like Hunsdon and Sir Francis Knowles[8] she took into her cabinet, derived their greatness from herself. Her unlucky, it may be almost called culpable, attachment to Leicester made marriage unconquerably distasteful to her, and her disappointment gave an additional twist to her natural eccentricities. Circumstances more than choice threw her originally on the side of the Reformation, and when she told the Spanish ambassadors that she had been forced into the separation from the papacy against her will, she probably spoke but the truth. She was identified in her birth with the cause of independence. The first battle had been fought over her cradle, and her right to be on the throne turned morally, if not in law, on the legitimacy of Queen Catherine's divorce. Her sister had persecuted her as the child of the woman who had caused her mother so much misery, and her friends therefore had naturally been those who were most her sister's enemies. She could not have submitted to the pope without condemning her father, or admitting a taint upon her own birth, while in Mary of Scotland she had a rival ready to take advantage of any concession which she might be tempted to make.

For these reasons, and not from any sympathy with the views either of Luther or Calvin, she chose her party at her accession. She found herself compelled against her will to become the patron of heretics and rebels, in whose objects she had no interest, and in whose theology she had no belief. She resented the necessity while she submitted to it, and her vacillations are explained by the reluctance with which each successive step was forced upon her, on a road which she detested. It would have been easy for a Protestant to be decided. It would have been easy for a Catholic to be decided. To Elizabeth the speculations of so-called divines were but as ropes of sand and sea-slime leading to the moon, and the doctrines for which they were rending each other to pieces a dream of fools or enthusiasts. Unfortunately her keenness of insight was not combined with any profound concern for serious things. She saw through the emptiness of the forms in which religion presented itself to the world. She had none the more any larger or deeper conviction of her own. She was without the intellectual emotions which give human character its consistency and power. One moral quality she possessed in an eminent degree: she was supremely brave. For thirty years she

---

[8] Henry Carey, first Lord Hunsdon, was appointed to the Privy Council in 1561, and Sir Francis Knowles (Knollys) in 1558.

was perpetually a mark for assassination, and her spirits were never affected, and she was never frightened into cruelty. She had a proper contempt also for idle luxury and indulgence. She lived simply, worked hard, and ruled her household with rigid economy. But her vanity was as insatiable as it was commonplace. No flattery was too tawdry to find a welcome with her, and as she had no repugnance to false words in others, she was equally liberal of them herself. Her entire nature was saturated with artifice. Except when speaking some round untruth Elizabeth never could be simple. Her letters and her speeches were as fantastic as her dress, and her meaning as involved as her policy. She was unnatural even in her prayers, and she carried her affectations into the presence of the Almighty. She might doubt legitimately whether she ought to assist an Earl of Murray or a Prince of Orange when in arms against their sovereign; but her scruples extended only to the fulfillment of her promises of support, when she had herself tempted them into insurrection. Obligations of honor were not only occasionally forgotten by her, but she did not seem to understand what honor meant.

Vain as she was of her own sagacity, she never modified a course recommended to her by Burghley without injury both to the realm and to herself. She never chose an opposite course without plunging into embarrassments, from which his skill and Walsingham's[9] were barely able to extricate her. The great results of her reign were the fruits of a policy which was not her own, and which she starved and mutilated when energy and completeness were most needed.

That she pushed no question to extremities, that, for instance, she refused to allow the succession to the crown to be determined, and permitted the Catholics to expect the accession of the Queen of Scots, has been interpreted by the result into wisdom. She gained time by it, and her hardest problems were those which time alone could resolve satisfactorily. But the fortune which stood her friend so often never served her better than in lengthening her life into old age. Had the Queen of Scots survived her, her legacy to England would have been a desperate and dreadful civil war. And her reluctance was no result of any farsighted or generous calculation. She wished only to reign in quiet till her death, and was contented to leave the next generation to settle its own difficulties. Her ten-

[9] Sir Francis Walsingham, appointed secretary to Elizabeth in 1573.

derness towards conspirators was as remarkable as it was hitherto unexampled; but her unwillingness to shed blood extended only to highborn traitors. Unlike her father, who ever struck the leaders and spared the followers, Elizabeth could rarely bring herself to sign the death warrant of a nobleman; yet without compunction she could order Yorkshire peasants to be hung in scores by martial law. Mercy was the quality with which she was most eager to be credited. She delighted in popularity with the multitude, and studied the conditions of it. . . . She was remorseless when she ought to have been most forbearing, and lenient when she ought to have been stern; and she owed her safety and her success to the incapacity and the divisions of her enemies, rather than to wisdom and resolution of her own. Time was her friend, time and the weakness of Philip; and the fairest feature in her history, the one relation in which from first to last she showed sustained and generous feeling, is that which the perversity of history has selected as the blot on her escutcheon. Beyond and beside the political causes which influenced Elizabeth's attitude towards the Queen of Scots, true human pity, true kindness, a true desire to save her from herself, had a real place. . . . Whatever might have been the indirect advantage of Mary Stuart's prospective title, the danger from her presence in the realm must have infinitely exceeded it. She was "the bosom serpent," "the thorn in the flesh," which could not be plucked out; and after the rebellion of the north, and the discovery of the Ridolfi conspiracy,[10] neither Philip nor Alva expected that she would be permitted to survive. It seems as if Elizabeth, remembering her own danger in her sister's lifetime, had studied to show an elaborate tenderness to a person who was in the same relation to herself. From the beginning to the end no trace can be found of personal animosity on the part of Elizabeth; on the part of Mary no trace of anything save the fiercest hatred.

But this, like all other questions connected with the Virgin Queen, should be rather studied in her actions than in the opinion of the historian who relates them. Actions and words are carved upon eternity. Opinions are but forms of cloud created by the prevailing currents of the moral air. Princes, who are credited on the wrong

---

[10] The plot, masterminded by the Florentine banker Ridolfi, was to have the Duke of Alva send an invading force to England. The Duke of Norfolk was to secure Mary or seize Elizabeth, and English insurgents were to rise to restore Catholicism.

side with the evils which happen in their reigns, have a right in equity to the honor of the good. The greatest achievement in English history, the "breaking the bonds of Rome" and the establishment of spiritual independence, was completed without bloodshed under Elizabeth's auspices, and Elizabeth may have the glory of the work. Many problems growing out of it were left unsettled. Some were disposed of on the scaffold at Whitehall, some in the revolution of 1688; some yet survive to test the courage and the ingenuity of modern politicians.

III THE VIRGIN QUEEN

Mandell Creighton

THE FORMATION OF HER CHARACTER

Like Froude, Mandell Creighton was led by his research to dislike of Elizabeth. He was born in 1843 at Carlisle in Northumberland, and received his formal education at Durham Grammar School and Merton College, Oxford. While a Fellow of Merton College he was ordained in 1873. He left Oxford in 1875 to become parson of Embleton, Northumberland, but returned to academic life as Dixie Professor of Ecclesiastical History at Cambridge in 1884. He accepted the bishopric of Peterborough in 1890, and of London in 1897. A master of narrative history, he was a founder and the first editor of the English Historical Review. *His major work is a multivolume* History of the Papacy *from the Great Schism (1377) to the Sack of Rome (1527). His biography of Elizabeth was first published in 1896.*

It is tempting to consider the influence of heredity on Elizabeth's character. In her great qualities of caution and prudence she reverted to her grandfather, Henry VII, while from her father she inherited the royal imperiousness and personal charm which always secured his popularity. To her mother she owed her vanity, her unscrupulousness, her relentless and overbearing temper. Anne Boleyn has been hardly judged. Indeed her position was impossible from the beginning; and none but a coarse, ambitious, and self-seeking woman would have struggled so desperately as she did for a prize which was sure to be fatal. Her hardness and coarseness passed to her daughter, in whom they were modified by finer qualities, and were curbed by a sense of duty. But Elizabeth always remained more truly the daughter of Anne Boleyn than of Henry VIII, though she never took any steps to clear the character of her mother, whom indeed she was anxious to forget.

The day after Anne's execution Henry married Jane Seymour, and Elizabeth was banished from her father's sight. She was committed to the care of Lady Bryan, a relative of her mother, and was assigned as a residence, Hunsdon House, in Hertfordshire, pleasantly situated on a hill overlooking the Stort river. With her was her half-sister Mary, now twenty years of age, devoted to the memory of her mother, and vainly endeavoring to soften the inhumanity of the king.

At first, Elizabeth was entirely neglected by her father. Lady Bryan was driven to write to Cromwell that the child was almost

From Mandell Creighton, *Queen Elizabeth* (London, 1920), pp. 5–18, 41–42, 303–307.

without clothes; she begged that provision should be made for her needs. Her remonstrance seems to have had some effect; and she did her best to discharge her duty to the child entrusted to her care. Elizabeth was well brought up. . . . Edward was also committed to the charge of Lady Bryan, and for some time the two children were educated together. They were willing pupils, for the Tudors were fond of learning. They rose early and devoted the first part of the day to religious instruction. Then they studied "languages, or some of the liberal sciences, or moral learning collected out of such authors as did best conduce to the instruction of Princes." When Edward went to exercise in the open air, Elizabeth, "in her private chamber, betook herself to her lute or viol, and, wearied with that, to practise her needle."

Their teachers were carefully chosen from the best scholars of the time. First came Richard Cox, who had been trained in Wolsey's new college at Oxford, and whom Elizabeth afterwards made Bishop of Ely, in remembrance of her Latin lessons. After Cox came the great Cambridge scholar, Sir John Cheke, who carried on their education in the classics. With him was Roger Ascham, who did not disdain to teach them writing, and formed that bold handwriting which characterizes them both, and was a product of a time when writing was still considered as a fine art. Besides them were learned masters in French and Italian. Elizabeth showed such proficiency in these languages that, at the age of eleven, she wrote an Italian letter to Queen Catherine Parr, and also sent a translation of a book of devotions, *Le Miroir de l'Ame pécheresse,* written by Margaret of Valois, sister of Francis I.

While she was thus carefully educated in mind and body, Elizabeth had no education of her affections. Her father seldom saw her and took no interest in her. She was separated from her brother Edward, and was settled by herself at Enfield. As soon as she could think for herself, she must have felt that she was surrounded by an atmosphere of suspicion, and was alone and friendless in the world. The death of Henry, in 1547, did not remove this isolation. The young Edward was separated from his sisters; and they were carefully kept apart. In fact, the accession of Edward VI opened the way for deep-laid political intrigues. The boy was sickly, and was not likely to come to years of discretion. It is true that Henry VIII had, by his will, made tardy reparation to the daughters whom he had so deeply wronged, and recognized their right of succession. But Henry's will was not of much value. The Council which he had provided was set aside by the influence of Edward's uncle, Edward Seymour, who took the rank of Duke of Somerset and the title of lord protector. Others, however, were not likely to acquiesce in his supremacy; and Mary and Elizabeth might be instruments in their hands.

Elizabeth was committed to the care of the queen-dowager, Catherine Parr; but she had a house of her own and a retinue of a hundred and twenty attendants. Her governess was a relative by her mother's side, Catherine Ashley, a foolish and imprudent woman, little capable of guiding the precocious girl amid the dangers which beset her. Elizabeth was soon to learn the lessons of life in a way which indelibly impressed them upon her mind. We may pity a girl exposed to such temptations; but we must admit that there was little intuitive modesty in a character which could not resist their grossness.

The matrimonial proceedings of Henry VIII had necessarily lowered the tone of morality amongst his courtiers. The coarse gossip which was prevalent was degrading and removed all sense of restraint. The great social revolution through which England was passing gave scope to unlimited covetousness. Men were low-minded, sensual, self-seeking, hypocritical, and unscrupulous. There was a feeling that they were sharing in a general scramble, and that he was cleverest who gained most. There was little sense of honor, or of family affection. The fact that Somerset had won the first place was resented by his brother Thomas, Lord Seymour of Sudeley, who was made lord high admiral. His first plan was to marry Elizabeth; but this required the consent of the king and Council, and he knew that their consent would not be given. He then approached the queen-dowager, whose lover he had been before her marriage with Henry VIII, and secretly married her within a few months after Henry's death. The marriage was reluctantly sanctioned in June 1547. Lord Seymour was now brought nearer to the young king, and had the guardianship of Elizabeth. He was a tall, handsome man; and Catherine was devoted to him. At first, she thought no harm of the familiarity with which he began to treat the young girl who was now thrown in his way. But it soon became evident, even to her, that Seymour was making love to Elizabeth in a corrupting way, and that Elizabeth showed no displeasure at his revolting attentions. Catherine

Ashley was an accomplice, discussed with Elizabeth the attentions of her admirer, and connived at water-parties by night on the Thames. Things went so far that, at last, the queen-dowager could endure Elizabeth's presence no longer, but dismissed her from her house in May 1548. This was done without any open scandal; the cause was kept a profound secret. Elizabeth was established at Cheshunt, and friendly correspondence continued between her and her former friends. Everything was done to repair past indiscretion and let it sink into oblivion.

Catherine, however, was deeply wounded and could not forget. On August 30 she bore a daughter, and died a week afterwards. . . .

Seymour, however, felt no remorse for his treatment of a wife who bequeathed him all that she possessed. Scarcely was she buried before he resumed his intrigues for gaining power by a new combination. He had bought from her father the wardship of the Lady Jane Grey, whom he kept in his house and designed to marry to the young king, while he himself married Elizabeth. He opened communications through Catherine Ashley, who told Elizabeth that Seymour, who would fain have married her before he married the queen, would soon come to woo. Elizabeth was certainly pleased at the prospect, and encouraged the proposal. But Seymour, ambitious as he was, could not conceal his projects, and Somerset was resolved to rid himself of his audacious brother. In January 1549, Lord Seymour was arrested on a charge of high treason. Elizabeth's governess, Catherine Ashley, and her steward, Thomas Parry, were carried away and imprisoned in the Tower. Elizabeth herself was confined to her house at Hatfield, under the guardianship of Sir Robert Tyrwhit, who was charged by the Council to examine her and discover evidence against Seymour.

It was a terrible position for a young girl who was not yet sixteen. Deprived of her only friends, not knowing what they might reveal, left alone to the mercy of an astute official, whose duty it was to examine her from day to day, and make her admit her guilt, she well might quail. Her honor, even her life, was at stake. She was at the mercy of her servants. She had not the unconsciousness of absolute innocence; and could only confide in the fidelity of her imprisoned attendants and in her own dexterity. At first, she burst into a flood of tears, and Tyrwhit thought that his task would be easy. He advised her to confess everything; the evil and shame would be ascribed to Catherine Ashley; she would be forgiven on the score of her youth. But Elizabeth soon regained her self-command in the face of danger. He could get nothing from her: "and yet," he writes, "I can see from her face that she is guilty, but she will abide more storms before she accuse Mrs. Ashley." The next day he succeeded no better, and could only repeat, "I do assure your Grace she hath a very good wit, and nothing is gotten of her but by great policy." Elizabeth would not commit herself, and in a week's time felt sufficiently secure of the reticence of her servants to write in a dignified strain to the protector, defending her reputation and protesting her innocence. "My conscience," she wrote, "beareth me witness, which I would not for all earthly things offend in anything, for I know I have a soul to save, as well as other folks have, wherefore I will above all things have respect unto this same."

As nothing could be discovered from Elizabeth, Tyrwhit turned his attention to her imprisoned steward, Parry, and extracted from him an account of the unseemly familiarities between his mistress and Lord Seymour. Catherine Ashley could not deny her knowledge of them, and furnished a few more particulars. Then Tyrwhit returned to Elizabeth and put the two confessions into her hand. She read them abashed and breathless. But when Tyrwhit told her that Catherine Ashley would say nothing till she was confronted with Parry, the Tudor rage broke forth. "False wretch," she cried, "he promised not to confess to death; how could he make such a promise and break it?" Yet, downcast as she was at reading the record of her indiscretion, she soon recovered her presence of mind. She saw that on the main points her servants had stood firm. They sacrificed Elizabeth's private character to maintain her political innocence. She had been a shameless flirt, but had never contemplated marrying Seymour without the consent of the Council. Elizabeth took her cue accordingly. Tyrwhit could extract nothing from her except scraps of foolish conversation about the possibility of such a marriage, in answer to which suggestions she always reserved the Council's assent. "They all sing the same song," said Tyrwhit wearily, "and so I think they would not do unless they had got the note before." After all his efforts, the girl of sixteen baffled the experienced man of affairs.

The Council proceeded against Seymour on other grounds, but administered a rebuke to Elizabeth in a letter which informed her: "Catherine Ashley, who hithertofore hath had the special charge to see to the good education and government of your person, hath shown herself far unmeet to occupy any such place longer about your Grace. Being informed that she hath not shewed herself so much attendant to her office in this past as we looked for at her hands, we have thought good somewhat to say roundly to her in that behalf." Elizabeth was informed that Lady Tyrwhit had been appointed in Catherine Ashley's stead, and was recommended to follow her good advice. At first, Elizabeth was furious. She would have no mistress save Catherine Ashley; she had not behaved so as to deserve the change. She wept all night, and sulked all the following day. Her mood was changed by a letter from the protector, which told her that Seymour's household was broken up, and enabled her to see that his ruin was imminent. Then Elizabeth's spirit began to droop, though she vigorously defended Seymour if anything was said against him. She wrote to the protector, remonstrating at the removal of Catherine Ashley as likely to corroborate the rumors which were current about her conduct. She asked that these rumors might be contradicted by a proclamation. This last request was gratified. But one of the articles against Seymour was that he had "attempted and gone about to marry the King's Majesty's sister, the Lady Elizabeth, second inheritor in remainder to the Crown." On March 20, 1549, Seymour's head fell on the scaffold.

This was a crushing experience for a girl of sixteen. It was undoubtedly the great crisis of Elizabeth's life, and did more than anything else to form her character. She learned, and she never forgot the lesson, that it was dangerous to follow her inclinations and indulge her affections. She dearly loved Seymour, with the ardor of a passionate girl. She was on the brink of a secret marriage with him, though she knew his coarse character and had been witness of the unhappiness of his former wife. She had a strong feeling of attachment for Catherine Ashley, and had trusted to her discretion. She learned the limitations of human trustworthiness, the inevitableness of personal responsibility. All this was an unwelcome revelation of life and its issues to herself. She must trust in herself and in herself only. Rigorous self-repression and self-restraint could

alone enable her to stand securely. Love, trust, confidence were all
beset with dangers. In the quietness which followed this period of
trial she thought out the meaning of what she had endured. She had
loved, and her lover had perished. She could ask herself what that
love had meant to her. Was it more than a temporary stirring of
the senses? Was it worth the risk which she had run, the imprudence
which she had committed? What would have been her future had
she married Seymour? Was he capable of loving her in return, or
was she merely a puppet in his hands, a piece in his game of political
self-seeking? She must have recalled his treatment of the queen-
dowager, whose tears she had seen flow, whose dying words of disappointment had been repeated to her. At the time, secure in her
own youthful charms, she had thought disdainfully of the middle-
aged queen. If she had become Seymour's wife, would she have
been any the happier? Would not she too have been abandoned
when her usefulness was past? She had seen the Lady Jane Grey,
an inmate of Seymour's house, another girl whose hand was of value
for an intriguer to dispose of. What place had love in such matters
as these? It was possible for a village maiden: it was an impossible
luxury for one who had a shred of claim to the throne of England.

We know how thoroughly Elizabeth understood these truths and
acted upon them later. Her success in so doing was due to the
severe teaching of experience. When she recovered from the shock
of Seymour's death and could look around her, she saw that it was
necessary to recover her character and restore her reputation. No
one could be better fitted to help her than Lady Tyrwhit, who was a
wise, sympathetic, and pious woman. She had formed one of the
household of the queen-dowager, knew what Elizabeth had gone
through, and could talk to her freely about the past. Under her
care Elizabeth once more lived a quiet and studious life, principally
at Hatfield. Ascham was summoned to be her tutor and was aston-
ished at the rapidity of her progress. When she had just entered
her seventeenth year she could speak French and Italian as well as
English; Latin with ease, Greek moderately. But her taste for literature
was genuine: she appreciated nice distinctions in the use of words,
and was a severe critic of style. She read with Ascham nearly the
whole of Cicero and Livy, Sophocles, and several orations of Iso-
crates, besides the Greek Testament, the writings of St. Cyprian and

the Commonplaces of Melanchthon. She was fond of music, but did not devote much time to it, nor to dress, in which she loved simplicity.

Her literary tastes were enduring; her love of simplicity soon passed away. Indeed, it was never real, and Ascham's mention of it shows that Elizabeth was acting a part. She had been detected as a shameless coquette; she adopted the attitude of a modest and pious maiden. It was the wisest thing which she could do; for the times were stormy, and their signs were hard to read. . . .

*   *   *

Few rulers ever ascended a throne better prepared for the task than did Elizabeth. The facts of her personal experience had corresponded with the experience of the nation. Her own life had been interwoven with the national life. She had been in imminent danger, both under Edward and under Mary. She had suffered, and had learned as the nation learned and suffered. She had lived amongst perils, and had been taught the need of prudence. Self-mastery and self-restraint had been forced upon her. Bitter experience had taught her how little she could satisfy her own desires, how little she could confide in the wisdom or discretion of others. She had spent long hours in enforced solitude and reflection as the drama of events passed before her. She had seen the failures of other lives, their disappointments, and their tragic end. And, in all this, she had been no idle spectator, but one whose own fortunes were deeply involved; and at each new turn of events men's minds had been more closely directed to her, so that her personal importance had been emphasized. She seemed to form part of all that the nation had passed through. Now she was called upon to amend the melancholy results of the ill-directed zeal of others, to bring back England to peace and security. For all men's hopes were set upon her as "born mere English, here among us, and therefore most natural to us." Men looked back to the days of Henry VIII, which loomed greater through the clouds of the past twelve years of misgovernment, to a time when at least there was an intelligible policy, and welcomed Elizabeth as the true inheritor of her father's spirit. Her training had been severe; but to that severity was due the character and the qualities which enabled her to face the work which lay before her.

She would not have had it otherwise, for it made her one with her people.

* * *

The character of Elizabeth is difficult to detach from her actions. She represented England as no other ruler ever did. For the greater part of her long reign the fortunes of England absolutely depended upon her life, and not only the fortunes of England, but those of Europe as well. If England had passed under the papal sway it is hard to see how Protestantism could have survived the repressive forces to which it would have been exposed. There were times when Elizabeth doubted if this could be avoided, times when any one, save Anne Boleyn's daughter, would have been tempted to make terms. In asking England to rally round her, Elizabeth knew that she could not demand any great sacrifices on her behalf. By cultivating personal loyalty, by demanding it in exaggerated forms, she was not merely feeding her personal vanity; she was creating a habit which was necessary for the maintenance of her government. By avoiding risky undertakings, by keeping down public expense, she was not merely indulging her tendency to parsimony; she was warding off from her people demands which they were unequal at that time to sustain.

Elizabeth's imperishable claim to greatness lies in her instinctive sympathy with her people. She felt, rather than understood, the possibilities which lay before England, and she set herself the task of slowly exhibiting, and impressing them on the national mind. She educated Englishmen to a perception of England's destiny, and for this purpose fixed England's attention upon itself. She caught at every advantage which was afforded by the divided condition of Europe to assert England's importance. France and Spain alike had deep causes of hostility; she played off one against the other, so that both were anxious for the friendship of a state which they each hoped some day to annex. England gained courage from this sight and grew in self-confidence. To obtain this result Elizabeth was careless of personal dignity or honor. She did not care how her conduct was judged at the time, but awaited the result.

It is this faculty of intuitive sympathy with her people which makes Elizabeth so difficult to understand in details of her policy. The fact was that she never faced a question in the shape in which it presented itself. It was true that it had to be recognized and discussed in that form; but Elizabeth had no belief in a policy because it could be clearly stated and promised well. Things had to be discussed, and decisions arrived at in consequence of such discussion; but action could always be avoided at the last moment, and Elizabeth would never act unless she felt that her people were in hearty agreement with her. Thus in her position towards her ministers she represented in her own person the vacillations and fluctuations of popular opinion. Ministers naturally wish to have an intelligible policy. Burghley laboriously drew up papers which balanced the advantages and disadvantages of alternative courses of action. Elizabeth read them and seemed to accept one out of two inevitable plans. She felt that, as a reasonable being, she could not do otherwise. But when it came to decisive action she fell back upon her instinctive perception of what England wanted. As she could not explain this, she was driven to all sorts of devices to gain time. She could not, on the other hand, fully take her people into her confidence. It was the unconscious tendency of their capacities which she interpreted, not their actual demands. She was eliciting from them their meaning, and educating them to understand it themselves. For this purpose she must seem to govern more absolutely than she did; but, on great occasions, she took them into her confidence, and fired them with a high conception of the greatness of their national life. She strove to focus and coordinate all their aspirations, and only repressed tendencies which were adverse to the formation of an English spirit; for she cared more for the spirit of the national life than for its outward organization.

Her private character is hard to detach from her public character. She behaved to those around her as she did to her people in general. She was surrounded by men representative of English life; they must be made to fall into line; and any method which served this purpose was good. Above all things she must impose her will equally on all. Personally, she was attracted by physical endowments, and let herself go in accordance with her feelings up to a certain point. But she was both intellectually and emotionally cold. In politics and in private life alike she cared little for decorum, because she knew that she could stop short whenever prudence made it needful.

It is easy to point out serious faults in Elizabeth, to draw out her inconsistencies, and define her character in a series of paradoxes. But this treatment does not exhibit the real woman, still less the real queen. Elizabeth was hailed at her accession as being "mere English"; and "mere English" she remained. Round her, with all her faults, the England which we know grew into the consciousness of its destiny. The process was difficult; the struggle was painful, and it left many scars behind. There are many things in Elizabeth which we could have wished otherwise; but she saw what England might become, and nursed it into the knowledge of its power.

Elizabeth Jenkins

A PSYCHOLOGICAL ASSESSMENT

Elizabeth Jenkins, a well-known English author, received her education at St. Christopher School, Letchworth, and Newnham College, Cambridge. Her special interest in biography is displayed in Jane Austen, a Biography *(1938) and* Henry Fielding *(1947). In addition to her widely read* Elizabeth the Great, *which attempts in part to probe the psychological makeup of the queen, Miss Jenkins has also written* Elizabeth and Leicester *(1961).*

On the king's death, Seymour proposed to the Council that he should marry Elizabeth, and Mrs. Ashley who thought the king himself had favored the idea was disappointed that the matter came to nothing. But Seymour received an unequivocal rebuff from the Council, and immediately renewed his old suit. The queen dowager, released from the sufferings of her marriage to Henry VIII, behaved like an enamored girl. She married Seymour secretly, and received his clandestine visits at her house in Chelsea, where her porteress let him in at five in the morning. The situation was full of submerged danger, for by the Council's permission Elizabeth was now living with her stepmother. Seymour, for all his geniality, was a man of

From Elizabeth Jenkins, *Elizabeth the Great* (New York: Coward-McCann, 1958), pp. 25–28, 80, 83–90, 95–96, 99–100. Copyright © 1958 by Elizabeth Jenkins. Reprinted by permission of the author.

ruthless ambition. He was twenty years older than Elizabeth, but as he was in his prime this meant only that he had the maturity a very young girl admires, and his attractions were of the kind to which she was susceptible all her life. He had been put into her head already as a possible husband, and now he was coming and going in romantic secrecy, in the first light of the May mornings, as the husband of her still-youthful stepmother.

Had Seymour left Elizabeth alone, no harm would have come of it; but one of his reasons for marrying the queen dowager was that Elizabeth had been consigned to her care. His brother had control of the king: he himself would have control of the king's enigmatic young sister. It was true that if she were drawn into any entanglement it might be regarded as high treason, and that the penalty for this was, for a woman, beheading or burning alive. Seymour knew these facts, but he preferred to disregard them.

The queen dowager's household was a charming one. Beyond it, indeed, matters were stormy. Seymour was perpetually at variance with his brother, refusing to accept his authority or to carry out his own duties as lord admiral, while the situation between the brothers was the more embittered by the hostility of their wives. The Duchess of Somerset, eminently strong-minded and disagreeable, had once been obliged to treat Catherine Parr with ceremonious respect; she now took pains to show her that the queen dowager was merely the wife of the protector's younger brother. This occasioned anger abroad, but at home all was pleasure, ease, and a delightful freedom from past restraints.

The princess's household formed a unit within the queen dowager's; it included Mrs. Ashley, the tutor, young Mr. Grindal,[1] and several ladies-in-waiting. There was also attached to it a man who would seem to have had more sense than all the rest put together: this was the princess's distant cousin John Ashley. In the months after the king's death he gave his wife a warning "to take heed for he did fear that the Lady Elizabeth did bear some affection to my Lord Admiral." He had noticed that she looked pleased and sometimes blushed when Seymour was spoken of. His wife was coarser-fibered; either she saw no danger, or in the congenial atmosphere of

---

[1] William Grindal, a friend of the humanist Roger Ascham; Grindal died of the plague in 1548.

ease and pleasure with the exciting undercurrent that Seymour's presence brought, she would not recognize it.

Seymour went openly to work. He began romping with the princess, and his wife did what many women do in such a case: to prove to herself and everybody else that there was no harm in the romp, she joined it herself. There was no doubt as to Elizabeth's state of mind—Ashley had recognized it at once; but with the passion there was considerable fear. Seymour's boisterous approaches were liable to be alarming to a girl of fourteen, and one with who knows what buried dread of men? Seymour would come into her bedchamber in the mornings. If she were up "he would strike her familiarly on the back and buttocks." If she were in bed he would open the bed curtain "and make as though he would come at her," while she "would go further into the bed." One morning he tried to kiss her in her bed, at which Mrs. Ashley, who slept in the princess's room, "bade him go away for shame." Elizabeth's bedroom, at Chelsea and at Seymour's town house, Seymour Place, was above the queen dowager's, and Seymour used to come up "in his nightgown, bare-legged in his slippers." Mrs. Ashley told him "it was a shame to see a man come so, bare-legged, to a maiden's chamber," but her protests were not taken seriously. The queen dowager, however, took to coming with her husband on his morning visits and one morning they both tickled the princess as she lay in her bed. In the garden one day there was some startling horseplay, in which Seymour indulged in a practice often heard of in police courts: the queen dowager held Elizabeth so that she could not run away, while Seymour cut her black cloth gown into a hundred pieces. The cowering under bedclothes, the struggling and running away, culminated in a scene of classical nightmare, that of helplessness in the power of a smiling ogre. Seymour had possessed himself of a master key, and early one morning at Chelsea, Elizabeth heard the privy lock undo, and, "knowing he would come in"— Seymour, smiling in his long red beard—"she ran out of her bed to her maidens and then went behind the curtains of the bed, the maidens being there; and my Lord tarried a long time in hopes she would come out." Afterwards, "she was commonly up and at her book" by the time Seymour came, and then he would merely look in at the door and say good morning. But he had overcome her initial resistance; the queen dowager, who was undergoing an uncomfortable pregnancy, could not bring herself to make her husband angry by protesting about his conduct, but she began to realize that he and Elizabeth were very often together; then one day in May, she went into a room unexpectedly and found Elizabeth in his arms.

There was no quarrel and no public appearance of her being sent away in disgrace, but it was decided she should remove with her establishment to the house of Sir Anthony Denny at Cheshunt. She and her train arrived there just after Whitsun, and Elizabeth wrote to her stepmother to say that at their parting she had been too much moved to thank her properly for her kindness, so sad was she to go away, leaving her "in doubtful health," and, she said, "albeit I answered little, I weighed it the more, when you said you would warn me of all evils you should hear of me, for if your Grace had not a good opinion of me, you would not have offered friendship to me that way."

The abrupt parting from Seymour, the disgrace and the contrition, and the warring of sexual excitement with deep-buried dread, all this coming upon her at the critical age of fourteen and a half, coincided with, if it did not bring on, an illness. In Mrs. Ashley's words: "She was first sick about midsummer." At times she was "sick in her bed," and so unwell for the rest of the year that Mrs. Ashley said she herself had never been more than a mile from the house.

For the next few years, the princess suffered from intermittent ill health; she developed migraine attacks and pains in the eyes, and by the time she was twenty it was a matter of common rumor, of particular interest to ambassadors, that her monthly periods were very few or none, a condition often accounted for by shock and emotional strain. In Elizabeth's history, the events of her mother's death, and that of her mother's cousin, and the engaging of her own affections by Seymour's outrageous siege, seem to have done her nervous system and her sexual development an injury from which they never recovered. . . .

The queen's suitors now included Prince Charles of Sweden, the Duke of Saxony, and the Archduke Charles; but the talk was all of Lord Robert Dudley. It was widely supposed that the queen was his mistress. Bishop Quadra, who had replaced Feria at the Spanish embassy, wrote to the latter: "I have heard great things of a sort that cannot be written about and you will understand what they must be by that." Sir Thomas Challoner was dismayed by reports that reached him at the imperial court. He considered them mere slander, but, he said, "so young a Princess cannot be too wary what countenance or familiar demonstration she makes more to one than another." Above all, what distressed him was this "delay of ripe time for marriage"; he saw no safety for the realm without heirs of the queen's body.

*   *   *

The queen had made an excellent beginning but those nearest to her who wished to gaze upon her with approval found their vision blocked by Lord Robert Dudley.

Protective and adoring, the master of the horse fulfilled his office thoroughly to the queen's satisfaction. He wrote to the Earl of Sussex in Ireland that the queen would like some Irish horses sent over, thinking that they might go faster than hers, "which," he said, "she spareth not to try as fast as they can go. And I fear them much, yet she will prove them." But to the anxious councillors the satisfaction he gave to the queen was far too great. In their view it accounted for her disinclination to marry, and her marriage was an object they desired with increasing fervor. During the negotiations in Scotland Cecil had written to her, praying that "God would direct your Highness to procure a father for your children . . . neither peace nor war without this will profit us long," and all the answer the queen had made was to reject the Scots' offer of the hand of the Earl of Arran. The queen's youth and her glamorous appearance, and the fact that Dudley's young wife was living apart from her husband, gave their intimacy a scandalous air. Amy Dudley had no children and no proper establishment of her own; she and her servants occupied part of a house at Cumnor, near Oxford, belonging to a man called Forster, who had been Lord Robert's steward. The house, isolated among fields and orchards, had originally been part of a monastery. Horse transport and bad roads made every rural district secluded and remote, but a surprising number of people knew about Lady Dudley in her lonely situation. Then they heard that on September 8, a Sunday, she had been found at the bottom of a staircase with her neck broken.

The scandal was appalling. In France, Mary Stuart said with a ringing laugh: "The Queen of England is going to marry her horse-keeper, who has killed his wife to make room for her." Throckmorton, the ambassador at Paris, wrote to Cecil: "I know not where to turn me, or what countenance to make."

Elizabeth sent Lord Robert away from Windsor at once, and he himself wrote begging his cousin Blount to go to Cumnor to take charge of everything: "The greatness, and suddenness of this misfortune doth so perplex me, until I do hear from you how the matter stands or how this evil doth light upon me, considering what the malicious world will bruit, as I can take no rest." He urged Blount to make sure that the coroner's jury were "discreet and substantial persons," who would sift the matter to the bottom.

The verdict at the inquest was accidental death, but in the general opinion it should have been murder, either at Dudley's instigation, or without his connivance but in his interest. The question, all-important though hardly to be framed, was whether the queen had been accessory before the fact.

De Quadra told Philip that the queen had said to him as she came in from hunting that Lady Dudley had fallen down a staircase and broken her neck, and asked him to say nothing about it. He made out that the queen had said this before the news of the death was brought to Windsor on the ninth. Had Elizabeth connived at the murder, it may be safely asserted that she would not have been so grossly stupid as to tell de Quadra the death had occurred, before she was supposed to know that it had. The explanation, suggested by Maitland and also by Pollard, is that de Quadra here employed "a deft economy of dates." Nor can it be taken for granted that Elizabeth wanted Amy Dudley out of the way. She wanted an engrossing romantic relationship with Robert Dudley; there is no proof that she wanted a marriage with him, only that other people supposed she wanted it. If she did not want the marriage, the death was for her an untoward event; now that it could be expected to end in a marriage, her delicious amusement was brought into the realm of state affairs.

When the news was known, Elizabeth had dismissed Lord Robert from the court with orders not to show himself there again till his wife was buried. A few weeks after the funeral, however, he returned; and Elizabeth had now to face the position that if she went on with the liaison she would be expected to marry her lover. The fear that she might, as Throckmorton put it, "so foully forget herself," made the ambassador say that if that day came, he himself would not wish to live. Indeed, the prospect of her wedding to Robert Dudley aroused general abhorrence. He was the son of a traitor,[2] he was suspected of wife-murder, it was believed that he had dishonored the queen already: all those sound reasons reinforced the inevitable ones of envy and jealousy. Yet there was one voice prepared to speak in his favor, that of Sussex, whose chivalry toward Elizabeth was pure, tender, and constant. He disliked Dudley to such an extent that their relationship was almost a standing quarrel, but he wrote to Cecil in October, saying that they were all agreed that a child of the queen's body was their greatest necessity. Therefore, said Sussex, let her choose after her own affection, let her take the man at sight of whom all her being was aroused in desire; for that was the way to bring them a blessed prince, and, he affirmed, "whomsoever she will choose, him will I love and honour and serve to the uttermost."

Whatever feelings were aroused at the idea of Robert Dudley's wearing the Crown Matrimonial, it was taken for granted that the queen must want him for her husband. The only question seemed to be, how far she would let I-dare-not wait upon I-would. It was not yet realized how keenly, how exquisitely Elizabeth enjoyed conducting courtships and marriage negotiations which she never intended to complete. The series of brilliant diplomatic maneuvers involving marriage alliances with the princes of the House of Valois, which were to be so invaluable for the next twenty years, carried conviction while they lasted because it was plain that the queen enjoyed every moment of them. To be the object of public and magnificent courtship, with ambassadors, letters, and presents, to be intensely desired in marriage, for whatever reason, was to her a fascinating, an absorbing diversion. To talk of love, to talk of marriage, above all, to listen while someone talked, or was talked of, as wanting to marry her, gave her an exhilaration that was the keener because such feelings had to do duty for others that had been put to death. But when she came to the edge of the precipice, and it looked as if she might have to endure a hard struggle to avoid being pushed over it, then nervous strain began to show itself. Sir Nicholas Throckmorton at Paris had sent his secretary Jones to

---

[2] i.e., John Dudley, Duke of Northumberland.

the queen to tell her, among other things, what the French view was of the rumors about Dudley. Jones reported on November 30: "The Queen's Majesty looketh not so hearty and well as she did by a great deal, and surely the matter of my Lord Robert doth much perplex her and is never like to take place."

The strange state of mind was the harder to recognize in connection with Robert Dudley because his presence, his lovemaking, his mere name mentioned in conversation, gave her such obvious delight. Therefore when, early in 1561, Sir Henry Sidney approached de Quadra with a secret proposal that the king of Spain should give his support to the marriage of the queen with Lord Robert Dudley, in return for Elizabeth's restoring Catholicism as the national religion, it seemed, even to de Quadra's intelligent mind, a plausible proposition. Sir Henry Sidney was the husband of Dudley's sister Mary; there was no doubt that he and Dudley were eager for the scheme, and there seemed on the face of it no reason to doubt that the queen's wishes were the same as theirs. The ambassador sent Philip a detailed account of a conversation with the queen, in which Elizabeth had said that she had indeed some affection for Lord Robert but had never decided to marry him, or anybody else. Nevertheless, de Quadra believed, from her avid enjoyment in talking of the matter, that she was prepared to make the match, and on the conditions proposed. To all of which Philip merely replied: "Get it in writing, with her signature."

On Midsummer Day, Lord Robert gave a water party on the Thames. As he, the queen, and de Quadra were all together on deck, Lord Robert, who was talking amorous nonsense to the queen, exclaimed that the bishop might as well marry them then and there. Elizabeth said she doubted if he knew enough English to perform the ceremony. De Quadra interposed gravely. He said, let the queen first free herself of Cecil and his gang of heretics; she could then do as she pleased, and he himself would gladly be the priest to marry her and Lord Robert. This brilliant scene on the midsummer Thames, with Lord Robert as the eager, almost assured lover of the queen, appeared decisive from the political standpoint. That it was, in itself, intensely enjoyable, and that since a marriage negotiation with Philip was no longer possible, one with his protégé was, diplomatically, of almost equal value, appeared to strike nobody.

The general view was that the queen was being carried away by her feelings to a marriage that would be catastrophic.

The urgent wish that Elizabeth should not make a ruinous marriage was paralleled by the anxiety that she should make a good one and as soon as possible. The pressure upon her to do this now received a sudden and painful impetus.

If Elizabeth died without heirs, her successor by Henry VIII's will was Catherine, the elder of the two surviving sisters of Jane Grey. This young woman was nineteen years old. Though gentle and feminine she had a strong sense of her own importance; she was easily influenced by anyone who paid her attention and easily offended by the appearance of a slight. Emotional and lacking in common sense, she was fated, in her dangerous situation, to be both a nuisance and a victim.

Elizabeth's experience of how the heir is courted at the expense of the reigning monarch had made her determine never to recognize a successor. The lesson had been seared into her memory and it was acted upon with all the force of her intellect. But Catherine Grey cared nothing for this; she resented the fact that Elizabeth had not at once accorded her the position of heiress-presumptive to the crown. Feria had found that she was "discontented and offended" because she had not been given this official status. The mere fact that she claimed it should have taught Catherine Grey to behave with the utmost discretion. It was generally understood that royal blood conferred a condition like that of hemophilia, in which one reckless contact might result in death. In Catherine's own family the truth had been driven home with shocking force. Her sister Jane at fourteen had been one of the most renowned young ladies in Protestant Europe; at sixteen she was a headless corpse. But Catherine understood her situation only in terms of how other people should behave to her; she had no idea of what it demanded of herself. To her, Elizabeth was merely her disagreeable cousin who had once been obliged to walk out of the room after Catherine's mother. She was heard to speak "very arrogant and unseemly words in the presence of the Queen." Feria saw that, married to the archduke, or to Don Carlos, this sprig of the English royal stem would be a valuable Spanish asset. He cultivated her closely, but no move was made, and when de Quadra replaced him, the latter reported that "the Queen was making much of Lady Catherine to keep her quiet." The Duchess of Suffolk was in her last illness, and with disastrous irresponsibility she encouraged a clandestine courtship between Catherine and the young Earl of Hertford, son of the late Protector Somerset. Hertford's sister, Lady Jane Seymour, a charming but delicate girl, was one of Elizabeth's favorite maids of honor; she was also Catherine Grey's best friend, and as Lord Hertford's dilatory and languid courtship caused Catherine much jealous misery, he was brought up to scratch by his frail but energetic sister. The wedding took place secretly in the winter of 1560, in Hertford's lodging. The clergyman whom Lady Jane had fetched in was unknown by name to the bride or bridegroom, and she herself was the sole witness.

In the following March this resolute girl died suddenly, and the queen, much distressed, ordered her a state funeral in Westminster Abbey. Soon afterwards Hertford was appointed to go to France. He made no move to avoid the mission, but before he disappeared, he gave his wife a deed of jointure,[3] settling on her £1,000 a year. This document was not only her sole claim to her husband's support; as the clergyman was unknown and the single witness dead, it was the one and only proof that the marriage had taken place. It is hardly necessary to say what happened: Lady Catherine lost the deed, so completely that she never afterwards "knew where it was become." This was the lady who was eager to take over the cares of government from Queen Elizabeth.

It was August and the queen was going on a progress through Suffolk and Norfolk. She had the look of someone greatly oppressed; so pale was she, it was said "she looked like one lately come out of childbed." The question of marriage, pressing heavily on her, sharpened her irritation at the sights which met her at Ipswich and Norwich, of the squalid and disordered state to which wives and children had reduced the cathedral and college precincts. On progress as she was, the queen at once wrote out an ordinance and sent copies of it for publication to the archbishops of Canterbury and York, forbidding the presence of women in cathedral or

[3] A deed of jointure provides for the joint holding of property by a husband and wife, with the estate passing to the latter in the event of widowhood.

college lodgings; it was an interruption of studies, she said, and contrary to the intentions of the founders.

Matthew Parker, Archbishop of Canterbury, had once been chaplain to Ann Boleyn. Scholarly, grave, gentle, and courageous, he had hoped to spend the rest of his life in a university. To be the primate of England was the last thing he himself would have chosen. Elizabeth, with her remarkable insight in making appointments, offered him the see of Canterbury, and when he declined it, she positively refused to take no for an answer. When Dr. Parker at last submitted, he told Cecil that one of the considerations which influenced him was that he could never forget what Ann Boleyn had said to him about her child, six weeks before her own death. He did not say what the words had been, but his tenderness for Elizabeth was obvious, in spite of the disapproval of some of her doings which, as he saw occasion, he courageously expressed. Elizabeth treated him with the bad behavior of a spoiled and irritable girl who knows she may say what she likes to an old friend of the family. She told him this summer that she disapproved of married bishops and wished she had not appointed any. Dr. Parker, a married man, did not say that he wished she had thought of this before she insisted on appointing him, but he gently reminded her that the idea of a celibate clergy was a Catholic, not a Protestant, one; whereupon the queen's self-control gave way. "She took occasion to speak in that bitterness of the holy estate of matrimony . . ." that the archbishop in his own words to Cecil, "was in a horror to hear her." In this frame of mind, Elizabeth was visiting the great houses of Suffolk, with Lord Robert Dudley in attendance and Lady Catherine Grey among the ladies-in-waiting.

The latter was now in miserable plight: she was pregnant, her mother was dead, and she could get no word from her husband in France, though other ladies had received presents from him. While the court was at Ipswich, she decided to make her case known to Lady Saintlow, a brisk matron who after several profitable marriages became known as the redoubtable Bess of Hardwick. Lady Saintlow's response was to call down curses on the wretched girl for making her party to such a secret. Lady Catherine's next bestowal of her confidence was even more unwelcome. At dead of night she glided to the bedchamber of her dead sister's brother-in-law, Lord Robert

Dudley, and poured out at his bedside the story of her deplorable mishaps. The possibility of the queen's hearing of a woman in his bedroom electrified Lord Robert; he obliged Lady Catherine to remove herself, and the next morning he told Elizabeth the facts.

The mere unfounded suspicion of a secret marriage had once brought Elizabeth herself into extreme peril, so gravely was such an act regarded in anyone who claimed to be in succession to the throne. That Lady Catherine should be removed that afternoon from Ipswich to the Tower, and Lord Hertford sent for, was a matter of course. But Elizabeth's fury had another source beside the uncovering of potential treason. She had been urged by the Privy Council and by Parliament to marry and become a mother, and this was the thing she could neither face nor bring herself to say she could not do. It remained to be seen whether her brilliance, her dedication, her hold on the public imagination would outweigh the lack of the one, primitive, essential service of bearing a child. Meanwhile, the heiress-presumptive was bearing one.

*   *   *

Among the suitors who were entertained and rejected, one still kept the field. Lord Robert Dudley intended to marry the queen and was pursuing his quarry with steady determination. Once, at least, it was said that he had succeeded. In June 1562, de Quadra had told the queen point-blank that he heard everywhere she had been secretly married to Lord Robert. The queen admitted that the rumor had somehow got about, and that when she had come back that afternoon from the Earl of Pembroke's house and entered her Presence Chamber with Lord Robert, her ladies had asked if they were to kiss his hand as well as hers. She had told them no, and that they must not believe everything they heard. In other walks of life, the matter was given a ruder turn. . . .

When she swore on what she thought was her deathbed "that nothing improper had passed between Lord Robert and her," and at the same time asked for a lavish pension to be given to the servant who slept in his bedchamber, she indicated the nature of their relationship, that it was a sexual one which stopped short only of the sexual act. No one who saw her among men doubted her extreme susceptibility to male attraction; it was in fact more than ordinary; but it would seem that the harm which had been done to Elizabeth as a small child had resulted in an irremediable condition of nervous shock. Saint Ignatius said: "Give me the child till he is seven, and afterwards anyone may have him"; and the discoveries of the present age have only confirmed the strength of the influence of early impressions. In a creature of such intensity and power, the emotions connected with a vital instinct were, inevitably, of tremendous force. Held up in the arms of her imploring mother to her terrible father as he frowned down upon them: hearing that a sword had cut off her mother's head: that her young stepmother had been dragged shrieking down the gallery when she tried to reach the king to entreat his mercy—these experiences, it would appear, had built up a resistance that nothing, no passion, no entreaty, no tenderness, could conquer. In the fatally vulnerable years she had learned to connect the idea of sexual intercourse with terror and death; in the dark and low-lying region of the mind where reason cannot penetrate, she knew that if you give yourself to men, they cut your head off with a sword, an ax. The bloodstained key that frightens the girl in "Blue-Beard" is a symbol merely of the sexual act; in Elizabeth's case, the symbol had a frightful actuality of its own. It was the executioner's steel blade, running with blood.

Even the ostensible fears, the loss of liberty and submission of will, were so strong that they made the prospect of marriage seem an alienation of herself. She told the French ambassador de Foix that whenever she thought about marriage, she felt as if someone were tearing the heart out of her bosom. Up to the point of capitulation, however, she enjoyed being made love to with an abnormal avidity that was the penalty of a deranged instinct; and as she never passed the point at which nature transforms the adoring suitor into the complacent lover, the element of worship that was incense to her vanity was perpetually prolonged.

John Ernest Neale

MARRIAGE AND
POLITICAL CONSIDERATIONS

One of the outstanding Elizabethan scholars of the twentieth century, John Ernest Neale was born in Liverpool in 1890. He was educated at the Universities of Liverpool and London, and taught at the University of Manchester, Oxford University, University College of North Wales, and the British Academy. From 1927 to 1956 he was Astor Professor of English History at the University of London. The recipient of numerous honorary degrees, Neale was knighted in 1955. He has served as a member of the Editorial Board of the History of Parliament. Among his many noted works are The Elizabethan House of Commons *(1949) and* Essays in Elizabethan History *(1958). His biography of Elizabeth was awarded the James Tait Black Memorial Prize for Biography in 1934.*

Elizabeth was far and away the best marriage to be had in Europe, a fact of which every eligible bachelor and widower was aware. Philip II realized it, and among the duties which brought Feria[1] to England on the eve of Elizabeth's accession, was the management of this market. Philip had not yet made up his mind whether he wanted to marry her himself, but Feria was to see that whoever obtained the tidbit received it at his master's hands. The ambassador imagined himself playing much the same role as Simon Renard[2] at the accession of Mary; and there was good reason for his expectations. In her sister's reign, as my Lady Elizabeth, the focus of discontent, Elizabeth had naturally been friendly with France, but times had changed, and unless she was to repeat Mary's blunder, she would have to live in the present, not the past. The present meant hostility to France, where a rival claimant to the English throne was the dauphin's wife. It meant also friendship with Spain; nay, possibly dependence on Spain, for England was in a dangerous state. Its finances were in disorder, its fortresses defenseless, its military forces negligible, while to emerge honorably from the peace nego-

From J. E. Neale, *Queen Elizabeth I* (New York, 1934), pp. 68–82. Reprinted by permission of Sir John Neale and Jonathan Cape Ltd.

[1] Gomez Suarez de Figueroa, Count of Feria, Philip II's first ambassador to the court of Elizabeth.
[2] The ambassador of Charles V and a confidant of Mary Tudor's.

tiations, closing Mary's unfortunate war with France, it must have Philip's support.

No wonder Feria was patronizing! He was surprised that Elizabeth did not see the situation as clearly as he did; but then, he remarked, "what can be expected from a country governed by a Queen, and she a young lass who, although sharp, is without prudence?" He was exasperated at the cool manner in which he was treated. Instead of being given a room at court and taken into counsel on every question, as he expected, he found himself in embarrassing ignorance of what was going on. "They run away from me as if I were the devil," he wrote; and their glib, irresponsible talk nearly drove him crazy. At first there was an arrogant confidence in his reports. On November 21 he thought that his master had merely to ask for Elizabeth in order to have her: "If she decides to marry out of the country she will at once fix her eyes on your Majesty." A month later his assurance had evaporated: "I am afraid that one fine day we shall find this woman married, and I shall be the last man in the place to know anything about it."

The warning made Philip apply the spur to his slow-moving mind. On January 10 he wrote to Feria that his doubts on the subject of marriage with Elizabeth were many: he could not be much in England owing to the claims of his other dominions; then Elizabeth had been unsound in religion, and marrying her would seem like entering upon a perpetual war with France, owing to Mary Queen of Scots' claim to the throne; again, he would find himself involved in costly entertainments in England, which his treasury was not in a state to afford; there were other difficulties, equally grave. However, it was important that England should not relapse into its old religious errors, and for this reason he was prepared to put aside all doubts and marry her, as a service to God. But it could only be on conditions: she must profess his religion and maintain it in her country; she must obtain secret absolution from the pope. In this way it would be evident to the world that he was serving the Lord in marrying her and that she had been converted by his act.

Pathetic illusion! It would be hard to imagine ruminations more remote from reality. If Englishmen in 1553 had loathed the prospect of a Spanish marriage, how much more did the tragic experience of Mary's reign make them loathe it now? The mere suspicion that Elizabeth was hesitating, brought a torrent of dissuasions from her councillors. They were needless. The lessons of yesterday were as clear in her mind as in anyone's. Did she not boast that she was "descended by father and mother of mere English blood, and not of Spain, as her late sister was"? But it was inexpedient to refuse Philip's offer at once, for the peace negotiations with France were still proceeding, and she was in an appreciably stronger position to bargain, with Philip as her suitor; moreover, Parliament was about to meet in order to reverse the religious settlement of Mary's reign, and there was a double service that Philip could perform. He could keep the pope quiet, and avoid giving the English Catholic opposition a lead.

Feria was therefore well received when he broached the subject. She must consult her parliament, Elizabeth said, but Philip could be certain that if she married at all she would prefer him. The lie earned a month's breathing space, at the end of which she again managed to evade an answer. Early in March, unable to prevaricate longer, she announced that she had no desire to marry. The advantages of the marriage to both sovereigns, she urged, could be attained by a continuance of their good friendship. With malicious humor, she asked Feria how she could possibly marry her sister's husband without dishonoring the memory of her father, he having repudiated his brother's wife. Some of her remarks looked so much like an echo of Philip's complacent letter of January 10 that the ambassador was left wondering whether his correspondence was tapped, and he was even more uneasy when at his next interview she turned the tables on Philip by declaring that she would not marry him as she was a heretic. That ended the wooing. Philip married the French king's daughter[3]—a diplomatic setback for Elizabeth, but unavoidable. She accepted the news with an easy air, now and again giving little sighs that bordered on laughter. Philip, she remarked, had a fortunate name. Feria tried to impress upon her a proper sense of her blunder; she retorted that it was all Philip's fault, for she had given no answer, and he could not have been much in love, since he had not had the patience to wait four months for her.

As a matter of fact, Elizabeth was far from blind to her interests, as Feria thought. She knew as well as he that she needed Philip's

---

[3] Elizabeth of Valois, eldest daughter of Henry II, in accord with the Treaty of Cateau-Cambrésis.

support, but she knew also that Philip was not a free agent, and that as the rival of France and the ruler of the Netherlands, commercially dependent upon England, he could not afford to desert her. She might exploit Philip just as much as he exploit her, and which should be the victim depended on their temper, wit, and acumen. Philip told his ambassador to frighten Elizabeth and make her thoroughly understand that she was ruined unless he succored and defended her; but this done, she was to be assured that he would never fail to help her, both on account of his great love and affection, which his marriage alliance with France would not weaken, and also for his own interests, which would be greatly injured if—as God forbid!—her kingdom were to fall into other hands. Could naivety go farther? Neither master nor servant was a match for the young woman at the diplomatic game of bluff. "I try all I can to keep her pleasant and in good humour," Feria wrote, "and although sometimes I speak to her very freely, as I ought to do, having right and truth on my side, yet I think that for this very reason she does not get tired of me, but likes to discuss matters with me." Like to discuss matters with him! there is no doubt that she did. She poured out nonsense and wit, shifted her ground and her sentiments, until, sometimes convinced of his great influence, at other times he was bewildered and angry. "In short," he wrote on one of the latter occasions, "what can be said here to your Majesty is only that this country after thirty years of a government such as your Majesty knows, has fallen into the hands of a woman who is a daughter of the Devil, and the greatest scoundrels and heretics in the land."

Philip was only one, the most transient and so the most fortunate, of Elizabeth's suitors. The king of Sweden's ambassador was in England offering his master's eldest son, Eric, as he had done a year before, and bestowing lavish presents on the ladies and gentlemen of the court, who took his gifts but laughed at his outlandish ways. The emperor, also, was bidding on behalf of his two younger sons, the Archdukes Ferdinand and Charles; and with Philip out of the market, the imperial and Spanish ambassadors joined forces to bring off yet another fortunate marriage for the House of Hapsburg. Feria was confident of success; confident, if only the emperor and his sons would understand, which apparently they would not, that the marriage was virtually in Philip's gift! At first, both sons were mentioned, but Ferdinand the elder was soon withdrawn, for his Catholicism was unassailable and his father had learned that Elizabeth was not sound in religion. It was distressing enough to offer Charles, whose youthful judgment was less firmly based; and the emperor confessed to his ambassador that without weighty political reasons he would not have thought of subjecting his son to the danger of forfeiting the eternal salvation of his soul.

At home, among Englishmen, two names were being canvassed, the Earl of Arundel[4] and Sir William Pickering. Arundel had nothing but rank and family to commend him. He was about forty-seven, not handsome, and rather silly and loutish; he had been married twice and had two married daughters. They were disabilities, which in that age of mercenary marriage customs and moving love lyrics, would have mattered little if the disparity of rank had been reversed. Pickering was about forty-two, tall, handsome, very much a ladies' man, and said to have enjoyed the intimacy of many. These qualities, not rank or fortune, gave him hope; and perhaps there was an old friendly attachment between the queen and him. Londoners rather favored his chances and took bets on them, while he himself, courted by councillors and others with their eyes on the future, lost his head and plunged into an extravagant life, giving himself airs by dining apart, with music playing. One day the talk went that he was sending a challenge to the Earl of Bedford for speaking ill of him. Six or seven weeks later he was quarreling with Arundel who had stopped him as he went through to the Chapel inside the queen's apartments, saying that he knew quite well that a man of his rank had no right to be there; his place was in the Presence Chamber. Pickering answered that of course he knew, as he also knew that Arundel was an impudent, discourteous knave.

Suitors, statesmen, everyone, talked of marriage. They assumed, as a matter of course, that Elizabeth would marry. All women did, who could; and the political reasons in Elizabeth's case seemed overwhelming. When Parliament met at the end of January 1559, the House of Commons urged this step on her. She answered that since reaching years of understanding she had chosen the virgin life, and if ambition, or danger, or the peril of death could have led her into marriage, she would not now be in that trade of life with

---

[4] Henry Fitzalan, whom Elizabeth appointed lord high steward and lord great chamberlain on the eve of her coronation.

which she was so thoroughly acquainted and in which God had preserved her. They could assure themselves, she went on, that whenever it might please God to incline her heart to marry, her choice would light upon one who would be as careful for the preservation of the realm as she herself; or if it pleased Him to continue her still in this mind to live unmarried, provision would be made for the succession to the throne. "And in the end," she concluded, "this shall be for me sufficient, that a marble stone shall declare that a Queen, having reigned such a time lived and died a virgin."

Being men of the world, the Commons did not think that there was anything alarming in this prating about virginity. Let political considerations or passion single out some man, and another protesting spinster would go the way of most flesh. Her virgin state, which Elizabeth ascribed to a godly vocation, might with more conviction be ascribed to politics, for she had been forced to eschew marriage in the past to avoid being a pawn for either Northumberland or Philip. Experience, no doubt, had left its effect. The Seymour affair, at the age of fifteen, had been her first cautionary tale: and as her many perils had grafted a wary mind upon an impulsive nature, so in regard to marriage she found herself thinking twice, and thinking yet again. Among the legion of her remarks on the subject, some false, some true, and some betwixt and between—and which were which no one really knew—she said that marriage was a matter of earnest with her and that she could not marry as others did. On the other hand, she confessed that "she was but human and not insensible to human emotions and impulses, and when it became a question of the weal of her kingdom, or it might be for other reasons, her heart and mind might change."

The weal of the kingdom or *other reasons:* the latter had to wait on fancy and the emotions, the former did not. In abstract the public good required marriage, but in practice everything depended upon the person, and principally whether he was to be a subject or a foreigner. Naturally, Elizabeth had the lessons of Mary's reign in mind when she faced the problem. The country had then wanted Courtenay[5] for king, a person, thanks to his Yorkist descent, whom Mary could have married without serious risk of arousing the

[5] Edward Courtenay, Earl of Devon, great grandson of Edward IV.

jealousy of her nobles. By the irony of fate England had then had a queen out of tune with her people, while now that the situation was reversed, there was no Courtenay. Perhaps the fevers of Padua, which took his life, were to give England a virgin queen. At any rate, there seemed to be some risk of this, for what Englishman was there to replace Courtenay? Pickering, whom, for lack of a better, many would have liked, was at daggers drawn with some of the nobility; and there was no other whom Elizabeth could have married without a fair certainty of setting her nobility by the ears. Celibacy might be the better of the two evils.

A foreigner offered no better prospect. Elizabeth was prejudiced by the knowledge that Mary's major blunder had been her marriage, and by the feeling that a foreign match would be unpopular. Her doubts might have disappeared if court and Council had given a unanimous lead; but some were for one candidate, some for another. The result was that she kept on hesitating, ever ready to dilate on the attractions of a maiden life, baffling everyone with her art and wit and coquetry. She had never purposed never to marry, she told them; but they must believe her when she said that she had never had a mind to marry.

Ambassadors kept up their siege. In October 1559, there were ten or twelve competing for Elizabeth's favor and eyeing one another in far from friendly manner. Cecil was just as perplexed as they were: "How he shall speed," he said of one envoy, "God knoweth and not I." Feria's successor, Bishop Quadra, rang every change of mood: one day he did not understand her; another day he was confident that the archduke would get her; another day he qualified his hopes; and then he was in despair and angry. "Your Lordship," he told Feria, "will see what a pretty business it is to have to treat with this woman, who I think must have a hundred thousand devils in her body, notwithstanding that she is for ever telling me that she yearns to be a nun and to pass her time in a cell praying." In another blue mood, he lost all hope in the affairs of this woman. "With her all is falsehood and vanity."

Elizabeth was not entirely to blame for all protracted wooings. She was a great prize, and hope is tenacious. It was incredibly tenacious in Eric of Sweden. After being formally turned down in May 1559, he announced in July that as soon as she gave the word he would hasten to her through seas, dangers, and enemies, confident that she would not chide his faith and zeal. A second, a third, a fourth rejection—and more; he nevertheless remained buoyant. His brother was in England from the autumn of 1559 till the following spring, a munificent but unsuccessful envoy. The following August he set out himself, and though turned back by the winds, started again, only desisting in the face of a storm that scattered and damaged his fleet. Fortune, he wrote to Elizabeth, had been harder than steel and more cruel than Mars; but as he had attempted to come to her through the stormy seas, so would he at her first summons rush through armies of foes.

Even Elizabeth found courtship wearing at times. But it had compensations, for during the year 1559, when the weak, poverty-stricken England of Feria's imagination was pursuing a policy that annoyed the papacy, troubled Philip, and threatened to lead to hostilities with France, it was no little advantage to have a number of princely suitors. Their hopes became a safeguard for her throne, and since of all the suitors, the Archduke Charles was politically the best match, she took care to retain him as a kind of insurance. Whenever the imperial ambassador's hopes ran low, she set herself to revive them. One evening in June, having met him rowing on the Thames, she offered him a seat in the treasurer's boat, laid her own alongside, talked at great length, and played for him on the lute. She invited him to court the next day, then to breakfast the following morning, and in the evening had him on the river in her boat, made him take the helm, and was altogether very talkative and merry.

There were two obstacles to marriage with Charles. Religion was the first. Although Elizabeth herself might be tolerant enough to allow the archduke and his suite to hold the Catholic form of worship at her court, "One king, one faith" was the essence of political stability, and she could risk neither the anger of her Protestant subjects at the spectacle of the Mass, nor the danger of taking a husband who might become the focus of Catholic discontent. The second obstacle was personal. Time and again Elizabeth declared that she would marry no one whom she had not seen. She knew very well, she said, how Philip had cursed the painters and envoys when he first beheld Queen Mary, and, as she politely put it, she would not give the Archduke Charles cause to curse. The imperial and Spanish ambassadors were eager to bring Charles to

England *incognito,* but the emperor would not hear of it. It was undignified; it was not the way princes wooed; it would make a laughing stock of them in case of failure; and Elizabeth's whims were notorious. She would not sacrifice a fraction of her freedom of decision to induce him to come. Equally, she would not marry him without seeing him. And this repugnance towards the unknown was becoming deeper because her fancy had been caught by one of her courtiers, Lord Robert Dudley. Until the problem of Dudley was settled, *other reasons* looked like being in the ascendant, and the *weal of the kingdom* in eclipse.

Dudley was a name of ill omen. Lord Robert's father was the Earl of Northumberland, his grandfather the notorious Edmund Dudley of Henry VII's reign; both had perished on the scaffold. His enemies gibed at his tainted blood, but with Elizabeth it was the man that mattered. In the gorgeous clothes of the time he was a magnificent, princely-looking person, tall and dignified, finely built, with clear-cut features, and long slender fingers such as the queen admired. He was an accomplished courtier, a good talker, and not uncultured, though to the regret of Ascham, who warned him that languages opened the way to politics, he had neglected Cicero for Euclid's pricks and lines. Like Somerset's unfortunate brother, Thomas Seymour, he was an expert jouster; the sort of man whom Elizabeth wanted for a husband, not, she said, one who would sit at home all day among the cinders. The queen and he were much about the same age and must have met frequently in their youth. During Mary's reign he had been one of her supporters and had sold some of his land to aid her in her troubles. On her accession he was one of the first to be appointed to office, becoming master of the horse, an honorable and valuable post which gave him a lodging at court.

It is not strange that a lively young woman of twenty-five, unmarried, and living, so to speak, as the hostess of an exclusive men's club—the court—should delight in the company of one of its most fascinating members. Nor is it strange that she felt an emotional response to his manhood. On the other hand, it was not discreet. "A young princess," wrote one of her ambassadors, "cannot be too ware what countenance or familiar demonstration she maketh, more to one than another." And when that one was a married man, tongues were bound to wag. Dudley had married Amy Robsart as long ago as 1550. Probably he was not a bad husband, but his affection for her was dead and there were no children to act as a bond between them or as a solace to the wife. Like other courtiers' wives, Amy Robsart had to live apart from her husband in the country for much of her time, while he attended on the queen at court; and she must have brooded on the gossip and foul rumors that gathered about her husband's name and the queen's.

The intimacy was first noticed in April 1559. "During the last few days," Feria wrote, "Lord Robert has come so much into favor that he does whatever he likes with affairs and it is even said that her Majesty visits him in his chamber day and night. People talk of this so freely that they go so far as to say that his wife has a malady in one of her breasts and the queen is only waiting for her to die to marry Lord Robert." By August things looked so bad that Kate Ashley implored her mistress on her knees and in God's name, to marry and put an end to disreputable rumors, as her affection for Dudley threatened to sully her honor and rouse discontent in her subjects. Elizabeth took the rebuke well. If she showed herself gracious to Dudley, she answered, it was because his honorable nature and dealings deserved it. She did not see how anyone could think evil of her conduct: she was always surrounded by her ladies of the bed-chamber and maids-of-honor, though indeed—she added with a flash of spirit—"if she had ever had the will or had found pleasure in such a dishonorable life—from which may God preserve her!—she did not know of anyone who could forbid her."

Such was the scandal that the imperial ambassador, to reassure his master, found it necessary to make inquiries about Elizabeth's virtue among those who had brought her up since childhood. They swore by all that was holy that she had most certainly never been forgetful of her honor. But gossip took no heed of truth. In December the English ambassador at Brussels felt compelled to write to his mistress and Cecil about the rumors current there, which were so bad that he did not dare to say all, even in a covering note for Cecil's own eyes. Some of the nobles and councillors, such as Cecil, were overwhelmed with anxiety, others lusted for Dudley's blood. Quadra told of a plot to murder him, and someone was said to have asked whether England was so poor that none could be found to stab him with a poniard. It was the imperial ambassador's opinion that if the queen married Dudley, she might one evening lay herself down as queen of England and rise the next morning as plain Mistress Elizabeth. Quadra heard people say that they wanted no more women rulers. It mattered little if a king's passions ran away with him, but a queen, like Caesar's wife, had to be above suspicion. In the summer of 1560 old Mother Dowe of Brentford was telling her acquaintances that Dudley and the queen had played at legerdemain and that he had given her a child. There was a similar rumor current in Hertfordshire. But far more sinister, in the light of what was about to happen, was a persistent report that Dudley intended to get rid of his wife—to poison her was the usual story.

On September 11 the Spanish ambassador, Quadra, had a very remarkable budget of news. Probably three days before, after a futile interview with Elizabeth on the subject of marriage, he had met Cecil, in the gloomiest of moods. Cecil had been away from court that summer, negotiating a treaty in Scotland, and on his return had found Dudley in high favor and the queen difficult. He was still inclined to treat Elizabeth as a young woman whose proper business was marriage and babies, not politics, and her refusal to follow his advice was the last straw to a jealous, disgruntled, and overwrought statesman. He went the astounding length of making a confidant of Quadra, telling him that he thought of retiring, although he expected to be cast into the Tower if he did. It was a bad sailor, he added, who did not put into port when he saw a storm brewing, and he clearly foresaw that Dudley's intimacy with the queen would be the ruin of the country. He was convinced that she meant to marry him. She was abandoning the government to him and spending her days hunting, to the great danger of her life and health. Twice he repeated that Lord Robert would be better in paradise than here, and begged Quadra, in God's name, to point out to Elizabeth the effect of her misconduct and persuade her to give some attention to business. In conclusion he remarked that Dudley was thinking of killing his wife, who was said to be ill, although she was quite well and would take very good care that they did not poison her.

The conversation probably took place on September 8, 1560. That very day Amy Robsart was found dead at the foot of the stairs in Cumnor Place, near Oxford. Cecil, however, was ignorant of the tragedy that was to lend such terrible significance to his petulant outpourings, nor was it until the following day that Dudley himself received the news at court. Returning from hunting, Elizabeth told

Quadra in confidence that Dudley's wife was dead, or nearly so; but the tragedy was not made public until further particulars had been obtained. On the eleventh the queen informed the court: "She has broken her neck," she said in Italian; and Quadra added the news in a postscript to his letter.

A coroner's jury which investigated the facts brought in a verdict of accidental death. At our distance of time, it is difficult to be certain, but so far as one can judge, it was a case of suicide. Several times Amy Robsart had been heard praying to God to deliver her from desperation, and on the fatal day, although it was Sunday and some objected, she had insisted on her household going to the fair at Abingdon. Apparently, neglect and the scandalous stories current about her husband and the queen had preyed upon her mind until at last, for all her prayers, desperation had mastered her.

Rumor had been prophesying murder too long for contemporaries to think anything else. Thomas Lever, the rector of Coventry, wrote to two councillors on September 17 of the mutterings in his neighborhood, urging that the truth should be earnestly searched out. To Elizabeth's ambassadors the news came as a thunderbolt. They had been ill enough at ease already in the face of unrestrained gossip; and their mistress seemed now to be on the edge of the abyss. The tragedy "so passioneth my heart," wrote Randolph[6] from Scotland, "that no grief ever I felt was like unto it." Throckmorton[7] in France wished himself dead. People, he declared, were saying things "which every hair of my head stareth at and my ears glow to hear." "One laugheth at us, another threateneth, another revileth the Queen. Some let not to say 'What religion is this, that a subject shall kill his wife, and the Prince not only bear withal but marry with him?'" All he could do was to pray God that this cruel hap might not be the messenger of a further disaster, namely, the marriage of Elizabeth and Dudley.

As for Elizabeth, discretion was her last thought. She believed completely in Dudley's innocence. Even if she had not been so fond of him, it is probable that pride, courage, and loyalty would have revolted at the idea of letting his enemies drive him from court and favor, as a result of the tragedy. Actually she wanted to marry him,

6 Thomas Randolph, ambassador to Scotland.
7 Sir Nicholas Throckmorton, ambassador to France.

imagining that she could best satisfy English humor by marrying a subject; and it was hard to bring herself to recognize that the scandal attaching to the death of Amy Robsart, coupled with the jealousy of her councillors and nobility, made the one marriage that appealed to her impossible. There were few as wise and tolerant as the Earl of Sussex[8] who wrote to Cecil in October suggesting that it would be best to let her follow her affections, since if she chose a man at sight of whom her whole being was suffused with desire, it would be the readiest way of getting an heir to the throne. Elizabeth herself blew now hot now cold, to the perplexity of everyone. She was inclined to defy all opposition and have her way, and yet there was a fundamental caution in her. While in her defiant mood, the opponents of her marriage, Cecil among them, were in eclipse, business was apt to come to a standstill, and it looked as though all was going to the dogs.

In November it was rumored that Elizabeth and Dudley had been secretly married at the Earl of Pembroke's,[9] for the queen's ladies, seeing them both return together from Pembroke's house, had momentarily jumped to this conclusion. But Elizabeth's mood changed, and when a patent, raising Dudley to the peerage, was ready for signature, she took a knife and cut it in two. Then her mood changed again. In January Kate Ashley's husband was in trouble for being too outspoken on the subject, while Cecil and a friend wrote to Throckmorton begging him to restrain his blunt expressions of opinion as they were doing more harm than good with his mistress. "What the Queen will determine to do, God only knows," Cecil added.

Thus the affair drifted on, with its ups and downs, and gossip ever busy. In February, Drunken Burley of Totnes was regaling his neighbors with the story "that the Lord Robert did swive the Queen." In March, the Earl of Bedford[10] wrote to Throckmorton the welcome news that "the great matters whereof the world was wont to talk are now asleep," and Cecil again in control of everything; but it is typical of the situation that ere he sealed his letter the great matter was alive again and flourishing. The peerage proposal once more

---

8 Thomas Radcliffe, Earl of Sussex, the lord deputy of Ireland.

9 William Herbert, Earl of Pembroke, a member of the Privy Council.

10 Francis Russell, second Earl of Bedford, a privy councillor and an outspoken Protestant.

cropped up, only to be rejected as before, Elizabeth remarking that she would not confer the title on those who had been traitors three descents. Dudley sulked, and her mood changed; Robin was clapped on the cheek, with "No, no, the bear and the ragged staff is not so soon overthrown"; he was in as great favor as ever. Some of her courtiers, who favored Dudley, took courage to urge his suit; she would only "pup with her mouth" and say that she would not be fellow with the Duchess of Norfolk, for when they were married folk would be coming and ask for her husband as "My Lord's Grace." In vain did the courtiers reply that the remedy was simple; she should give Dudley the title of king. She would never agree to the suggestion.

By the summer of 1561, although the romance was by no means at an end and continued spasmodically to trouble Cecil and others for years, the crisis was past, and Elizabeth was proving that her intelligence could control her emotions. This was the significance of the episode. At one time it had looked as though the second woman ruler, like the first, would take the bit between her teeth and let passion have its ruinous way. But while not unfeminine or sexless, Elizabeth was a less emotional type than her sister. Experience had added caution to a quick and active mind, and she was consumed with ambition to be a great popular ruler like her father. Momentarily she had sacrificed her good name and popularity; that is a measure of her infatuation for Dudley. But in the long run it was *the weal of the kingdom* and the limits of practical politics that directed her judgment.

If ever she married, she remarked a few years later, it would be as a queen and not as Elizabeth. She had not yet, in 1561, abandoned all hope of marrying as both—that is, of marrying Dudley with the approval of her nobles and people. But even if Dudley had been less envied and hated by his fellows, the tragedy of Amy Robsart was too black a cloud over his reputation with Englishmen to permit marrying him: And so, having decided not to marry simply as Elizabeth, it was certain that, unless another man appeared to stir her emotions, she would never marry except as queen—as queen alone. And that, she said, she would only do from stern necessity.

IV AFFAIRS OF STATE

The Early Years

Neville Williams

THE EARLY YEARS—
AN UNREMARKABLE FAILURE

Neville Williams, former deputy keeper of public records, studied at Oxford University. He is a member of the Council of the Royal Historical Society and a Fellow of the Society of Antiquities. A prolific author, his works include a biography of Thomas Howard, Fourth Duke of Norfolk *(1964) and lavishly illustrated portrayals of* Henry VIII and His Court *(1971) and* The Life and Times of Elizabeth I *(1972).*

1569, the year of conspiracy and revolt, began with an attempt by Leicester and Norfolk to dislodge Cecil from the position of dominance he had held since Elizabeth's accession, continued with a series of intrigues involving some of the greatest in the land, and culminated in the rebellion in the north. This succession of plots and counterplots, some bringing the threat of foreign intervention in England and all connected with Mary Queen of Scots, was a direct challenge to Elizabeth and her whole system of government. She was in "manifest danger," such as she had not experienced since the spring of 1554.

The attempt to remove Cecil was made simply because his opponents could not in the context of the Tudor constitution criticize the queen herself. As there was no official "opposition" in the modern sense, it was the duty of those who opposed official policy to intrigue, and Cecil as secretary was the principal instrument of policies which were becoming increasingly unpopular. No minister of later days could have stayed in office in the face of such unpopularity, but ministers who retained Elizabeth's confidence could only be removed by backstairs methods, and the success of such intrigues depended entirely on how the queen herself reacted. "Many did

From *Elizabeth the First: Queen of England* by Neville Williams, pp. 157–178. Copyright © 1967 by Neville Williams. First published in the U.S.A. by E. P. Dutton & Co., Inc. in 1968. Reprinted by permission of E. P. Dutton & Co., Inc. and George Weidenfeld & Nicolson Ltd. (Footnotes omitted.)

rise against his fortune, who were more hot in envying him than able to follow him, detracting his praises, disgracing his service and plotting his danger," wrote a biographer of Cecil in his own lifetime. Elizabeth recognized the maneuver for what it was, an attempted coup against her.

The seizure in Plymouth Sound of the Spanish ships with £85,000 treasure aboard in November 1568 had provoked a serious commercial crisis with Spain and the Netherlands and brought England to the brink of war. English property in the Netherlands was seized in retaliation and an embargo on trading was imposed—economic sanctions which brought the ports to a standstill. As the situation became blacker Cecil's unpopularity grew. Other critics were alarmed at the growing estrangement from Spain on political grounds, because they feared that England would be drawn into an alliance with her old enemy, France. In the country at large the severity with which the laws against Catholic recusants were being enforced, following Mary's flight, was laid at Cecil's door, and in the Council itself he had few friends. Leicester regarded him as the man who had prevented him from becoming Elizabeth's consort; Norfolk saw him as the sworn enemy of Mary Queen of Scots, whom he was now bent on marrying; Pembroke and Northampton disliked his Protestantism as evinced in his partiality for the Suffolk claim[1] and in his supporting the Huguenots in France and the rebels in the Netherlands; while Arundel, Northumberland, and Westmorland, all staunch Catholics, looked for his dismissal as the first step in a grand design for the restoration of the old faith. Together they made an incongruous, though formidable team. "Although Cecil thinks he has them all under his heel," wrote de Spes[2] who was in the secret, "he will find few or none of them stand by him."

---

[1] William Parr, Marquis of Northampton, a member of the Privy Council. The Suffolk claim was based on the marriage of Henry VIII's youngest sister, Mary, to Charles Brandon, Duke of Suffolk. Their eldest daughter, Frances, married Henry Grey, Duke of Suffolk. The three daughters of this marriage fared unhappily: Lady Jane Grey's fate is well known; Katherine Grey (d. 1568) married Edward Seymour, Earl of Hertford, but the couple was imprisoned and the marriage declared invalid; Mary Grey (d. 1578) married Thomas Keys, Elizabeth's sergeant porter, but the queen kept the couple separated. The younger daughter of Mary and Charles Brandon, Eleanor, married Henry Clifford, Earl of Cumberland. Their daughter Margaret, with only a weak claim to the succession, married Henry Stanley, Lord Strange, later the Earl of Derby.

[2] Guerau de Spes, the Spanish ambassador, who was expelled from England in 1571 for his role in the Ridolfi plot.

The plan was a time-honored one. Cecil was to be charged in the Council chamber with being an evil adviser and, once in the Tower, "means to undo him would not be far to seek." But Elizabeth saw straws in the wind and, sensing danger, summoned a Council meeting at which she would be present. Her suspicions were confirmed when Cecil's opponents severally made excuses for their absence, and she grasped an opportunity of dealing with them informally on Ash Wednesday. A group of them were in her chamber before supper when she went out of the way to rebuke Leicester for the unbusinesslike attitude of the Council. This provoked the earl to launch a vigorous attack on Cecil whom so many people thought was ruining the country, and at this the queen cast aside her mask, praising the Secretary warmly and making a great tirade against Leicester. . . . So their plans misfired and Elizabeth's handling of the affair should have brought home to her rebel councillors that she was not prepared to sacrifice Cecil and that if they were bent on a change of policies they would need a change of queen. Though murmurings against Cecil continued, the clique was too dismayed by Elizabeth's attitude to act swiftly and by Easter the move to replace him had petered out, but in the aftermath of Ash Wednesday other distinct, yet simultaneous, schemes were being launched, no less far-reaching in their consequences to queen and country.

Leicester now put his weight behind the project, brought forward by Maitland of Lethington,[3] for Norfolk to marry Mary as the only realistic solution to the Scottish problem, in which he was supported by Pembroke and Throckmorton. Mary's abdication was to be revoked, Darnley's murder conveniently forgotten, and a divorce from Bothwell obtained, so that after marriage with the duke she would be restored to her throne, ratify at long last the Treaty of Edinburgh[4] and be pronounced as Elizabeth's heir. The curtain could be rung down on the great drama of matrimonial maneuvers with Hapsburg dukes and French princes, and Dudley himself would achieve his ambition of being Elizabeth's consort. After discreet

---

[3] William Maitland of Lethington, the Scottish secretary of state.
[4] The Treaty of Edinburgh (1560) provided for the withdrawal of French and English troops from Scotland, established a council of nobles to govern Scotland, and stipulated that France recognize Elizabeth as the lawful queen of England. Francis II and Mary rejected the latter point, and France did not ratify the treaty. Hence it became a point of dispute for years between Mary and Elizabeth.

pondering Norfolk was prepared "to sacrifice himself" in this way for his own sovereign's benefit. On paper it looked a tidy scheme, but the drawbacks were Cecil's preference for the Suffolk line and Elizabeth's increasing aversion to Mary. For the moment, however, Leicester felt confident he could sway the Council and force a decision on the queen.

There were other plans afoot which also hinged on a marriage between Mary and the duke. Arundel and Lumley[5] devised a desperate design, with the full support of Northumberland and Westmorland, for liberating Mary and enthroning her in Elizabeth's stead; this was to be achieved through Spanish aid and lead to the restoration of Roman Catholicism. Mary also had her own schemes, negotiated by the Bishop of Ross with both sets of English conspirators and with the Scots, which varied from month to month, but in every case her first requirement was to be free and she grasped at the idea of marrying Norfolk as an essential means to achieve this. She told Leicester she would in all things follow Elizabeth's advice, but at once began courting Norfolk by proxy.

Throughout that summer Elizabeth sensed something was afoot and regarded the usual faces at court with growing unease. . . . Though ignorant of the identity of the conspirators and of the scope of their plans, the queen took precautions by ordering systematic musters of the militia in each shire and requiring the Council in the North to take special heed of the state of the north, which she rightly regarded as the most vulnerable quarter. Norfolk had raised the problem of Mary's marriage at a meeting of a quorum of the Privy Council in Cecil's absence, when those present agreed to his proposal that the Scottish queen should be set at liberty on condition she married an Englishman, and he now hoped Leicester would confront Elizabeth with this resolution; the French ambassador was sure she dare not oppose it. Yet to Norfolk's dismay Leicester did nothing.

The signs were not propitious. Elizabeth, he heard, "had been out of quiet," and then some of the women at court babbled their hearsay—that the arrangements with Mary had already been concluded. The queen taxed Leicester with daring to proceed with these plans without first consulting her, but he more or less satisfied her

---

[5] John Lumley, son-in-law of Henry Fitzalan, Earl of Arundel.

there was nothing in these tales, though her attitude was sufficient warning to tread warily. Time and again he insisted to the duke that only he, Leicester, could successfully raise this topic with his sovereign. She at last took the initiative by asking Norfolk when he joined her in the garden at Richmond what news her cousin had to tell her. He mumbled that he knew of nothing. "No," she cried out, "You come from London and can tell no news of a marriage?" But instead of speaking out, Norfolk excused himself. Nothing had come into the open before Elizabeth left Richmond for her summer progress. She gave the duke another chance of being straightforward with her at Sir William More's house at Loseley, near Guildford, and in mid-August, at Farnham, called him to her dinner table, but once again he remained tongue-tied, partly from timidity, partly from fear of upsetting Leicester's plans, and at the end of the meal the queen gave him a nip, saying "that she would wish me to take good head to my pillow" (an allusion to their interview the previous December). "I was so abashed at Her Majesty's speech," the duke later confessed, "but I thought it not fit time nor place there to trouble her." Elizabeth had given him three chances of making a clean breast of the whole affair, which he had rejected, and she had every reason for feeling he had forfeited her confidence. He left the progress at Southampton, feeling he had committed himself too deeply to Mary's cause to withdraw, and back in London approved a plan for Northumberland and Leonard Dacre[6] to rescue Mary from Wingfield once he should give the signal. From Northumberland came the proud message that "the whole of the north" was at his devotion, while from Pembroke, still with the court on progress, came the suggestion that the queen dare not refuse her permission to the marriage for there was not a person about her who would dare to give her contrary advice.

That same day, however, Hunsdon wrote to Elizabeth speaking out most strongly against so dangerous a proposal and forthwith she summoned the duke to come to her. Before he had time to obey, Leicester had taken to his bed with a feigned sickness at Titchfield and when the queen came to his bedside, anxious and full of sympathy, he revealed to her the detailed plans for the Norfolk-Mary marriage. His own loyalty, he assured her, was never in ques-

6 The Dacres were members of a powerful Border clan. Leonard was Catholic and the nephew of Thomas Percy, Earl of Northumberland.

tion, yet he craved her forgiveness. Later that day in the gallery at Titchfield she rated the duke, charging him on his allegiance "to deal no further with the Scottish cause." She knew that in the current political unrest the projected marriage would be disastrous for her; within four months of it taking place, she said, *she* would have been in the Tower. The six-week delay in bringing their plans to her notice had made Leicester, Norfolk, and their supporters appear as a body of whispering conspirators who would never come into the open, though had they moved speedily in July there might have been some chance of forcing the marriage scheme on Elizabeth. After ten miserable days at Titchfield, where Leicester treated him with cold disdain and the other courtiers followed suit, the duke left for London, but there were too many rumors for his own peace of mind. Elizabeth feared that his withdrawal from court was the prologue to a general rising, uniting under one banner all the opponents of her regime. Already, her most formidable enemies, the religious malcontents in the north under Northumberland and the political malcontents in the ranks of the Privy Council, were in alliance and civil war seemed possible. In this manifest danger Elizabeth swiftly made her dispositions. She closed the ports, alerted the militia, and sent Huntingdon[7] to supersede Shrewsbury as custodian of Mary, with orders for her removal from Wingfield to Tutbury. She herself would move to Windsor Castle, prepared to stand a siege if necessary. Meanwhile she still hoped she could call Norfolk's bluff and required Leicester and Cecil to write a joint letter to him, ordering him to repair to Windsor and submit. He wrote that he was not well enough to travel . . . but hoped to be at Windsor by September 26. Other messages reached the duke, including a warning note from Leicester that it was likely he would be sent to the Tower, and with failing courage he rode off that night to his country residence, Kenninghall Palace, feeling home was the only safe place.

The queen did not realize this was a retreat in fear, but took it as an open act of defiance, the signal for revolt. "All the whole court hung in suspense and fear lest he should break forth into rebellion," wrote Camden; and it was determined if he did so, forthwith to put the Queen of Scots to death. But Norfolk was indeed ruined "by his own pusillanimity"; instead of taking the field and

---

[7] Henry Hastings, Earl of Huntingdon.

rallying his many supporters, he lay low, terrified that he had become "a suspected person," and saw the shadow of the Tower, as he wrote to Elizabeth, "which is too great a terror for a true man." She commanded him on his allegiance to submit, telling him she never intended "to minister anything to you but as you should in truth deserve," and when he still disobeyed telling him to come straightway, in a litter if need be. . . . At last he listened to reason, and left home to throw himself onto his royal cousin's mercy, to all intents a prisoner, on October 1. But before he left he dispatched a messenger to the northern earls at Topcliffe to call off their projected rising, "for if they did, it should cost him his head"; he specially asked his brother-in-law of Westmorland to remain loyal, even if Northumberland should rise. But for the earls, the duke's withdrawal to Kenninghall had been the signal for which they had awaited all summer, an overt action which the later message could not effectively cancel. They had brought the partisan hopes of their supporters to fever-heat, and their rising planned for October 6, though postponed was not cancelled.

The Percys, Nevilles, and Dacres ruled a patriarchal society and could count on their tenantry in the Palatinate of Durham and the North Riding of Yorkshire to follow them with blind devotion once they were ready to strike their blow for the old religion and Mary's right to the succession. "He is a rare bird," said Sussex, the Lord President at York, when the standard was finally raised, "that hath not some of his [kin] with the two Earls, or in his heart, wisheth not well to the cause they pretend." As Sadler[8] noted, "if the father came to us with ten men, his son goes to the rebels with twenty." Throughout the summer they had been preparing for battle, holding meetings "to allure the gentlemen," right under Sussex's nose. There was overwhelming sympathy for Mary and men told tales of their fathers' bravery in the Pilgrimage of Grace, which had so seriously threatened the monarchy of Henry VIII.

Because of his friendship with the duke, Sussex was under a cloud in September, and both queen and secretary thought he knew more of Norfolk's plans than they did and felt he was not acting vigorously enough against the dissidents; were he to side with the earls the north would indeed be lost. He did his best to assure the

---

[8] Sir Ralph Sadler, privy councillor and chancellor of the Duchy of Lancaster.

queen that despite his affection for Norfolk, whom he was sure was an innocent conspirator, this high personal regard counted as nothing beside his devotion to his sovereign, "for he had always hitched his staff at her door." He wished he could come to London to justify himself, rather than write, and there was indeed talk of recalling him for examination, but the rapid development of events made it imperative for Elizabeth to pin her faith on him, and he did not disappoint her. He was above all calm, refusing to believe the thousand rumors, and wanted to treat the problem in his own way without interference from court. He called the earls of Northumberland and Westmorland to York on October 9 to require their help in ending rumors and sent them home to be on hand to deal with any hotheads. "I trust the fire is spent with the smoke," he told Cecil— "a great bruit of an intended rebellion, the cause of which is yet unknown and which I think is now at an end." Any premature action on his part would make the dying embers flare up; he knew the men he was dealing with and realized that those at Windsor could not possibly grasp the intricacies of the local problems. Elizabeth was aghast at his complacency and his underestimating of the gravity of the situation and feared he was treating the earls with far more sympathy than they deserved. She decided she would deal with them as she had dealt with the duke and on October 24 she ordered Sussex to send for them at once and in her name summon them to court. At the same time, so doubtful was she of Sussex's loyalty, that she asked other members of the Council in the North to report individually on the situation.

Sussex told Elizabeth that his Council was unanimous that it was best to postpone an examination of the cause of the recent disaffection and to delay sending for the earls until dead of winter, but since she had come to different conclusions he would do as she had bidden. The causes of the present discontents, he reported, were various and confused—"some specially respect the Duke of Norfolk, some the Scottish Queen, some religion and some, perhaps, all three." . . . All at York agreed that the best policy for avoiding further troubles was to turn as blind an eye as possible to recent events. But the queen at Windsor could not share Sussex's calm, and forced him into employing tactics which he knew to be fundamentally wrong.

The earls feared that if they submitted, as Norfolk had done, they would like him be sent to the Tower. At first both excused their attendance at York and then Sussex sent them a *pursuivant,*[9] charging them on their allegiance to report to him. Northumberland promised to come in a day or so, when his business was settled, but Westmorland stoutly refused to obey: "I dare not come where my enemies are, without bringing such a force to protect me as might be misliked; therefore I think it better to stay at home and use myself as an obedient subject." His wife had stiffened his resolution and warned him against putting his head in a noose. The lord president had now to write again, setting down what he had proposed to tell them in person, namely to repair to court on their allegiance. They were to beware of the counsel "of such as would show you honey and deliver you poison, and stand, as noblemen, upon your honour and truth, for it will stand by you." They were not to be scared of their own shadows but to submit with humility to the queen's clemency, otherwise a show of willful disobedience might provoke her into acting with extremity. But while Sussex's messenger, who carried this letter, was still at Topcliffe, Northumberland's home, towards midnight on November 9, he heard the bells of the church ring backwards, as the signal to raise the standard of revolt. Northumberland rode south to Brancepeth to join Westmorland and found him at a council of war with the sheriff of Yorkshire, Richard Norton, and his sons, the Markenfields, Tempests, and Swinburnes who had assembled with bands of armed retainers. They discussed whether they should flee the realm, fight to the finish, or submit. A letter from Sussex gave them one final chance before proclaiming them as outlaws, yet when they were about to return to their homes Lady Westmorland, Norfolk's sister Jane, swayed them into action. In tears she goaded them: "We and our country were shamed for ever, that now in the end we should seek holes to creep into." This was decisive and next day, to show their hand, the earls rode off to Durham, stormed the cathedral, tore up the prayer book and English Bible and attended mass. After eleven years of peace England was plunged into civil war.

Whatever their earlier hesitations and disagreements, the rebels

---

[9] A warrant officer.

now made plain that they rose in defense of the Catholic faith, for the religious issue was the only one that could command widespread support; the earls could hide their own disobedience to their sovereign under the cloak of religion, though in all their edicts they maintained they were acting as true and faithful subjects of the crown. When they went in solemn procession to mass in Ripon Cathedral the earls' men bore on their backs crusaders' crosses to show they had armed themselves for a holy war, and followed the cross, borne by old Sheriff Norton, with the banner of the five wounds of Christ and the words *In hoc signo vinces.*[10] In the earls' first proclamation they stated that they and others of the ancient nobility were charged to determine "to whom of mere right the true succession of the crown appertaineth," but their proclamation at Ripon, addressed to all members of the old Catholic religion, had nothing in it about Norfolk or Mary. It ran:

> *Forasmuch as divers evil-disposed persons about the Queen's Majesty have, by their subtle and crafty dealings to advance themselves, overcome in this our realm the true and Catholic religion towards God and by the same abused the Queen, disordered the realm and now lastly seek and procure the destruction of the nobility, we therefore have gathered ourselves together to resist by force, and the rather by the help of God and you good people, to see redress of those things amiss, with restoring of all ancient customs and liberties to God's Church and his whole realm.*

The rebels' proclamation underlined the manifest danger to the queen personally and tore to shreds the unity of her kingdom. Glib phrases about rescuing the crown from evil advisers and restoring ancient liberties had been the stock in trade of English rebels for centuries. There was no comfort for her in the reports that men from the Palatinate and north Yorkshire were flocking to the earls in their thousands, a near feudal tenantry, knowing no prince but a Percy or a Neville, regarding their liege lord with more awe than their anointed queen. She, who had never traveled further than the southern Midlands, was amazed at the persistence of inbred loyalties:

> *A potent vassalage to fight*
> *In Percy's and in Neville's right.*

[10] "In this sign conquer," part of Charlemagne's vision.

She cursed as she heard that Sussex, with a gravely depleted militia, had not attempted to stop the rebel army's progress south and now pinned her faith in Hunsdon's main army, which had been hastily collected from the Midland shires to oppose them. By November 24 they were at Selby, within striking distance of Tutbury, and in London the chance of their rescuing Mary Queen of Scots seemed very great. The rebels now had Hartlepool in their hands, at which Alva might disembark his Spanish troops. The papists were predicting that Alva would be in London with Spanish troops by Candlemas and force Elizabeth to hear mass in St. Paul's Cathedral. She ordered Mary to be removed for greater security to Coventry and prayed for cousin Hunsdon's success.

Overnight on November 25 there was a complete *bouleversement,* for at Tadcaster the earls decided they must turn back; the way to the south was blocked by Hunsdon, news reached them of supporting armies led by Clinton and by Warwick, and the only course left was a strategic retreat to give battle on their own ground. The heart was taken out of the rebellion at this withdrawal, and as the earls rode north their army dwindled in the face of wintry weather and internal strife, until they reached Brancepeth, broken and dispirited, on the last day of the month. Though Westmorland succeeded in taking Barnard Castle, largely through the garrison's treachery, the rebellion was petering out. In Durham, at mid-December, the earls decided to flee while there was still time and with a few horsemen rode across the Pennines to the Dacre fortress of Naworth and from there into Scotland.

* * *

In February . . . Elizabeth issued a declaration on the rebellion, surveying the developments in church and state since her accession, portraying herself as "the natural father over her children" and bluntly pointing to the "manifest danger" of the past months. The queen also celebrated the suppression of the rebellion in verse:

The doubt of future foes exiles my present joy,
And Wit me warns to shun such snares as threaten my annoy,
For falsehood now doth flow, and subjects' faith doth ebb
Which would not be if Reason ruled, or Wisdom move the web,
But clouds of toys untried to cloak aspiring minds,
Which turn to rain of late repent by course of changed winds.

The top of hope supposed, the root of ruth will be,
And fruitless all their grafted guiles, as ye shall shortly see.
Those dazzled eyes with pride, which great ambition blinds,
Shall be unsealed by worthy wights, whose foresight falsehood blinds.
The daughter of debate, that eke discord doth sow,
Shall reap no gain where former rule hath taught still peace to grow.
No foreign banish'd wight shall anchor in this port;
Our realm it brooks no stranger's force, let them elsewhere resort;
Our rusty sword, with rest, shall first his edge employ,
To poll their tops that seek such change, and gape for joy.

She was merciless in her revenge. Sussex had sent the Privy Council his proposals about punishment, suggesting the execution of a handful of insurgents as an example and imprisoning those captives with lands to escheat to the crown, but the queen commanded much harsher reprisals to be made, and as a result some 750 rebels were executed according to martial law, while a further 60 awaited special sessions at Durham, York, and Carlisle. "You may not execute any that hath freehold, nor noted wealthy, for so is the Queen's Majesty's pleasure," Sussex told his henchman, Sir George Bowes—in other words pardons and reprieves were only to go to those who could afford them; at least the fines and forfeitures would help reduce the heavy bill for suppressing the revolt. Over 2,000 of the smaller fry who had followed the earls paid a fine according to their means and, providing they took the oath of allegiance, were pardoned, but the poorest were in danger of the scaffold. The vast estates of the two earls, of Dacre, the Nortons, Swinburne, and Tempest became forfeit to the crown and while some properties, such as Raby, were retained for strategic reasons, most of these lands were parceled out by grants and leases to Hunsdon and his followers. This redistribution of property in the north country was much more extensive than the leases and sales of monastic estates of the previous generation and brought to the area a class of land-lords who broke the old particularism. Parallel to these upheavals, the Court of High Commission in the province of York and the church courts in each diocese were active in seeking out offenders, so that hundreds of the clergy were deprived of their benefices. The north country was never the same again.

Despite his share of blame for provoking the northern rebellion, Elizabeth found she could not charge Norfolk with high treason. That her own cousin and the head of her nobility should have behaved as he had done was the greatest blow she had suffered. She called him "traitor," and when Cecil sent her extracts from the Treasons Statute of Edward III's reign to show he was innocent of such a crime, an interpretation with which the Council agreed, she was almost beside herself. She cried out that she could cut off his head of her own authority, and then appeared to faint. . . . Elizabeth could clearly not countenance the duke's release, but she did not know how to deal with him any more than she knew how to deal with Mary.

A new twist to the whole affair came with the publication of the bull *Regnans in Excelsis,* by which Pope Pius V deposed Elizabeth and absolved her Catholic subjects from allegiance to her. Rome moved in a mysterious way, and tardily. Had the bull arrived to coincide with the rebellion in the previous November it might have brought many waverers to the northern earls and stiffened the resistance of those who gave up the fight after Tadcaster. But its publication by John Felton at the gates of the Bishop of London's palace in St. Paul's in May, three months after Dacre's flight, was an anachronism. More than the rebellion itself, the bull provoked a spate of penal legislation against Roman Catholics which was to be rigorously enforced, and turned every practicing papist into a traitor. For the queen Pope Pius's action was a piece of insufferable insolence. "Deprived of her pretended right to the realm," indeed! "A heretic and an abettor of heretics," without dominion, dignity, and privilege whatsoever, a price was put on her head and for her Catholic subjects the strain of having to choose between sovereign and pope was intolerable. Not a few became fugitives, joining those rebels who had escaped from justice in England to the Continent; for all of the faith who continued to obey the queen were liable to sentence of anathema.

At midsummer Norfolk had made a fulsome submission in writing, craving the queen's forgiveness for his offense in following the will-o'-the-wisp of the match with Mary, to which he had been persuaded "for Your Highness benefit and surety," and vowing "never to deal in that cause of marriage of the Queen of Scots, nor in any other cause belonging to her, but as Your Majesty shall command me." . . . In the event, because of the duke's ill health and the danger from the plague to which all inmates of the Tower were liable, he was allowed to continue his confinement in his own residence,

Howard House, formerly the Charterhouse. Here before long he became trapped in the snares of the Florentine financier Roberto Ridolfi, the man from whom Felton had obtained copies of the papal bull.

Ridolfi concluded from the events of 1569 that the English were too inexperienced to plan their own revolutions. By nature an inveterate plotter, he was thick with the Spanish ambassador, the Bishop of Ross, and others with schemes for rescuing Mary Queen of Scots. Her only hope was in a concerted rising of her English friends, strongly aided by money and arms from the Catholic powers. Ridolfi was convinced that every other Englishman was an ardent Catholic at heart who would fervently take arms in obedience to the pope and reckoned that as many as 33 peers of the realm could be counted on, who could muster between them 39,000 men. He drafted letters in Norfolk's name to Pius V, the Duke of Alva, and Philip of Spain to support their holy cause, and though the duke shrank from signing them, he gave his verbal assent. Spain was to provide an experienced general commanding an army of 6,000 trained soldiers who would land at Harwich, merge with an English force raised by the duke and his friends, rescue Mary, capture Elizabeth, and take the capital. With his letters allegedly from Norfolk and authority from Mary, Ridolfi went to Brussels, Madrid, and Rome to canvass potential allies, but Alva thought the proposals foolhardy. Fighting a hard campaign against William of Orange he had neither men nor money to spare for so doubtful an enterprise; and he predicted that failure would increase the plight of the English Catholics and almost certainly provoke Elizabeth into executing Mary. Alva wrote to Philip, warning him off the scheme: Queen Elizabeth "being dead (naturally or otherwise) or else a prisoner, there will be an opportunity which we must not allow to escape." But the initiative must come from the Catholics in England; only when they had shown they were capable of achieving their coup should Spain send aid. But Ridolfi with his ciphered messages, babbling his way across Europe, failed to appreciate that realist statesmen thought his grand design a piece of wishful thinking. His cipher was not even foolproof, and others of his team were recklessly careless.

Ignorant of the web of intrigue being spun by Ridolfi, Elizabeth was again seriously considering whether Mary's restoration to

Scotland might not be the way out of the dilemma. She knew that so long as Mary remained on English soil she would be the center and soul of opposition to her. The sympathy Mary was winning from stout Englishmen was alarming, and the pressure from France and Spain for obtaining her release was increasing; indeed, the Duke of Anjou, whom Elizabeth was beginning to court, warned her that unless she took steps to restore Mary to her proper dignity and meanwhile treated her "in a kind and honourable manner, he should send forces openly to her assistance." The complications of Scottish politics had increased by the assassination of the Regent Murray in January 1570, and before she could begin fresh negotiations she decided to send Sussex to harry the Borders and beyond, as a reprisal for raids into England by fugitives from the rebel army of the northern earls. Sussex's men sacked fortresses, burned villages, and slew with a new vengeance on this, the last of a long series of punitive expeditions from the Marches that stretched to remote times. That accomplished, Elizabeth again put to her Council the question of Mary. Most councillors, led by Cecil, opted for unstinted support of the infant James's party, which meant sending more English money to Edinburgh; but Elizabeth preferred a new attempt at negotiations with Mary, through the Bishop of Ross. James was to be sent to England as a hostage to be educated for kingship away from rival factions and the influence of the kirk. At long last Mary was prepared to renounce her claim to the throne of England in favor of Elizabeth and her issue—"her lawful issue," insisted the other, whereat Elizabeth growled to Cecil, "she may, peradventure, measure other folk's dispositions by her own actions." But when the commissioners of the infant James arrived in February 1571, stalemate was soon reached and they excused themselves by saying they had no powers to sign a treaty without first calling a Parliament in Edinburgh. Before further progress could be made came the dénouement of the Ridolfi plot, which changed the entire situation.

*   *   *

For Elizabeth the manifest danger was past, now that the Ridolfi conspiracy had been unraveled, but she could take little comfort in the details of the examinations and confessions of those in the Tower, for they showed how many of her nobles had been involved in Norfolk's schemings to a greater or lesser degree. As she looked round the court, as she eyed the bearded figures at her Council table, whom could she trust beside Burghley, the faithful secretary she had at long last raised to the peerage in February? Already Lumley was locked in the Marshalsea Prison, Southampton,[11] another zealous Catholic, was in custody at Cecil House, and Arundel was under house arrest. Cobham[12] was soon to be arrested and the young Earl of Oxford, about to become Burghley's son-in-law, was behaving as irresponsibly as ever. At least one of Derby's sons and a stepson of Shrewsbury were in the plot,[13] while over the water and north of the border were others intriguing for all they were worth. She could not easily forget Leicester's share as the unauthorized broker in bringing Norfolk and Mary together in the summer of 1569, and now there were tales, by no means unfounded, that Sir Christopher Hatton, a rising favorite, was uncertain in his loyalties. Apart from Burghley she could only rely upon Bacon, Knollys, Sadler, and Hunsdon among her inner circle of councillors and none of these was popular, least of all Burghley. Since Norfolk was connected by descent or marriage with the whole body of the ancient nobility, there were moments when she doubted whether they would in fact find him guilty when he went before them. She had already moved into Whitehall for Christmas by the time the law officers had finished preparing their case, and she felt that a state trial in Westminster Hall, so near at hand, would cast a gloom over the traditional festivities.

She need not have worried about the outcome of the state trial, for at the end of the long day's hearing on January 16, without equivocation every peer present found the duke guilty of high treason. After sentence he wrote to her abjectly repenting and asking that she might look tenderly over his children and step-children. She sent a message next day agreeing to his suggestion that Burghley should become their guardian, and this care of hers "for my poor unfortunate brats" moved him deeply. Elizabeth signed his death warrant on February 9, but next day canceled it, as she

---

[11] Henry Wriothesley, Earl of Southampton.
[12] William Brooke, Baron Cobham, the warden of the cinque ports. Sir Henry Cobham, the latter's younger brother, was also arrested.
[13] Sir Thomas Stanley and Sir Edward Stanley, younger sons of Edward Stanley, Earl of Derby, were involved in plotting against Elizabeth. George Talbot, Earl of Shrewsbury, was for a time keeper of Mary Stewart. His second wife, Elizabeth ("Bess of Hardwick"), had three sons by a former marriage, the eldest of whom, Henry Cavendish, was partial to Mary's cause.

professed "a great mislike that the Duke should die." Indeed she could not make up her mind whether or not to allow the law to take its course. One day, as Burghley told Walsingham with feeling, mindful of her own peril, she was determined that justice should be done, yet the next, when she considered Norfolk's "nearness of blood, of his superiority of honour she stayeth." Until now no peer of the realm in her reign had suffered on Tower Hill and she desperately wanted to show clemency to her cousin. She looked back to her own days in the Tower, "much suspected" and to the affair with Seymour, earlier still, which had cost him his head, even as Norfolk's courtship of Mary by proxy had brought him the sentence of traitor.

When Parliament assembled on May 8 member after member demanded Norfolk's speedy execution and Mary's own trial. He was "a roaring lion" and she "a monstrous and huge dragon" who would plague the realm so long as there was breath left in either of them. As their names had been tragically linked together in love, so should their persons suffer together as attainted. A Clytemnestra, who had killed her husband and committed adultery, Mary was convicted by the evidence of Norfolk's trial of treachery by the laws of England and must suffer as those laws required. Elizabeth, said one member, should "cut off her head and make no more ado about her." And had she so acted then men would have thought her fully justified. "You saith she [Mary] is a Queen's daughter and therefore ought to be spared. Nay then," argued Thomas Norton,[14] "spare the Queen's Majesty that is a King's daughter and our own Queen."

Then at last Burghley persuaded Elizabeth that sentence against the duke could be delayed no longer. "The adverse party must needs increase when they see justice forbear against the principal and him spared to set up the mark," he had written, and he knew that unless he got his own way over Norfolk, there would be little hope of persuading the queen to come to grips with the problem of Mary. She could not hold out indefinitely against the logic of statecraft and at last, after five months' procrastination, she signed the warrant. For years to come her cousin's death would gnaw at her conscience and she would lay the blame for it on Burghley. Norfolk's

---

[14] Norton was an outspoken M.P. who staunchly opposed Mary Stuart and was critical of the bishops. A lawyer and a translator of works by Continental reformers, he sat for Gatton in 1559, Berwick in 1563, and London in 1571, 1572, and 1581.

blood made Parliament clamor the more mercilessly for Mary's. So long as she lived "the manifest danger" to Elizabeth remained. "If you strike not at the root," thundered John Knox in Edinburgh, "the branches that appear to be broke will bud again," and the bishops in Westminster, drawing on St. Paul as well as the Old Testament, set out to persuade their queen that it was her inescapable Christian duty to administer justice severely and uprightly; she "must needs offend in conscience before God if she do not punish" Mary according to the full terror of her offense. But Elizabeth stopped Parliament single-handed from proceeding against Mary by a bill of attainder, and instead a measure was brought in depriving her of her pretended title to the throne, declaring anyone who suggested her claim in any way to be guilty of treason, and making her liable to trial by the peers of the realm if she plotted further against the queen. The bill "concerning Mary, daughter of James the Fifth, late King of Scotland, called the Queen of Scots" passed both houses, yet the detailed drafting and the fiery debates had been in vain, for on the last day of the sessions, four weeks after Norfolk's execution, Elizabeth vetoed this effort at her own preservation.

She had reigned for nearly fourteen years and was still single and had deliberately left the problem of her succession still in the air. She was at odds with her Council, with both Houses of Parliament, and with Convocation, and the unity she had striven for in religion had been shattered. England was still isolated, without an ally in Christendom, a negligible country, weak, poor, and divided against itself. Had Elizabeth died in 1572 she would have gone down in history as an unremarkable failure, who had broken faith with all who had put their trust in her at the joyous moment of her accession and had been proved by events to be incapable of living up to the promise expected of her father's daughter. But there was soon a new spirit abroad and it stemmed from the sovereign herself.

Wallace MacCaffrey

THE EARLY YEARS—THE SHAPING OF THE REGIME

A leading American authority on Elizabeth, Wallace MacCaffrey was born at LaGrande, Oregon, in 1920. He studied at Reed College and Harvard University. Before becoming professor of history at Harvard in 1968, Mac-Caffrey taught at the University of California at Los Angeles and Haverford College. He was a Guggenheim Fellow in 1956/57, and an Overseas Research Fellow at Churchill College, Cambridge, in 1968/69. A Fellow of the Royal Historical Society, MacCaffrey is the author of several highly acclaimed works, including Exeter, 1540–1640 *(1958) and* The Shaping of the Elizabethan Regime *(1968).*

Most of the circumstances which shaped English politics in this decade [1558–1568] did not arise from English initiative, but English responses in each of the successive episodes were molded by the actions of a few dominant and very powerful personalities. In each episode the center of decision is to be found in the powerful but opaque personality of the queen. In the first few months of her reign a good deal could already be predicated about the new ruler. She was clearly her father's daughter; she had displayed the same personal qualities: courage, determination, a quick intelligence, a somewhat overpowering charm, a sardonic wit, and a commanding —indeed, an imperial—presence. Like Henry she had little interest in the more creative ranges of statesmanship although she possessed the same shrewd capacity for selecting advisors such as Cromwell or Cecil, who did possess these qualities.

But she soon showed the sharp differences which set her off from both Henry VIII and Mary Tudor. She shared neither Henry's zest for theological disputation nor her sister's simpler, but more potent, piety. There was in her a complete absence of the rather conventional ambitions of her father; obviously, she could not seek the laurels of a great commander, but, unlike her cousin of Scotland, Elizabeth entertained no ambitions for a marital alliance which would lift her to a greater throne than that of England. She was quite content to be queen of England and Ireland, and no more. Nor did she seek to magnify English power. In this she disappointed those enthusiasts who cast her as the English Deborah and—like Throckmorton—longed to see her mingle the glories of a Protestant champion with those of a renewed English leadership in Western European affairs.

More startling still was the absence in the queen of any marked dynastic sense. As there was no urge to magnify the dynasty's power, so there was none to perpetuate it. The lack of this particular motive, so dominant a trait among her predecessors and such contemporaries as Catherine de Medici, set off the English sovereign in an unusual way from her Continental peers. It gave to her political outlook a certain detachment and freed her advisors from some of the most vexing preoccupations of Continental ministers. On the other hand this very lack of ambition, dynastic or personal, left a kind of vacuum in her political attitudes since they were not oriented toward the usual goals of action. Nor did she share the religious enthusiasms which were the springs of action in so many of her contemporaries. She was in fact coldly—at times, hostilely—indifferent to religious concerns, pietist or *politique.*

The queen was, of course, deeply and happily involved in politics. She had an intensely political personality and loved the business of politics. She throve on the thrust and riposte, the matching of wits, and the confrontations—either on paper or face to face—which made up the everyday matter of political life. But her enjoyment stopped short at the door of the Council chamber. Once the focus of action moved to the distant frontiers of Scotland, or, worse still, beyond the seas, she was seized with doubts, anxieties, and hesitations. Necessarily, such actions could be carried out only by men; the limitations of her femininity came unpleasantly home to her at these times.

This sense of her limits of control was one of the factors which made Elizabeth in many respects a profound conservative, since it caused her always to long to contain events within the range of her immediate power as far as possible. There were other elements; her education was, in a sense, old-fashioned; she was as firm, though less learned, an exponent of divine-right monarchy as her Scottish successor. Monarchy, to her, was an instrument for protecting a standard of certainty in a political universe always threatened by instability. Certainly she did not see it as a tool for the selective and purposeful exercise of power. These views heightened the instinctive feelings for the unique dignity of her great office and its inviolability which worked steadily in her. Hence she was deeply resentful of any attempts to guide, to push, or even to persuade, since they seemed to impugn her capacities to fill that office. Open and independent initiatives such as those of the left-wing Protestants of course awakened her bitterest anger. And perhaps underlying this jealousy for her power was the suspicion that her masculine courtiers never quite believed in the royal capacities of a mere woman. This deeply buried sense of insecurity added another stratum to a complex character.

All these things working together made of the queen a ruler reluctant to act and suspicious of change. She always preferred to wait on events. At the best this produced an intelligent, cool-headed opportunism, which offset the sometimes overexcited nervousness of her ministers, to the benefit of the state. At the worst it led to a kind of *immobilisme* and a dangerous absence of imaginative leadership at the topmost level—the kind of leadership which goes out to meet a crisis, or at least prepares alternative solutions in advance.

In any case the conception and initiation of policy was frequently left to the royal councillors; it became their business to devise the best possible mode of proceeding in each individual contingency of state. It remained for the queen to accept, reject, or modify their proposals; there could be no question that final decision remained a royal prerogative. Often the result was a somewhat spasmodic working of the state machinery. In 1559–1560 Cecil propounded the scheme for countering the French in Scotland; it took months of unwearying patience to jog his mistress step by weary step along the path of action. At the worst, English policy came near to paralysis, as in the troubled months after Mary Stuart's fall when the queen's instincts, profoundly outraged by the Scottish nobles' treatment of their ruler, led her to insist on a policy which cut athwart all other considerations of English interests at this point. Her deep-rooted abhorrence of all rebels against constituted authority —monsters in nature—made for a constant bias in her attitude in a whole series of major decisions. Cooperation with rebels, Scottish,

French—or later, Dutch—went too much against the grain of her beliefs to make such policies easy for her. Yet this complex royal personality included not only an element of high-flown, metaphysical dogmatism but also the easy flexibility and moral neutrality of the practicing politician.

For the latter role the queen possessed great qualifications. First of all—a very masculine attribute—was the sheer force of her imperious personality, which she used ruthlessly in subordinating to her will both court and Council. She thus made effective her unchallenged control of all decisions. Yet by itself this might not have served had Elizabeth not also displayed two other traits. One was a self-mastery which enabled her at crucial moments to put political goals ahead of personal preferences. The great testing-time for this quality came in 1560–1561 when she tacitly turned away from marriage with Dudley. But that mastery was not always complete. In her relations with Mary Stuart, for instance, personal biases alternated uncertainly with political calculation, and her ministers had always to reckon with the influence of these half-buried but intensely felt instinctive reactions.

Secondly there was the keen political acumen which the professionals of her court came to appreciate. They continued to be dismayed and exasperated by what seemed to them a lack of seriousness about the ultimate goals of politics. But they came to have confidence in her as a virtuoso in the game of politics. They trusted her judgment as a player in making individual moves on the board. This respect for her professional skill made possible a working relationship between the queen and her ministers although it did not remove altogether their mutual misunderstandings. She, on her side, had no comprehension for their ideological involvements or for the goals which they pursued. They, on theirs, could not understand what seemed to them an ultimately wayward frivolity about the highest ends of state. Nevertheless, the combination of awestruck fear and professional admiration which the queen commanded in the highest political circles stood her in good stead when her control of policy was seriously challenged in 1569. It was the foundation of the political stability which obtained in the years to follow.

*   *   *

The course of events during these years [1568–1572] reflected in large part the attitudes of . . . three great actors; it was they who shaped the pattern of English development. The queen was almost always content to wait on events, to play for time, and run as few risks as possible; Cecil, pessimistic but resolved, brooded watchfully, ready to pounce when the opportunity offered, while Leicester became the spokesman of the activists, pushing for involvement and commitment. The bold gamble in Scotland in 1559–1560 which paid off so handsomely was largely Cecil's doing. But it was Dudley who was responsible for the intervention in Normandy two years later, an unwise speculation which ended in failure, but there was no harm done to vital interests of the English crown and no liabilities for the future were contracted. There followed some years of quiet isolation from Continental matters, a state of affairs which suited both the queen and her secretary. But in 1568 Cecil believed that impending dangers to English security made it absolutely necessary to resume the initiative and persuaded his mistress into the risky gamble of seizing Alva's treasure. The crisis that followed was frightening and for a moment in the succeeding spring royal confidence in the secretary may have wavered. But his skill in carrying through a policy which conceded nothing to Spain and yet avoided war assured the advancement of his career. Thereafter, in relations with France, Dudley once more came to the fore as the leading exponent of Anglo-French cooperation, but the final achievement of alliance involved Leicester and Burghley in a common enterprise.

At the very moment of agreement on the Treaty of Blois[1] the revolt of the Sea-beggars in Holland opened a new phase in English relations with the Low Countries, Spain, and France, but it found England in a relatively strong and advantageous position vis-à-vis all parties concerned. Relations with Scotland were also about to enter a new stage. In May 1573 the regent Morton, using artillery provided by the English, battered his way into Edinburgh Castle and smashed the last remnants of Marian power in Scotland. The final victim of the Stuart enchantress, Secretary Maitland, met his tragic end in the wake of this event. Scotland's future was as unpredictable

---

[1] The Treaty of Blois was concluded in April 1572, between France and England. It provided for mutual assistance if either country was attacked by a third power, for the establishment of a "staple" in France to compensate England for the loss of her Flemish trade, and for a mutual effort to establish peace in Scotland. The first two provisions were never enacted.

as ever, but at least the present situation was one which the English government could regard with some satisfaction.

At home the queen's preference for Dudley had skewed the shape of politics for many years. Even after she turned away from marriage with the favorite, there was a long duel between him and his enemies. Cecil played a discreet but important role in their plan to find a husband for their mistress, preferably the Austrian archduke. Their failure to achieve this had been followed by privy conspiracy of a mischievous kind—the effort to provide for the succession by marrying Mary and Norfolk. In this scheme the favorite in a characteristic move switched alliances, and played a key role, this time as a backer of the match and coconspirator in a plot to ruin Cecil. The failure of this scheme, the suppression of the earls' rising, and the successful detection of the Ridolfi plot had proved the enduring vitality of the regime and confirmed beyond all question the queen's sovereign control over English politics. Leicester had survived his adventures, essentially unscathed but reduced in importance and thoroughly tamed to a more domestic mode of political action than he had pursued in the past. Burghley had grown mightily in political stature, obtained new office, and risen to a new height of dignity and influence. Each rival had successively failed to dislodge the other, and they now were driven to an armistice and to tacit acceptance of the other's political existence.

Out of these events emerged the reestablishment of basic political stability, such as England had not enjoyed since Henry VIII's conscience was first troubled at the end of the 1520s. There had been at least two major causes for that prolonged instability. One, more urgent but essentially more superficial, had been felt only since the death of Henry in 1547. This was the absence of effective leadership at the very top. The political machinery of the English state was geared to operate only under firm royal direction, and this had been lacking under the boy-king Edward and his half-sister, Mary. And even though Elizabeth's personality was an imperiously commanding one, there was through the first decade of her reign an underlying lack of confidence in the political future. The second obstacle to renewed stability was more complex and far more difficult to surmount. It arose from a new phenomenon in English political life—the presence of a large body of organized, coherent, and very articulate public opinion on the great political questions of the age, shaped by the new faith and shared by a large segment of the aristocracy, which it was impossible either to ignore or effectively to control.

The first problem, although the simpler of the two, was far from easy to deal with. During Edward's time it became clear that the royal power of the Tudors could not be safely delegated during the incapacity of the monarch. The bitter infighting among the rival councillors led to conspiracy, coup d'état, and ultimately to Northumberland's attempt to replace the dynasty. Mary's swift recovery of power was reassuring, but she failed in the long run to win the enduring confidence of the political elite and by the end of her reign royal control was shaky and a real threat of civil strife shadowed the future.

Elizabeth reasserted effective royal control over the court and the aristocracy but the terrifying uncertainties of an unsecured succession, the plausible ambitions of Mary Stuart, and the ambiguities of the wider European religious and political scene made for continuing malaise and lack of confidence. Elizabeth's own flirtation with Robert Dudley did nothing to reassure those who were apprehensive of feminine rule, especially since the experience of Mary's reign. Deep unease arose from the unmarried condition of the sovereign. Men looked to the marriage of the queen not merely as a normal incident of her personal life but also as a necessary condition for effective royal leadership. Only a man could provide the weight of personality, the decision, and the judgment which would win general loyalty and trusting obedience. And only a man would display the ambition and driving energy which would give direction and purpose to political life. Elizabeth surprised her courtiers by the range of masculine qualities which she commanded, but, effective as her personal leadership was, it still lacked that very element of personal or dynastic ambition which men thought an essential ingredient in serious politics. For a long time they expected her to take a husband; until that event took place all political calculations seemed to them to have a merely provisional character.

In the end a partial but workable solution was found. The queen did not marry but she acquired surrogate husbands. Her collaboration with Cecil and Dudley—and to a lesser extent with the whole Council—served to fill out the missing dimensions of effective leadership. Leicester no doubt provided some of the personal emotional support which the queen would have found in actual marriage with him. But both secretary and favorite came to act in the less personal, the public and official roles, which a royal consort would have played. By providing those masculine elements of ambition and of drive toward a goal which even their versatile mistress could not encompass, they became a good deal more than mere ministers, offering advice and executing commands. They became in fact sharers in supreme power. In the total process of decision, the queen was very much the first person in this secular trinity, but, if the final choice was hers, the ingredients which went into it, the specific contents of decisions, were the ministers'. By this oblique participation in supreme power they slowly bent the shape of English policy into forms of their desiring.

The arrangement was a makeshift one and subject to strain. It depended on the cooperation of three powerful personalities, and, as we have seen, two of these, Cecil and Dudley, devoted much of their energy in the 1560s to attacking one another. The queen's steady but measured support, first of Dudley in the years when the Howard clan sought to oust him, and then of Cecil in the crisis years of 1569 and 1570, finally steadied the triple relationship and made regular the orbits of movement of the two lesser lights. The Elizabethan political world now had about it an air of permanence and predictability which had been lacking for the past fifteen years. The queen would not marry, but her confidence in Burghley and Leicester was now a reliable landmark. Men could make their political calculations accordingly, possessing at last a political map which was clearly marked. They knew which were the thoroughfares to favor and advancement and they knew that these highroads would be open so long as the political principals remained alive.

The second great obstacle to a stable political order was of a different magnitude from the first, nothing less than a mutation in the very nature of English politics. . . .

*   *   *

The problem which required attention was how to regularize relations between a conservative and traditionalist monarch and those determined advocates of a forward [Protestant] policy. By an ironic turn of history the political activism which the queen's father had introduced to the English scene when he used the royal power to overthrow Rome's authority was now taken over by a political elite which, while loyal to the crown, drew its strength and convictions from sources quite independent of the monarchy. The crown in its turn had reverted, under Elizabeth, to a conserving and balancing role in society, consolidating the general position which Henry had secured rather than moving toward any new ground.

The risks of open defiance of the crown were limited by the ironclad necessity which bound the queen and her Protestant subjects in permanent embrace. Neither could do without the other; for her there was no turning back from the decisions of 1559, however much she would have liked to blur the fact. For them she was the only possible occupant of the throne. Nevertheless, the radical Protestants did not allow even their rejoicing in Elizabeth's providential accession to hinder their determination to have their own way on the religious settlement. In 1563 they made themselves felt in Convocation, where they were narrowly defeated, and in 1566 in Parliament. They were unremitting in their efforts to obtain harsher anti-Catholic laws and further reform of the English church. They also took up a determined stand on the succession and were resolved to block Mary's claims. After 1559 they never were very successful in securing additional religious reform, but they jostled the government into an evermore extreme anti-Catholic stance and effectually checked Mary Stuart's hopes for the succession. In the Hapsburg wooing they made clear their disapproval of a marriage which would exempt the royal consort from the penal laws. In all these things what is important is their cheerful determination to oppose their judgments to the queen's whenever their convictions so dictated. The traditional view that great decisions of state were solely the business of the crown was being shunted firmly aside.

Elizabeth's responses to these pressures varied from haughty rejection of their demands to politic evasion, but she took few pains to conceal her dislike for the religious reformers and rarely shared even the *politique* Protestant enthusiasms of Burghley. In addition she resented what seemed to her an assault on her inviolable prerogative by these clamant, self-appointed counsellors, thrusting their proposals on her at every possible opportunity. Since neither side was likely to yield much in its views, there seemed to be an impasse.

What imperceptibly evolved was an arrangement characteristically makeshift, clumsily intricate, and just workable. The Council eventually provided the necessary bridge. That body, as it was constituted by 1572, had a good deal of homogeneity. All its members—save Croft[2]—were committed adherents of the new religion and agreed with one another on the major lines—if not the details—of national policy. They were dominated by the two major figures of Burghley and Leicester. This relatively harmonious and compact body enjoyed the full confidence of the queen; most of its members were her own choice; the lord admiral[3] was by now the sole holdover from her sister's reign. But they were also men who had close and sympathetic relations with the countryside and most particularly with the gentry of an advanced Protestant outlook. With the possible exception of Smith,[4] none of them was solely a courtier or a bureaucrat; each had his landed base and regional status—Leicester in Warwickshire, Burghley and Mildmay[5] in Northamptonshire, Bedford in the West, Knollys in Oxfordshire, to cite only a few. They were thus ideally suited to serve as transformers between the high political voltage of many of Elizabeth's more prominent subjects and the very low political voltage of the queen herself. They were able to mediate between the cool indifference of the monarch and the ardent Protestant activism of her subjects. The two centers of initiative within the nation—the crown and the party of the new faith—were brought into a clumsy but viable working relationship. The presence of such outspoken supporters of the advanced Protestant cause as Leicester, Bedford, or Knollys, or of the more discreet but no less committed Burghley, gave a sense of confidence to the gentlemen of left-wing persuasions in the counties.

This cumbersome arrangement had relatively narrow working limits; in the next generation even the more moderate Puritan hopes for reform were doomed to disappointment. But that lay in the future; in 1572 reformers could afford to be more cheerful. There

[2] Sir James Croft, comptroller of the royal household.
[3] Lord William Howard, appointed lord admiral in 1553 and lord chamberlain in 1558 (by Mary) and 1559 (by Elizabeth).
[4] Sir Thomas Smith, who also served as secretary and ambassador to France.
[5] Sir Walter Mildmay, chancellor of the exchequer.

was a line of communication between the crown and a restless, opinionated elite. So long as the Privy Council retained a broadly representative function, so long as it was not solely a "court" body but also in some sense a "country" one as well, there would be some protection against a dangerous rift between the rival foci of loyalty and action—the crown and the Protestant interest.

The years between 1568 and 1572 were crowded with melodramatic events, tumbling one upon another in rapid succession, bewildering and alarming to spectators. Yet, veiled by their turbulent confusion, a number of clear-cut and far-reaching changes were rapidly taking place. What was most visible to contemporaries—and most comforting to them—was the fact that the new regime had finally won through to a hopeful prospect of lasting stability. Rather more slowly they came to realize that the longer and even more dangerous era of instability which had opened when Henry VIII led the country into the Reformation was now past. Lastly, an even greater shift in the deep currents of English political life was just beginning to make itself felt as England moved out of the classical age of dynastic politics. The nation was leaving behind the relative simplicities of a time when the great decisions of state had been determined largely by the interests and ambitions of the royal house. Ahead lay a troubled time when royal authority would be challenged by opinionated and ambitious subjects with their own strong views on national policy. It was the beginning of the long and painful transformation from personal monarchy into an aristocratic parliamentary polity. In this new era the traditional currents of personal and family interest would be crossed by the strong tides of ideological conviction.

But in 1572 what was most immediately apparent was that the Elizabethan regime had at last attained its majority.

The Exercise of Royal Authority

Conyers Read

THE PARTNERSHIP WITH BURGHLEY AND THE FATE OF MARY STEWART

Born in Philadelphia in 1881, Conyers Read studied at Harvard and Oxford. In a distinguished academic career he taught at Princeton (1909–1910), the University of Chicago (1910–1920), and the University of Pennsylvania (1934–1951). He served as executive secretary (1933–1941) and president (1949) of the American Historical Association, and was a Corresponding Fellow of the Royal Historical Society and a member of the American Philosophical Society. Moreover he was also president of the textile firm, William F. Read & Sons. In addition to his extensive two-volume study of William Cecil, his works include Mr. Secretary Walsingham and the Policy of Queen Elizabeth *(3 vols., 1925) and* The Tudors *(1936). He died in 1959. Read's careful analysis of Elizabeth's actions prior to Mary's execution sheds light on her relationship with Cecil and with Parliament, as well as the extent of her responsibility for Mary's death.*

She disclosed early that she had, like her father before her, a fine eye for a competent man and a genuine devotion to the interests of her country. But it does not appear that she had any pattern of action. Cecil, who was closest to her, never could be quite sure what she would do next. He was always ready to tell her what to do, but he never could and never really attempted to dominate her. She was always the mistress, he always the loyal servant.

As she became increasingly aware of his competency and his integrity, she gave increasing weight to his counsels. It would be difficult to decide whether, during this first critical decade of her reign, he did more to influence her, or she to influence him. What emerged was a partnership in which his wide knowledge and worldly wisdom tempered her feminine impulses and her versatility forced him to cast off the shackles of precedent. Together they carved out their own errant way without any particular respect for established patterns of procedure, turning now to religious now to secular considerations, resorting now to flirtations, now to the more orthodox methods of diplomacy, as the exigencies of the occasion seemed to demand. Since they were not hampered by guiding principles, they had operated with great flexibility. What they both wanted was a strong and a secure England; all other considerations, religious as well as secular, were subordinated to that end. They were to go together through many a perilous passage before they achieved it. But during this first decade they defined their objective and made a fair appraisal of the obstacles they had to surmount on the way to it.

*   *   *

All that remained to be done [in 1586] with Mary Stuart was to proceed to her execution. But that turned out to be the hardest task of all. Even the verdict was not proclaimed until after confirmatory action by Parliament.

Meanwhile, both the French and the Scottish ambassadors were interesting themselves on Mary's behalf. Two days before the verdict was reached in Star Chamber, the French ambassador, being denied audience, wrote a letter to Elizabeth for the stay of proceedings against Mary. "But it was answered," Walsingham wrote to Stafford, "by her Majesty, that it was not convenient to stay the proceedings and [she] hoped that the King, his master, would not be an intercessor in that behalf, and if he should, she could not but take it unkindly at his hands."

James of Scotland had sent a special envoy to intercede for his mother. But both Elizabeth and her councillors were convinced that the Scottish king was chiefly concerned about his presumptive rights to the English succession. That accounts for the explicit statement on the subject by the commissioners and the judges at Westminster.

Burghley undoubtedly took an active part in dealing with the Scottish and the French delegations, of which a few fragments are recorded. We hear of him wining and dining Archibald Douglas,

FIGURE 3. William Cecil, Lord Burghley. Attributed to Marcus Gheeraerts. (*National Portrait Gallery, London*)

James's quasi-ambassador in London, sometime parson of Glasgow, who had played some part in the murder of the king's father and was at the moment playing some part in betraying the king's mother, but who temporarily enjoyed the king's favor. We hear also of a long debate between Burghley and Pomponne de Bellièvre, one of the French king's ablest councillors, who had been sent to intervene for Mary on points of law involved, interlarded with quotations from Cicero and the *Corpus Juris* and historical precedents. . . .

Bellièvre, after his return to Paris, made some complimentary remarks about Burghley to the English ambassador there. He knew nobody, he said, of the Council of England so impassioned as Burghley, saving only the queen herself. He complained, however, that Burghley seemed to be counting upon an early peace with Spain, an indication that Burghley seized upon the occasion to play upon the old rivalry of Hapsburg and Valois.

It cannot be doubted that Elizabeth herself was somewhat concerned about both the Scottish and the French attitudes—though mainly because she herself was more than doubtful about the expediency of the final step and therefore disposed to overemphasize all objections to it. Davison reported to Walsingham on October 29 that he had long arguments with her on the subject.

> *She laid before me the same objections she had used before to yourself, which I did repel with all the reason I had and in the end, as I conceive, left her satisfied. The most material point she urged was the danger she stood in of the son, after the mother should be taken away, to whom all her [Mary's] friends would be ready to offer themselves. I let her see the fear to be utterly vain if she list to take such a course, as in honour and surety and good policy she ought, that her [Mary's] friends consisted of our enemies in religion, which could have no hope in him, remaining as he is. . . . Another scruple was that yet the King of Spain, having a title, might affect the kingdom for himself. The affecting of it I granted, but the likelihood of attaining it I impugned. . . . This and a great deal more passed between her and me yesternight.*

Burghley and his colleagues all felt that the best way to strengthen Elizabeth's resolution was by Parliament. As early as September 8 he had written to Walsingham: "We stick upon parliament which her Majesty misliketh, but we do all persist to make the burden better borne and the world abroad better satisfied."

The Parliament called in 1584 was still in being, and by its last prorogation was to meet again on November 15. The Privy Council held that this was too late and persuaded the queen to dissolve it on September 19 and to summon a new parliament. In order, however, that the personnel of the Parliament in being should be preserved as far as might be, the Privy Council sent off letters to the constituencies urging them to favor the sitting members. The new parliament was summoned for October 15, but the delays attending upon Mary Stuart's trial led Burghley to the conclusion that October 15 was too early. He dug up a precedent from Elizabeth's first parliament which justified a postponement of the day of assembling and instructed Walsingham to prepare a warrant accordingly. Burghley suggested that October 22 would be a good day. Elizabeth thought this hardly allowed time enough, and actually Parliament did not meet until a week later. Obviously a verdict had to be reached on Mary before Parliament could be asked to consider her further fate, the sole reason for its summoning.

The Parliament of 1586–1587 was a momentous one. At this point we are only concerned with its first session which adjourned on December 2 and did not reassemble until Mary had gone to her reckoning.

On October 16, Burghley wrote to Shrewsbury: "Tomorrow the parliament shall be prorogued until Saturday, at which time her Majesty will come from Lambeth to Westminster, return to Lambeth until Monday forenoon and then, having allowed of the Speaker, return to Richmond." Evidently Elizabeth's original intention was to open Parliament in the usual fashion. But she changed her mind between Wednesday and Saturday.

As it turned out, she absented herself from the opening ceremonies, and remained at Richmond, not wishing, as she herself said later, to participate in the proceedings against her kinswoman. Instead she appointed a committee of three, Whitgift and Burghley and the Earl of Derby, to act for her.

Up until the adjournment on December 2, Parliament devoted its attention almost exclusively to the Queen of Scots. There were eloquent denunciations of her in the Commons, the best of them by Sir Christopher Hatton; analogous denunciations in the Lords with Bromley[1] and Burghley and principal speakers. Of Burghley's we

---

[1] Sir Thomas Bromley, appointed lord chancellor in 1579.

know no more than the brief entry of it in the *Lords Journals:* "The which, by Wm., Lord Burghley, Lord Treasurer of England, as one unto whom the said Queen of Scots' whole proceedings were better known by reason of his long service done unto our most gracious sovereign Lady, since the beginning of her reign, were more fully dilated."

The burden of all the speeches was that Mary should "suffer the due execution of justice according to her deserts."

Both houses then proceeded to prepare a petition to the queen. Burghley evidently played an important part in the drafting of the petition. The gist of it is as follows:

> We beseech your Majesty that declaration of the said sentence *[against the Scottish queen]* and judgment be made and published by proclamation and thereupon direction be given for further proceeding against the said Scottish Queen according to the effect and true meaning of the Statute of 1584–5.

It was presented to the queen at Richmond on the twelfth. She was evidently restless to receive it, asked Burghley if he could get it to her on the eleventh. He had to point out to her that it could not be arranged. Nothing which was done seemed to suit her. Burghley wrote to Davison on the eleventh:

> Yesterday in the parliament chamber grew a question whether it were convenient for the two archbishops and four other bishops to accompany the Lords temporal in the petition to her Majesty for the execution of the Scottish Queen. Some scruple I had whether her Majesty would like it because in former times the bishops in parliament were wont to absent themselves. But yet I do not think *[it]* unlawful for them to be present and persuaders in such causes as the execution of the sentence tends to the state of the church as it does.

He bade Davison consult the queen's pleasure.

He wrote to Shrewsbury on the twelfth that the petition was to be presented the same day at Richmond "by 21 Lords temporal, 6 Lords spiritual and 40 of the Commons." But at the last moment again Elizabeth decided otherwise, and the clergy did not appear. Burghley needed all his sangfroid to adjust himself to these royal whims. "I still find by experience," he wrote to Walsingham "that such direction must be taken as princes shall give, after counsel given."

The petition was presented on the twelfth with speeches by the Lord Chancellor and the Speaker of the House. The queen's reply is among the more notable of her public utterances.

She began with an expression of her gratitude to God for his mercies. She rejoiced in the good will of her subjects, "which, if haply I should want, well might I breathe but never think I lived." In this connection she referred to the Bond of Association as eloquent testimony of their devotion. She declared that she was not unwilling to die if she might serve her people that way. She swore that she was without malice to Mary and would gladly have pardoned her if she had confessed her faults. And finally she asked for time to consider—to seek divine guidance. But she promised a speedy answer.

Burghley described the speech "as princely wise and grave . . . not only to the admiration of all that heard it but to the drawing out of the tears out of many eyes."

In reporting Elizabeth's answer to the Commons on the following Monday (November 14), Hatton mentioned something which the queen had forgot and which she had charged him to declare to them. It was to the effect that she would be glad to spare the "taking of her [Mary's] blood, if by any other means to be devised by her Highness' Great Council of this realm, the safety of her Majesty's own person and of the state might be preserved."

This suggestion was debated during the ensuing week in both houses and the answer was unanimous—Mary must die.

The parliamentary committee was called again to wait upon the queen on November 24, to give their answer and to receive hers. Elizabeth's speech on this occasion followed very much the same lines as her earlier one. She had hoped they would find another way out. She complained that having winked at so many treasons she should now be forced to take action and spill the blood of her own kinswoman. She was not so much concerned to prolong her own life as to save both their lives. She spoke of her accession, of the religion in which she was born, of her determination to maintain it. She claimed that she had been a just ruler. She appreciated their advice which she took to be wise and honest and conscionable. But she was still in doubt.

"Therefore," she concluded, "if I should say I would not do as you require it might peradventure be more than I thought—and to say I would do it might perhaps breed peril of that you do labour to preserve."

It was, as she herself described it, an answer answerless.

What she did intend at this juncture is past finding out. Her immediate intention was clearly to disclaim all desire to bring Mary to her reckoning, and at the same time to make manifest her devotion to her subjects, to their faith, and to their interests. It is not improbable that she hoped that someone of those who had signed and sealed the Bond of Association would take the law into his own hands. In that connection her effort to have the bond mentioned in the petition and her own emphasis upon it in her speech are significant. In any case, she proceeded to rid herself of further parliamentary pressure by a sudden decision to prorogue Parliament.

Elizabeth's speeches were rushed into print. They appeared in pamphlet form before the end of the year. John Stow set them forth in what was virtually the last item in the second edition of Holinshed which came out early in January 1587.[2] A French version was published in the same year. There is sound reason to believe that the editor was Robert Cecil, Burghley's youngest son, who sat in the Parliament of 1586. Robert was only twenty-three years old at the time, but precocious beyond his years. Accepting his authorship, it may be conjectured that Burghley prompted the publication. He was a firm believer in propaganda of that sort. Certainly Elizabeth herself approved. She even went so far as to correct the copy in her own hand before it went to press.

But Burghley was far from happy at Elizabeth's noncommittal attitude. He wrote Davison on November 24, the same day upon which Elizabeth delivered her "answer answerless":

> *I pray you remember her Majesty to send in writing the manner of the speech that my Lord Chancellor shall use tomorrow at the prorogation of the parliament. I know her Majesty meaneth to thank them for their pains, and especially for their care and continuance therein for her safety, but if they have not some comfort also to see the fruits of their cares by some demonstration to proceed from her Majesty, the thanks will be of small weight to carry into the countries [i.e., counties]. And then the realm may call this a vain parliament or otherwise nickname it a parliament of words. For there is no law made for the realm and if also*

---

[2] The antiquarian and chronicler John Stow revised Raphael Holinshed's *Chronicles,* an early record of English history.

there be no publication presently of so solemn a sentence, the sentence against the Queen of Scots will be termed a dumb sentence, whereof the nobility that have given it and all the parliament that have affirmed it may repent themselves of their time spent.

The sentence is already more than a full month and four days old.

If her Majesty will sign it this day both the ambassador of Scotland may be prevented this day in that point, as done to satisfy the importunity of all the noblemen [of] the Commission and of all the States in the parliament. And tomorrow also my Lord Chancellor may declare the same, to the liking of parliament.

And for hope of the last part for execution, if her Majesty shall be content that it be said that therein she will prefer no other men's advice, being strangers, afore her own people, she shall leave hope of execution. And to that hope I beseech God give full perfection.

Thus you see I cannot but utter my opinion, long afore daylight, for I have been up since five.

Burghley's reference to the Scottish ambassador is explained by a letter which he wrote to Shrewsbury on the twelfth, in which he referred to a request by Mr. Keith, the Scottish envoy, for "a stay of proceedings against the Queen of Scots, and that nothing be done to the prejudice of any title of the King." "The latter," Burghley wrote, "is granted; the former can hardly be granted without her Majesty's peril and discontentation of all the parliament, wherein the sentence against her is already confirmed."

Elizabeth, at the last moment, postponed prorogation for a week and, in deference to Burghley's objections, shortened the period of recess to February 15.

But she could not be persuaded to proclaim the sentence against Mary until after Parliament had risen.

Burghley got word of this latest royal volte-face at nine o'clock in the morning when the Lords were already assembled and the Commons on their way to join them for the prorogation. It arrived at the last possible moment in the queen's own illegible hand—so illegible that Burghley had to write it out for the lord chancellor's perusal. He observed in a letter to Davison that Bromley "also misliked such a sudden warning." He added: "These hard accidents happen by her Majesty being so far from hence"—a shrewd thrust at Elizabeth's deliberate retreat to Richmond.

Instead of prorogation, Elizabeth ordered that the Parliament be adjourned for a week. She was evidently sparring for time, uncertain about her next step. Meanwhile, Burghley pressed forward. On the twenty-ninth the commissioners of the trial assembled at Star Chamber to subscribe the sentence against Mary. The following day Burghley wrote to Shrewsbury, apologizing for not writing sooner. "Truly," he added, "the impediment is lack of leisure, being of late time and yet still more toiled with a care of her Majesty's affairs than I was these many years. . . . The sentence was subscribed yesterday by all the Commissioners. . . . I left a place for your name. The session shall be prorogued on Friday next [December 2] as I think, but I must ride tomorrow to Richmond and thereupon her Majesty will conclude."

The following morning he wrote to Walsingham: "I passed through the city and Southwark afore daylight, which served me to small purpose, for though I came [to Richmond] about 8 yet her Majesty did not stir before ten."

He had with him his draft of the proclamation.

I had good hap to please her fully to all respects, as she affirmed before my L. of Leicester and Mr. Secty. Davison, with that which I brought to be proclaimed. And so having caused it to be engrossed, which could not be before three. . . . Whereby I could not have time to bring the warrant signed, as I desired, that it might have been proclaimed tomorrow. But she will not have it published before Saturday.

"What will follow," Burghley wrote to Shrewsbury, "a few days will declare. Her Majesty is greatly pressed by the French and Scottish [ambassadors] to stay from the action. God must direct her therein which I most desire to be for her honour and her safety."

The sentence was proclaimed on Sunday, December 4, two days after Parliament was prorogued. Burghley had worked hard to have it announced in Parliament, but Elizabeth would not have it so. She evidently felt that its publication in Parliament would unduly intensify her commitments. Possibly one reason why she released it for publication at all was the opportune return of Leicester from the Low Countries on November 24, who for over a month had been urging upon her the necessity of disposing of Mary.

Burghley hoped that the proclamation of the sentence would be followed at once by an order for Mary's execution. He and Walsingham together drew up an order accordingly, with the idea that it should be dispatched the day after the sentence was proclaimed. On the tenth, Burghley, in Elizabeth's name, drafted orders to

Paulet to proceed to the execution. But once again she declined to
act.

It was probably with the idea of prodding her to action that a
conspiracy was hatched early in January, in which Des Trappes, one
of the servants of the French ambassador, was named as the *agent
provocateur,* and William Stafford, renegade brother of the English
ambassador in France, the assassin. The objective was twofold,
first to frighten the queen into action, second to cut off the communications of the French ambassador and so prevent further
French intervention until action with Mary was taken. We have a
long account in Burghley's hand of a conference with Châteauneuf
at his house, at which Leicester and Hatton and Davison were all
present. Châteauneuf admitted that Stafford had come to him with a
plot to murder the queen but that he had refused to have any part
in it. Burghley observed that, if that were so, Châteauneuf should
have felt morally obligated to reveal the conspiracy. He refused to
admit the obligation. And so the conference ended.

On January 11, Burghley wrote to Sir Edward Stafford: "I am
right sorry of an unhappy accident . . . whereof the ambassador
will complain, though we have cause to complain of him. But hereof
you shall hear more very shortly. I am commanded not to write to
you at this time, although I think the messenger will give you some
taste, which, though it may seem somewhat sour at the first, yet you
shall have no cause for yourself to doubt any sinister opinion, either
by her Majesty or any impassionate Councillor." The final sentence
here of course refers to Stafford's renegade brother.

Shortly afterwards William Waad was dispatched to the French
king with an official account of the plot. We need not pursue the
matter further. Châteauneuf was denied audience until after Mary's
execution. He was then by degrees received back into favor. Des
Trappes was released and in March Walsingham told Châteauneuf
that he was convinced that the whole business amounted to nothing
more than an effort on William Stafford's part to extort money from
the French ambassador. Walsingham blamed Davison, by this time
the established scapegoat for all the sins of the English government.
In any case the conspiracy served its turn.

Of Elizabeth's attitude towards Mary we hear little or nothing
after the proclamation of the sentence against her on December 4.
Months later Burghley wrote that she was being constantly urged

by her Privy Council to proceed to the execution of the sentence, "but [they] were dismissed unsatisfied with no other reason but that it was a natural disposition in her, utterly repugnant to her mind." This probably was true, though, when Burghley wrote it, his purpose was to convince the king of Scotland that Elizabeth had nothing to do with Mary's execution.

The events which followed, Davison set forth at length in a long letter to Walsingham. By his account Elizabeth had ordered Burghley to draw up a warrant for Mary's execution shortly after the sentence against her had been proclaimed. This warrant Burghley left with Davison with directions to have the queen sign it. After some delay, occasioned by the intervention of Scotland and France, she decided to sign it, and on February 1 she directed Lord Admiral Howard to order Davison to bring her the warrant. He did so. She called for pen and ink, signed it and told Davison to take it to the lord chancellor to receive the Great Seal, charging Davison to keep the matter secret, but suggesting that he show it to Walsingham, who was sick in bed in his London house. " 'The grief thereof,' she merrily said, 'would go near killing him outright.' " She then went on to speak of the execution. It should be as secret as possible and be done in the hall at Fotheringhay. At the same time she complained that others might have eased her of the burden and suggested that a letter be written to Paulet and Sir Drue Drury[3] sounding out their disposition to take the law into their own hands and, in accordance with the Bond of Association, dispose of Mary without warrant. Davison argued strongly against such a course. But Elizabeth retorted that it had been suggested to her by wiser persons than himself. Beale said later that Leicester had inspired the idea, which seems not improbable. In any case Elizabeth would have it so.

Davison went at once to Burghley and related what had passed, thence to Walsingham to whom he passed on Elizabeth's instructions about the letter to Paulet and Drury, and so to the lord chancellor who had the Great Seal attached to the warrant.

Next day early Elizabeth sent Henry Killigrew to him with orders not to have the warrant sealed until she had spoken to him. He went to her and explained. She protested against his haste, declared

---

[3] Drury assisted Sir Amyas Paulet in the care of Mary at Fotheringay.

that it might have been done in some other way and finally dismissed Davison impatiently with the remark that she wanted to hear no more of it until it was done.

Davison then went to Hatton, the vice-chamberlain, told the whole story, disclosed the queen's wavering attitude and said he could do no more. He and Hatton together then went to confer with Burghley, and the three of them decided to lay the problem before the Council. Burghley read to Hatton the instructions which he had drafted for the execution, which Hatton thought went into too much detail. Burghley undertook to rewrite them and, when the Council assembled later in Burghley's chambers, Burghley submitted the revised copy.

Davison went on to say that Burghley then addressed the Council. The queen, he said, had done everything she could do. He was aware of the fact that she was wavering in her decision, but he called to mind that she had told Davison that she wanted to hear no more of it until it was done. For his part he was prepared to bear his share of the burden without troubling her further. The Council agreed, and they selected Robert Beale to carry the orders to Fotheringhay.

The following morning Elizabeth spoke to Davison again, told him of a bad dream she had, a bad dream about Mary. Davison asked her whether she was resolute to go through with the execution of the warrant. "Her answer was yes, confirmed with a solemn oath in some vehemency." But she once more raised the question of disposing of Mary some other way, and in the afternoon she asked whether he had heard anything from Paulet. He told her no. But he heard from Paulet a little later in the day, and took his reply to the queen the following morning.

It is a well-known letter. The essence of it is contained in two sentences:

> My good livings and life are at her Majesty's disposition and I am ready to so leave them this next morrow if it shall so please her. . . . But God forbid that I should make so foul a shipwreck of my conscience or leave so great a blot to my poor posterity to shed blood without law or warrant.

It was a noble letter from a noble man, but Elizabeth did not find it to her liking. She complained of his daintiness, of his disregard of the Bond of Association which he had signed, stormed against "the niceness of those precise fellows [as she termed them] who in words would do great things but indeed perform nothing." And she went on to name "one Wingfield" who with some others would undertake it. Finally she grew weary of the debate and retired.

It is only fair to Elizabeth to point out that her preferred alternative was later endorsed both in Scotland and in France. But it was not English, not even sixteenth-century English. Most of Paulet's countrymen would have shuddered, as Paulet shuddered, at the idea of assassination. To this day it is a foul blot upon the memory of the Virgin Queen.

The next morning she had another change of heart, and declared to Davison that "it were time this matter were dispatched," swearing a great oath that it was a shame that it was not already done, considering that she had for her part "done all that law or reason could require of her."

This, according to Davison, was his last speech with her. The next day news came of Mary's execution.

Years later, Robert Cecil, in describing the perils of the secretary's office observed: "Only a Secretary hath no warrant or commission in matters of his own greatest peril but the virtue and word of his sovereign." Davison has given us his report of his interviews with Elizabeth, but it depended upon her virtue and word to validate them. It does not appear that she directly contradicted him. All she remembered, or chose to remember, of what passed between her and Davison was that she had told him to keep the matter secret and he had disobeyed. His answer was that the lord chamberlain knew, the lord chancellor knew, and she had herself told him to tell Walsingham. Under these circumstances he interpreted her injunction as not including her most intimate councillors. But the queen insisted that he had broken faith with her, and on those grounds he was sentenced to a fine of 10,000 marks and thrust into the Tower. He was released after eighteen months, his fine apparently was remitted and he continued to receive his secretary's salary until his death twenty years later. But he never recovered the queen's favor.

Robert Beale's account of his part in the business took up the story where Davison left it. Beale was Walsingham's brother-in-law, the same Beale who was one of the stoutest defenders of the Puritan position both in the court and in the Commons. We need not follow his narrative in detail. He told how Davison called upon him at eleven o'clock on the night of February 2, met him the next morning at Walsingham's house and notified him that the Privy Council had selected him to carry the death warrant to Fotheringhay.

Beale went to Greenwich the next morning and appeared before a meeting of the Privy Council in Burghley's chambers. Eleven councillors were there, including Burghley, Leicester, Howard, Hatton, and Davison. Walsingham was too sick to attend. Burghley presided. He explained the situation to Beale, impressed upon him the need for great speed and secrecy, the danger to the queen if his errand were known, and gave him detailed instructions as to his procedure. In order to cover Beale's real mission, he was provided with a commission to investigate hues and cries in Hertfordshire and thereabouts. He was also provided with letters to Shrewsbury and to Paulet, which Burghley drafted, Davison wrote, and all the councillors signed. Walsingham's signature was even obtained in his sick bed.

These instructions given, the councillors then promised among themselves not to reveal to the queen the sending down of the warrant "before the execution were past."

Some time before Beale left for Fotheringhay, Burghley and Walsingham together seem to have given some thought to the ritual of the execution. We have a memorandum in their two hands on the subject. Opposite Walsingham's note, "To consider what speeches were fit for the two Earls to use at the time of the execution," Burghley has written, "To express her many attempts both for the destruction of the Queen's person and the invasion of this realm, that the hope and comforts she hath given to the principal traitors of this realm, both abroad and here at home, are the very occasions of all the attempts that have been against her Majesty's person, and so confessed, and yet do continue, so as sure by the laws of God and man she is justly condemned to die. The whole realm hath often time vehemently required that justice might be done, which her Majesty cannot longer delay."

Opposite Walsingham's note, "To direct the Earls what to do in case she shall desire any private speech," Burghley has written,

"Not to refuse it so it be to three or two at the least." Other details had to do with her servants, her jewels, her burial. Burghley noted that she should be buried in the parish church in an *uppermost* place. One interesting question was raised by Walsingham as to what should be done if the sheriff of Northants, in direct charge of the execution "by some great impediment cannot attend." Burghley answered: "The Lords at the Court to give out that there will be no execution." A strange query and a strange answer.

Beale carried out his orders, and the execution proceeded as arranged. It has been well said that nothing in Mary's life became her so well as the leaving of it. When it was all over, Beale sent an account of it to the Privy Council. Preserved among Burghley's papers at Hatfield is a résumé of this account in his own hand. It may have been made for the queen's perusal. That may explain why, though Burghley followed the text of the report fairly closely, he left out altogether the following passage: "She demanded to speak with her priest, which was denied unto her, the rather for that she came with a superstitious pair of beads and a crucifix."

This brutal intolerance smacked of Puritanism. Elizabeth would not have liked its flavor.

Reviewing the events of the momentous week which lay between Elizabeth's signing of the death warrant and Mary's execution— and there can be little doubt about the facts—it appears that the immediate responsibility for Mary's execution lay squarely on Burghley's shoulders. He must have concluded that Elizabeth favored Mary's death but disliked to assume the responsibility for it. Long experience must have taught him that, so far as Mary was concerned, she would never take the straightforward course. And he decided to act for her. It was a calculated risk and he took it, though he made sure that all the essential orders bore the signatures of the Privy Council. It is tempting to assume that the whole procedure was by prearrangement with his mistress and that even her indignation was feigned. But the subsequent course of events does not bear out that interpretation. In any case, his decision was one of the most heroic events in his career, and it seems to have come as close as anything he ever did to accomplishing his downfall. At least he seems to have thought so. This much at least is fairly certain; had he not acted as he did, Mary would have been spared to plague Protestant England as long as she lived.

John Ernest Neale
ROYAL AUTHORITY AND PARLIAMENT

Serious business started on January 21 [1581]: quietly enough, with an exhortation from the Speaker[1] "to use reverent and discreet speeches, to leave curiosities of form, to speak to the matter"; "not to spend too much time in unnecessary motions or superfluous arguments." It was his mistress's voice. Decorum was not forgotten: there was a charming motion about that. Thereupon, while late-comers filtered in, they read a bill. Discipline then broke.

In 1576 it had been Peter Wentworth who at a similar moment set the sobersides shaking. This time it was his brother Paul. He "made a motion for a public fast, to the end that it might please God to bless us in our actions better than we had been heretofore, and for a sermon to be had every morning." We do not possess the text of his speech, but the words in our diarist's report—"better than we had been heretofore"—suggest a Pistor-like[2] lamentation or an echo of brother Peter's diatribe on the profane and deplorable proceedings of past parliaments. Whether or not he elaborated the point, members doubtless took it.

This apart, the motion was far from innocent and harmless, as we might suppose. Fasting was a conspicuous characteristic of Puritan practice; and the official attitude to it may be judged from the following admonition given to Bishop Chaderton by the Archbishop of York in the following May. "My Lord, you are noted to yield too much to general fastings. . . . There lurketh matter under that pretended piety. The devil is crafty; and the young ministers of these our times grow mad." What is more, to prescribe a public act of worship was the exclusive right of the supreme governor of the church and her ecclesiastical advisers. Coming directly after the royal injunction not to meddle in matters of religion, it seemed a

From *Elizabeth I and Her Parliaments, 1559–1581,* by John Ernest Neale (New York, 1958), pp. 378–92. Copyright © 1958 by Sir John Neale. Reprinted by permission of Sir John Neale and Jonathan Cape Ltd.

[1] John Popham, the solicitor general.
[2] Tristram Pistor, Puritan M.P. for Stockbridge, Hants., in Elizabeth's parliaments beginning in 1571.

blatant defiance of authority. When we reflect on Lewkenor's[3] premeditated call to prayer three days before, we are tempted to suspect that once more a group of Puritans had concerted their strategy, intending to launch an attack on the shortcomings, if not on the structure of the church, in the aura of daily revivalist excitement. Indeed, from an obscure passage in a later speech by Sir Christopher Hatton we might even infer that Wentworth in his motion had linked the fast with such a program.

The godly Knollys, though ready to fast with the best of them, was shocked. As leader of the House he rose at once to oppose the motion. . . .

The motion "was long argued": "*pro* and *con.*" . . . Fast, the majority of members were evidently determined to do. The opposition therefore tried to ride off on an amendment, that it "be private, everybody to himself." On this issue—public or private—the House divided: 115 voted for the former, 100 for the latter. . . . Conscious that they had been greatly daring, the House turned diplomatic and agreed that their councillor-members should nominate the preachers for the fast, "to the end they might be such as would keep convenient proportion of time and meddle with no matter of innovation or unquietness."

Next morning the Speaker was absent. He did not turn up until after 11 a.m., and then, having read the usual prayer, omitting the Litany for the shortness of time, adjourned the House. He had been at the court, summoned to attend on her Majesty. And the following day, when the assembly was full, they heard about it.

The Speaker expressed his sorrow for the error they had committed and showed her Majesty's great misliking. He had feared this would happen. He advised them to apologize, and for the future to confine themselves to "matters proper and pertinent for this House to deal in," suggesting that, as "of old time," all bills be submitted first to the scrutiny of a standing committee of four, and no motions be made except for privilege or good order. What a drubbing he must have received: "Such," to quote his own words, "as himself could not bear."

Vice-Chamberlain Hatton then delivered a message from the

---

[3] Edward Lewkenor, a Puritan M.P. from Suffolk, had earlier been associated with Peter Wentworth.

queen. He showed "her great admiration of the rashness of this House in committing such an apparent contempt against her Majesty's express commandment, very lately before delivered unto the whole House by the Lord Chancellor . . . ; blaming first the whole House, and then Mr. Speaker." "No public fast could be appointed but by her, and therefore [their action] impeached her jurisdiction." She herself "liked well of fasting, prayer, and sermons," and used them; but, as St. Paul enjoined, "Good things must also be well done." From reproof Hatton turned to set forth "very eloquently and amply . . . her Majesty's most honourable and good acceptation of the zeal, duty, and fidelity of this whole House towards religion, the safety of her Highness's person, and the state of this Commonwealth (in respect whereof her Majesty hath so long continued this Parliament without dissolution)." To their great joy and comfort he declared further "that her Majesty, nevertheless, of her inestimable and princely good love and disposition . . . construeth the said offence and contempt to be a rash, unadvised, and inconsiderate error . . . proceeding of zeal and not of the wilful or malicious intent of this House or of any member of the same; imputing the cause thereof partly to her own lenity towards a brother of that man which now made this motion": a thrust at Peter Wentworth. "After many excellent discourses and dilations" on the queen's concern for the welfare of religion and the state, he announced that she had already deeply consulted on these matters and prepared fit courses for them, ready to be delivered to the House in the proper way. He thought it very meet that the whole House or someone on its behalf should make humble submission, and ended with a rebuke to the Speaker, telling him that her Majesty liked his opposition to Wentworth's motion, but misliked his venturing to put it to the question, "being no bill."

The comptroller, Sir James Croft, followed, to the same effect, but—added our clerk in the secrecy of his rough notes—"urged and enforced the fault of the House with much more violence." Though the tide had turned, there was not lacking one courageous man. Nicholas St. Leger,[4] "with a great deal of discretion and moderation"—appreciation that comes from the clerk—extenuated their fault. He spoke of their deep affection for the queen and the sin-

---

[4] Nicholas St. Leger, M.P. for Maidstone, Kent, in 1572 and 1581.

cerity of their intention; then of the imperfections and sins to which states as well as men were subject, needing prayer and humiliation. This merged into an attack on the slackness of bishops; concluding "that he trusted that both her Majesty and all her subjects would be ready to express their true repentence to God in humbling themselves in sackcloth and ashes." Seintpole[5] followed: he was on the side of authority. Then Mildmay, urging submission: a judicious speech, one infers. Seckford, master of requests, joined the official chorus; and Sergeant Flowerdew recanted. After these rose George Carleton, the dyed-in-the-wool Puritan, quite unabashed, ready to speak his conscience: or so it seems Speaker and House anticipated, for they interrupted him and the Speaker put the question.

"With whole consent" it was resolved that the vice-chamberlain should tender to the queen "the most humble submission of this whole House, with their like most humble suit unto her Majesty to remit and pardon their said error and contempt." This carried, "Mr. Carleton offered again to speak, saying with some repetition that what he had to move was for the liberty of the House." But Speaker and House "did stay him": or, as our diarist reports, "Mr. Speaker [did] rise and would not tarry."

If Paul Wentworth's motion was really intended as the opening move in a concerted Puritan campaign, then it was a tactical blunder. . . . Members' nerves were shattered before the crucial issues over religion were raised, and when these appeared the House moved with propriety as it had done in the previous session. In contrast, Elizabeth's prompt counteroffensive proved astute and successful.

The following day, January 25, Sir Christopher Hatton reported on his mission. In place of storm there was sunshine. The queen accepted their submission "very lovingly and graciously," and was pleased "freely and clearly" to remit their offense and contempt. To avoid misunderstanding of her action, she wished not only the House but all her subjects to know that it was not the matter— "fasting and prayer being godly and virtuous exercises"—that she misliked, but the manner: "tending to innovation, presuming to indict a form of public fast without order and without her Majesty's privity, intruding upon her Highness's authority ecclesiastical." She hoped

---

[5] Thomas Seintpole, M.P. in 1576 and 1581.

this would be sufficient admonition to them to employ their endeavors more advisedly, "according to their special vocations in this service."

In the congenial atmosphere thus engendered, Sir Walter Mildmay rose to make the set government speech for supply: a speech carefully prepared, ranging over general policy as well as finance, and in its felicity of phrase and emotional appeal a great oration. It was divided into three sections: "of the present state we be in; of the dangers that we may justly be in doubt of; what provision ought to be made in time to prevent or resist them."

> *That our most gracious Queen, even at her first entry, did loosen us from the yoke of Rome and did restore unto this realm the most pure and holy religion of the Gospel . . . is known to all the world and felt of us to our singular comforts. . . . From hence, as from the root, hath sprung that implacable malice of the Pope and his confederates against her. . . . They hold this as a firm and settled opinion that England is the only sovereign monarchy that most doth maintain and countenance religion. . . . This being so, what hath not the Pope essayed to annoy the Queen and her state, thereby, as he thinketh, to remove this great obstacle that standeth between him and the overflowing of the world again with Popery?*

For proof Mildmay instanced events from the Northern Rebellion to the recent invasion of Ireland; "the Pope turning thus the venom of his curses and the pens of his malicious parasites into men of war and weapons to win that by force which otherwise he could not do."

"Though all these are said to be done by the Pope and in his name, yet who seeth not that they be maintained underhand by some other princes, his confederates? . . . The Pope of himself . . . is far unable to make war upon any prince of that estate which her Majesty is of," having lost "those infinite revenues which he was wont to have out of England, Scotland, Germany, Switzerland, Denmark and others, and now of late out of France and the Low Countries. . . . The Queen, nevertheless, by the almighty power of God standeth fast maugre the Pope and all his friends." Here Mildmay instanced "the Italians and Spaniards, pulled out by the ears at Smerwick in Ireland, and cut in pieces by the notable service of a noble captain and valiant soldiers. . . . This seemeth to be our present state: a blessed, peaceable, and happy time."

But, "seeing our enemies sleep not, it behoveth us also not to be careless." The storm is but partly over, the main tempest like to fall upon us; and "this realm shall find at their hands all the miseries and extremities that they can bring upon it. . . . If they can, they will procure the sparks of the flames that have been so terrible in other countries to fly over into England and to kindle as great a fire here."

In the mean season, the pope, by secret practices, leaves nothing unproved, "emboldening many undutiful subjects to stand fast in their disobedience to her Majesty and her laws. . . . The obstinate and stiff-necked Papist is so far from being reformed as he hath gotten stomach to go backwards and to show his disobedience, not only in arrogant words but also in contemptuous deeds. To confirm them herein, and to increase their numbers, you see how the Pope hath and doth comfort their hollow hearts with absolutions, dispensations, reconciliations, and such other things of Rome. You see how lately he hath sent hither a sort of hypocrites, naming themselves Jesuits, a rabble of vagrant friars newly sprung up and coming through the world to trouble the Church of God; whose principal errand is, by creeping into the houses and familiarities of men of behaviour and reputation, not only to corrupt the realm with false doctrine, but also, under that pretence, to stir sedition." In consequence, not only former recusants, but many, very many who previously conformed, now utterly refuse to be of our church.

Turning to remedies, Mildmay commented on the contrast between the persecuting church of Mary Tudor's reign and the clemency of her Majesty's merciful reign. "But when by long proof we find that this favourable and gentle manner of dealing . . . hath done no good . . . it is time for us to look more narrowly and straitly to them, lest . . . they prove dangerous members . . . in the entrails of our Commonwealth." Severer laws were needed to constrain them to yield at least open obedience in causes of religion, so that, "if they will needs submit themselves to the benediction of the Pope, they may feel how little his curses can hurt us and how little his blessings can save them from that punishment which we are able to lay upon them."

The next requirement was the provision of forces sufficient to answer any violence that may be offered, here or abroad. "God hath placed this kingdom in an island environed with the sea, as with a natural and strong wall, whereby we are not subject to those sudden invasions . . . which other frontier countries be. . . . What the Queen's navy is, how many notable ships, and how far beyond the navy of any other Prince, is known to all men." This involved great charges. Land forces were also necessary, but her Majesty does not need, "as other Princes are fain to do, to entertain mercenary soldiers of foreign countries, hardly gotten, costly and dangerously kept, and in the end little or no service done by them; but may bring sufficient forces of her own natural subjects . . . that carry with them willing, valiant, and faithful minds, such as few nations may easily compare with." This too required treasure, the nerve of war; and Mildmay went on to explain that the taxes, granted five years ago, had not even covered half the extraordinary charges incurred since then.

His patriotic eloquence then soared to new heights.

The love and duty that we owe to our most gracious Queen, by whose ministry God hath done so great things for us—even such as be wonderful in the eyes of the world—ought to make us more careful for her preservation and security than for our own: a princess known by long experience to be a principal patron of the Gospel, virtuous, wise, faithful, just; unspotted in word or deed, merciful, temperate, a maintainer of peace and justice amongst her people without respect of persons; a Queen besides of this realm, our native country, renowned through the world, which our enemies gape to overrun, if by force or sleight they could do it. For such a Queen and such a country, and for the defence of the honour and surety of them both, nothing ought to be so dear unto us that with most willing hearts we should not spend and adventure freely.

"Let us think upon these matters as the weight of them deserveth," he concluded, and provide for them in time both by laws and by provision.

When Mildmay had finished, Norton rose, "pursued the same admonition," and moved for a committee "to consult of bills convenient to be framed." He was assuming the leading role among nonofficial members. Also he was setting the stage for one of the main bills of the session, to come not from the government—as would certainly have happened in earlier years—but from a committee of the House. He was proposing to steal the legislative initiative for the House: another significant moment in this great theme of Elizabethan and early Stuart parliamentary history.

A grand committee was appointed, consisting of all privy councillors and fifty-seven others. Philip Sidney was one, Peter Wentworth and Lewkenor others: not, however, Paul Wentworth or George Carleton. They met that afternoon in the Exchequer Chamber. Our clerk was there and wrote an entry in his rough notes. Once more, it seems, Norton seized the leadership. He "spake very well" to the matters contained in Mildmay's speech that morning; "and did thereupon exhibit certain articles to the like purpose which were by the committees considered, and some others added unto them." He and four lawyers . . . were ordered to digest into article form the points agreed upon and exhibit them at the committee's next meeting. At subsequent meetings it was Norton alone who was entrusted with the drafting.

Two bills emerged from this committee: the subsidy, and what they referred to as "the bill for religion." The latter ultimately became the "Act to retain the Queen's Majesty's subjects in their due obedience"—the notorious law which ushered in the period of severest persecution of the Catholics. Behind the scenes in its passage lies a remarkable story of royal intervention; and for that reason we must follow it with a degree of detail which in the end will bring reward.

The committee was ready with its report on February 7, and on the following day its bill, entitled "For obedience to the Queen's Majesty against the see of Rome"—a far sterner measure than the one finally passed—was read the first time. Sir Christopher Hatton then informed the House that the Lords had before them a bill tending to many of the things contained in theirs. He suggested that they seek a conference; and this was agreed to by both Houses.

The bill to which Hatton alluded was . . . "For the coming to church, hearing of divine service, and receiving of the Communion," amended and extended—if an undated State Paper represents its provisions—to fit the deepening crisis. In its main clauses it was a rather severer version of the 1571 bill which had been vetoed by the queen: failure to attend church once a quarter incurred a penalty of £12; failure to receive Holy Communion twice a year involved fines ranging from £20 for the first offense to £100 for the fourth. The bishops, one supposes, had been at it again.

Except for the compulsory attendance at Communion, which had not been included in the Commons' bill—perhaps because the councillors on the committee knew that Elizabeth would not consent to it; perhaps because Puritans such as Wentworth, holding their own Communion services, were no longer enamored of it—the Lords' bill was a very pale affair indeed compared with its rival. It would have been fatal to let the upper house proceed along such mild lines, if councillors thought as the Commons did, and were already finding the queen far too merciful for their liking. Any hope of screwing up their mistress to the Draconic provisions of the bill in the lower house lay in presenting her with a solid front of Lords and Commons. This may have been the principal reason for Hatton's motion about a conference.

The representatives of both houses—eighteen peers (six of them bishops) and the whole of the grand committee from the Commons —met several times. A new, a longer and amended bill emerged; but the main provisions and penalties remained much the same. In other words, Lords and Commons—including the privy councillors of both houses—were agreed in wanting an extremely drastic penal code against Catholics. It is a crucial point in our story, and is corroborated—at least as regards the temporal Lords—by a later comment from Thomas Norton.

The new bill was read in the Commons a first time on February 18. It was still at that stage when on February 27, after an interval which in itself almost suggests that something was amiss, there came a message from the Lords appointing a new meeting between the committees of both houses. This was indeed extraordinary, for with the bill in their possession, the right of initiative lay with the Commons. They reinforced their already large committee, as though to meet an assault.

On March 4, as the result of a fresh batch of meetings, Sir Francis Knollys, on behalf of the representatives of the Commons, brought into the House a third bill. It was read once, and then, with a vote on the motion which implies opposition, was pressed to an immediate second reading. "After many speeches"—alas! unrecorded—it was sent to be engrossed. It passed at the next sitting, sailed through the Lords without any apparent fuss in three consecutive days, and in due course received the royal assent.

What had happened? What caused the representatives of both houses to scrap their agreed bill and replace it with a new, and, as we shall see, a very much milder measure? The only explanation that seems to fit the background of detail and make sense is that the queen had intervened to scale down the severities. She had been told about the preliminary Commons' bill: that we know. She must have been shown the provisions of the second bill. The halt of nine days after its first reading may have been due to paralysis at court while councillors tried to overcome her misgivings. When she had come to a decision, she appears to have transmitted her wishes to the House of Lords: both the expedient and the more fitting way of attaining her purpose. Such interference by the crown may seem to us despotic; but while the royal veto remained a live institution, it served the same practical purpose as a conference between both houses, indicating the limits to which one of the essential parties was prepared to go in a bill that no one wanted to lose. The sovereign held the trump card. After Elizabeth had spoken, Parliament might grumble but had to submit. The "many speeches" noted in the *Commons Journal* probably reflect the chagrin of the House and the fighting retreat of its more outspoken members.

And now to discover what changes resulted from this intervention. The bill as finally enacted falls broadly into two sections, the first concerned with the work of the Catholic missionaries, the second stiffening the penalties for ordinary recusancy or refusal to attend church. As historians have pointed out, it drew a statesmanlike distinction between being and becoming a Catholic: or, to express this more pungently in the language of today, it directed its greater severities against recruitment for the fifth column.

By its main provision, whoever withdrew the queen's subjects from their natural obedience, or converted them *for that intent* to the Romish religion, were to be adjudged traitors, as were those who willingly allowed themselves to be thus withdrawn or converted. Those significant words, *for that intent,* made the approach political and secular: as a modern scholar expressed it, "The law refrains from plainly defining conversion to Catholicism as treason, it was rather conversion accompanied by withdrawal of allegiance which was condemned."[6]

In the two earlier bills, our three important words did not exist. The bills were framed as an extension of the statute of 1571 against the papal bull of deposition, which—quite reasonably in view of the nature of the bull—had made it treason to reconcile or be recon-

[6] A. O. Meyer, *England and the Catholic Church under Queen Elizabeth,* trans. J. R. McKee (1916), p. 148.

ciled to Rome by virtue of such instruments. This statute and its penalties were now applied to Jesuits and seminary priests and their converts. It was thus treason to reconcile or be reconciled to Rome by virtue of the missionaries' priesthood. Lords and Commons had been concerned, not with principle but with the stark perils of ideological warfare. Alarmed and irate Protestants, they were facing a dilemma which in a milder way is with us today. To them conversion to Catholicism was in itself synonymous with treason.

Thus in its main provision the bill as finally enacted changed a principle. It did not change the penalty. Elsewhere this was done. The first two bills dealt with the saying and hearing of Mass by making the former felony (involving the death penalty) and for the latter imposing a fine of 200 marks and (in the second bill) imprisonment for six months at the first offense, and the pains of praemunire (imprisonment during pleasure and forfeiture of lands and goods) at the second offense. In striking contrast the statute, based on the third bill, reduced felony to a fine of 200 marks, while the fine for hearing Mass was scaled down to 100 marks: there was no increase for further offenses. These were indeed changes of substance: mercy it would, no doubt, be misleading to call them.

Perhaps the best-known clause in the final statute is the one imposing a fine of £20 a month for nonattendance at church. Though the modern critic is apt to forget that there was many a slip twixt Tudor law-making and law-enforcing, it was certainly for most recusants a ruinous penalty when enforced. But compared with the two earlier bills it was as whips to scorpions. Both of these drew a distinction between Catholic recusants and others—that is, Protestant sectaries, for whom Puritans entertained no sympathy. Catholic recusants were to incur the staggering fines of £20 for the first month, £40 for the second, £100 for the third, and the pains of praemunire for the fourth. Non-Catholic recusants, who were dealt with at the end, almost as an afterthought, were subject to a scale of £10, £20, £40, and nothing higher.

There were many other provisions in these two parliamentary bills: thirty-eight in all in the second. It would be tedious to describe them, but there was a group which had the significant purpose of excluding Catholics from positions of influence in society; and here again we cannot fail to note the parallel with our own times. Lawyers guilty of recusancy and refusing thereupon to take the oath of supremacy were deprived of the right to practice or hold any office; to save the youth of the country from contamination, all schoolmasters and tutors were obliged not only to take the oath but also to subscribe to the Articles of Religion as limited in the Act of 1571 (that is, the doctrinal articles—a Puritan touch, this!); and the oath of supremacy was also imposed on all law students and anyone connected with the ecclesiastical or civil courts. That this group of clauses was dropped after the intervention of the queen is in some ways even more impressive than the remarkable censorship of the rest of Parliament's proposals.

Assuming that the queen was responsible for these striking changes—and no other explanation seems feasible—what light they cast on her hostility to extreme doctrinaire policy! Better than anyone she kept her head in the fanatical atmosphere of the time. Of course, there must have been individuals about her who advised moderation. They hardly detract from the personal quality of the decision, especially as Burghley was probably not among them. The attitude of this great statesman is a conundrum. Like other eminent fellow-councillors, he wrote his periodic passages in the book of lamentations against the clemency of his mistress. Though during this session he seems to have been absent—presumably with gout—from many meetings of the House of Lords, we know that both the early severe bills passed through his hands, as did the third and last bill. His many corrections in the draft of the third bill point to his being on the joint committee of both houses and in charge of the bill. He may have played the same role on the occasion of the second bill, and if so, he must either have agreed in general with its provisions, or—which is hardly likely, and certainly Norton does not hint at lay discord—have found the committee's zeal beyond his control. Moreover, if he disliked the parliamentary proposals he must have been out of line with other privy councillors; and yet there are indications that they were pursuing a concerted policy.

Failing any direct evidence, it looks as if we might assume that Burghley was in favor of a measure planned to eradicate Catholicism from England by making life intolerable even for its peaceful and loyal adherents. Once the queen had finally decided against this policy, doubtless he became the instrument of her wishes, and

Philip Hughes

ROYAL AUTHORITY AND THE SUPPRESSION OF LIFE AND RELIGIOUS LIBERTY

Monsignor Philip Hughes was born in Manchester, England, in 1895. He received the Licentiate in Science from the University of Louvain in 1921. Louvain, the National University of Ireland, Villanova, the University of Portland, Seton Hall University, the College of St. Thomas, and Notre Dame University have bestowed honorary degrees on Father Hughes. In 1955 he was appointed professor of history at Notre Dame. His works have established him as the foremost Catholic scholar of the English Reformation. He died in 1967.

Queen Elizabeth put to death, solely because of their religion, between the years 1577 and 1603, 183 of her Catholic subjects. Of these, 123 were priests, one was a friar not yet ordained, and fifty-nine were layfolk, three of them women. Three of the priests were men ordained before the beginning of the queen's reign; the rest were products of the new seminary movement. Four of them indeed, after beginning their studies in the seminaries of Douay and Rome, went to join the Society of Jesus; another six were received into the Society after their ordination, while serving on the English mission or while they awaited their fate in the queen's prisons, as, in this way, another priest became a monk and yet another became a Dominican. Of the 123 priests put to death, all but four had passed through the seminaries, and 115 had been wholly trained there. Two of the three women martyrs were gentlewomen, the third came out of the upper-class merchant society that ruled the northern metropolis, York. The occupation or social standing of seven of the fifty-six men is not known; twenty-five are listed as gentlemen, one was a student of Douay College, there are five schoolmasters and four men servants and four yeomen. And there is one of each of the following: printer, bookseller, glover, tailor, dyer, joiner, husbandman, ostler, waterman; and one merchant, an Irishman from Waterford.

*   *   *

From *The Reformation in England* by Philip Hughes (rev. ed.; first published in the United States in 1963 by The Macmillan Company), vol. 3, pp. 338–49. Reprinted with permission of Macmillan Publishing Co., Inc. (Footnotes omitted.)

The 123 priests came from all classes of society, so far as we can judge from our scanty information about their families. Contemporary accounts of their lives give twenty-six as of gentle birth. The vast majority, naturally enough, had never exercised any other profession than their ministry, but of a small group of twenty-one who came late to their priestly vocation, eight had been schoolmasters, five fellows of Oxford colleges, two had been students at the Inns of Court, four had been married, one had been a clothmonger, of Wakefield in Yorkshire, and one had been the college shoemaker at Rheims.

Sixteen of these priests were tried and condemned under the statute of 1352, which is still our law of treason. The rest owed their death to laws enacted under Elizabeth, the purpose of which was to wipe out the Catholic religion in this country—the Acts of 1559 and 1563 explicitly demanding, under an ultimate penalty of death, recognition of the supremacy of the crown in religious matters; the Acts of 1571 and 1581 making reconciliation to the Church treason, and so punishing with death those who returned to the Catholic faith and all who had a hand in bringing this about; the Act of 1585 making treason, and so punishing with death, the very presence in the country of a seminary priest or Jesuit, and also whatever was done by others to shelter or assist the priests so proscribed.

And so five priests and seven laymen are hanged, drawn, and quartered for denying that with the queen lies the last word, for Englishmen, in all that belongs to the Church of Christ. One priest and two laymen suffer death for having said that the queen is a heretic. A priest suffers the penalties of treason for having in his possession a papal bull (that has no special reference to England, the matter of which is wholly spiritual; a bull, moreover, that has expired), and a layman for procuring a papal license to marry his cousin. A priest goes to the gallows for bringing into the country 500 copies of Allen's reply to Burghley, and with him a layman who helped to circulate the book; a printer also is executed for reprinting a tract by Gregory Martin exhorting Catholics to abandon the hypocrisy of attending services they considered to be heretical, and a bookseller for having similar works among his stock. Two priests suffer the penalties of treason because, having once conformed to the religion established by the queen's authority, they have since been reconciled, and three other priests for bringing about reconciliations; seven laymen were put to death for being reconciled, and another five for persuading others to be reconciled. And 94 out of the 123 priests were put to death simply because, being priests ordained abroad since June 24, 1559, they had returned to England: thirty-four laymen went to death with them, for giving them assistance in one way or another.

The statute of 1581 that made reconciliation treason, whatever the means by which it was brought about, spoke of this reconciliation as being a withdrawal of subjects "from their natural obedience to" the queen; it was reconciliation "with that intent" which was the treason. But, in practice, this reservation was mere words—as the reservation "maliciously" had been a mere word in the Act of Henry VIII punishing as traitors those who denied maliciously the king's supreme headship of the Church. All reconciliation was treated as, by the fact, a withdrawal of allegiance and an adherence to the queen's enemy.

But what exactly was reconciliation? A sinner is reconciled to God whenever, and as soon as, in repentance, he makes what theologians call an act of perfect contrition, or when he receives the sacrament of penance, i.e. goes to confession. Reconciliation is also used to mean the return to the Catholic Church of one who had left it to join some other religious body. And, since there is but one baptism, reconciliation is used to mean not merely the coming back of such wanderers, but the conversion to the Catholic Church of men who, though baptised, have never been bred as Catholics, have never lived as Catholics. To be reconciled could mean, in 1571 and in 1581, to go to confession (on the part of a good Catholic), or to give up the outward show of being of the queen's religion (on the part of a Catholic who had lapsed from Catholicism), or to be converted from belief in Protestantism to belief in the Catholic faith. In practice the statutes were used to punish as treason all three acts.

*   *   *

The Act of 1585—and the fact that it brought to their death men and women whose only "treason," admittedly, was their resolution to persevere in the ancient faith, and to bring to others the spiritual means of a like perseverance—has been the occasion of much apologetic on the part of the modern historians. The statute is, in itself, so peculiarly ferocious that they are "appaused" by it, as

Foxe says of Stephen Gardiner. Its very ferocity has sometimes, indeed, been taken as the proof, and the measure, of the government's dilemma: the natural consequence of honest belief (caused by plots) that the new priests are traitors in the natural sense of the word, agents who throughout England will prepare and organize the Catholics for the great day of the invasion planned by Allen and Persons.[1] The missionary priests, however, were never so employed: nor were they given the training that would suit them for such a purpose. There was no link—this is certain—between the real business of Allen's life, the presidency of Douay College, and his occasional activities as an advocate, with princes, of schemes for the overthrow of Elizabeth's government by force of arms.

The contrary, of course, has often been suggested, and it used to be taken for granted. The charge was openly made, at the time, by Burghley, that the seminaries were schools to train apostles of treason, and that to persuade men to turn traitor was one of the missionary priest's duties in England. The answer Allen then gave—in the *Defence*—ought to have stifled the slander as it was born; it would have done so, had not the government very effectively prevented the circulation of the book.

The justification, to Allen's conscience, of all these political maneuvers in which he had his part, was the papal sentence of 1570 excommunicating the queen. This was his authority for promoting activities that would otherwise have been, not merely treasonable in law and in fact, but mortally sinful: we shudder at assassination, the cowardliness of it appalls us, but treason is more sinful still. And how could the priests have brought the Catholics to organize for such a notoriously sinful activity, unless by teaching them that, the queen being excommunicated, the acts were no longer sinful? The meaning and effects of the papal excommunication of reigning princes must, by necessity—on this hypothesis—have been a major subject in the Douay curriculum. Whereas, "the governors of the students always of purpose [prohibited] . . . that in the course of our school questions and controversies concerning

---

[1] Robert Persons (Parsons), a Fellow of Balliol College, Oxford until 1574, entered the Society of Jesus in 1575 and was ordained in 1578. He was sent to England in 1580 as part of the English Mission. Before being forced to flee to France in 1581, he secretly printed Catholic tracts and was associated with the Spanish ambassador Mendoza. From 1581 on he was engaged in various plots for the invasion of England, notably the Great Enterprise of Philip II.

the Pope's pre-eminence, no matter of depriving or excommunicating princes should be disputed; no, not so much as in generalities, and much less the particularising of any point in our Queen's case."

Here is a stock question of divinity, Allen says, a routine problem that all authorities discuss, the problem what is to be done about rulers who are apostates from the faith of Christ; it is a problem, he notes, that Calvin considers and Zwingli too, and which both solve as the Catholic divines solve it. "Yet," this problem, "because it is incident to matter of state (as now our country most unfortunately standeth), and consequently might be interpreted by the suspicious to be meant of her, whose case men liked best to deal in, it was thought best to pass over all with silence." So little, then, are the seminaries schools where treason is systematically taught, and professional traitors formed and apologists for assassination.

That Allen spoke truly is confirmed by the way the unfortunate priests answer their inquisitors when taxed about these matters. They do not reply in any uniform way, giving a stock answer to the subtly phrased questions that Burghley's civil law experts have drafted. They blunder about, with answers that are contradictory, and that land them in further difficulties, as a man not taught must always blunder about, when he is suddenly asked riddles that only the technically trained can solve.

The priests were innocent. And the government was as innocent as the priests—so the historians nowadays seem to suggest, who invite us to lament an inevitable tragedy of good Englishmen now locked in mortal conflict.

Against the a priori view that the government really believed— and with reason—that the priests were ipso facto traitors in the proper sense of the word, it may however be urged that had they so believed they would have used their powers to the full, have rounded up and killed every priest in the country; that they would, at least, never have let any priest go free once they arrested him, let alone priests tried and found guilty, and sentenced to death as traitors. Yet Elizabeth banished priests by the dozen, among them priests sentenced to death for treason: and continually issued proclamations commanding priests to depart the realm—which is an odd policy towards subjects believed to be plotting the invasion of the country and the deposition and murder of the sovereign.

It is a more likely view, one more in keeping with sixteenth-century methods, that sees the famous statute of 1585 as intended to strike terror: to cow the many converts, and the neo-Catholics of the rebirth evident to all as the fruit of the seminary movement.

In procuring the enactment of this statute of 1585 the government, however, has not suddenly—and inexplicably—become more cruel. The new law does not differ in spirit from those of 1581 and 1563 and 1559; it is but a means to make easier the extirpation intended already by these earlier acts, a simplification that will bring to his death more expeditiously the priest guilty of refusing to acknowledge the crown as the lawful lord of all religious life. The death penalty has been there all along. In these twenty-six years, the government has been overcoming, step by step, the hindrances which the fact of strong opposition in the first parliament of the reign put in the way of its original purpose, namely to ensure the Elizabethan Settlement by means of statutes as bloody as the laws of Henry VIII. Public feeling, shocked by what is now about to happen, that priests will (for example) be captured as they land, even be taken from boats in the harbor, and then be hanged, drawn, and quartered for being found priests in England—should such feeling exist—can be silenced by bold propaganda. If Burghley's famous tract was a defense of the executions under the Statute of Treasons, was it not also a defense in advance, a preparation of the public mind for other executions to come?

Nor are these cruelties simply a ripost, savage perhaps, but not incomprehensibly so if we remember that the country is fighting an aggression which imperils its life. In all these twenty-seven years the real aggression—whether political or religious, whether the other party is Philip II or the pope—is wholly on the side of England. And the great movement of which Elizabeth used to be held, in a popular way, the patron saint; the movement, not to correct abuses in popular religion, but to bring about the acceptance of a new theory of salvation, of a new set of religious habits deriving from this, a new idea of God, therefore—to say nothing of such a detail as a new theory of the place of the state in a man's religious life: all this great movement is in itself an aggression, surely, when introduced to the ordinary man's notice—as it is—not by sweet reason, or evangelical preaching, but by acts of state, commanding obedient acceptance under threats against liberty and against life itself.

It can hardly be repeated too often—for attention is hardly ever drawn to the fact—that, from the beginning of the reign, a man's mere failure to conform his conduct to the new arrangements about religion which the state has devized and sanctioned is, itself, a high crime: a crime which, if a man persevere in it, must mean his ruin and may mean his death. As to these priests who were now put to death in such numbers under the Acts of 1581 and 1585, and the laymen whom they converted or who helped them in their work, and who for this suffered with them, neither directly nor indirectly had any single one of them any share in the activity of those Catholics beyond the seas whose aim was the overthrow of Elizabeth, whether in the activities of foreign princes or of English exiles. Nothing of this sort was ever proved against them in the treason trials; nothing of this was even charged against them in the rest. The great accomplishment of the Act of 1585 was that, henceforward, nothing of this needed even to be charged, in order to be rid forever of the missionaries whose success in spirituals spelled ruin to the creation of 1559—nothing except the fact that being priests they were, and had remained, within the queen's dominions.

Richard B. Wernham

MILITARY AIMS AND METHODS

*The distinguished English historian Richard Wernham was born in 1906
and educated at Oxford. In 1933/34 he was lecturer of modern history at
University College, London, before becoming a Fellow of Trinity College,
Oxford (1934–1951). From 1946 to 1948 he was University Lecturer of
Modern History at Oxford, and since 1951 he has been professor of modern
history at Oxford and a Fellow of Worcester College. As well as being a
specialist in Elizabethan foreign relations, he has been engaged in significant
editorial work. In 1933 he was appointed editor of the* State Papers, Foreign
Series, *and he has served as editor of volume III of the* New Cambridge
Modern History *(1968).*

> *If the late Queen would have believed her men of war as she did her
> scribes, we had in her time beaten that great empire in pieces and made
> their kings kings of figs and oranges as in old times. But her Majesty did
> all by halves and by petty invasions taught the Spaniard how to defend
> himself, and to see his own weakness which, till our attempts taught
> him, was hardly known to himself.*

So did Sir Walter Raleigh, looking back from James I's reign,
reflect upon Elizabeth I's conduct of her war against Spain. His
criticism won a wide acceptance from later historians and the picture of the war presented in most modern histories is still recog-
nizably of his school. Nevertheless, the criticism was never accepted
without some modification and recently the modifications have begun
to affect the main lines of the picture. Today we realize more clearly
that the men of war did not all speak with one voice and we are less
sure (or less agreed) which of them the queen should have believed
We also know much more about the nature of the queen's general
policy and the limitations of her resources, as well as about the
Continental, military side of the war; and knowing more, we are
inclined to forgive more. How far, then, does Raleigh's verdict still
stand?

That verdict contains both an assumption about Elizabeth's
war aims and a criticism of her methods. Let us begin by examining

From R. B. Wernham, "Elizabethan War Aims and Strategy," *Elizabethan Government and Society: Essays Presented to Sir John Neale,* ed. S. T. Bindoff, J. Hurstfield, and C. H. Williams (London, 1961), pp. 340–68. Reprinted by permission of
Professor R. B. Wernham and the Athlone Press of the University of London.

the assumption, for until we are sure about the queen's aims we cannot safely criticize her methods, and it does seem certain that her aims, rightly or wrongly, were not those that Raleigh would have had her pursue. It was never her aim to destroy Spain and "break that great empire in pieces." England, she believed, needed a powerful Spain to countervail the power of France. For Elizabeth, and the older generation of her scribes, had grown up in a Europe dominated by the French monarchy and the house of Hapsburg. Each of those two great powers far overtopped Tudor England in size, population, resources, and military strength. But, of the two, it was France that until recently had appeared the more dangerous.

In part this was because France was England's traditional rival, the ancient enemy of the Hundred Years' War. But the center of French power also lay much closer to England than the center of Spanish power; indeed, during the century before Elizabeth's accession it had come uncomfortably close. The French had conquered Normandy and Picardy from the English and their Burgundian allies. They had absorbed Brittany, another of England's old allies, in 1492. They had captured Calais from Mary Tudor in 1558. They had thus won control of the entire southern coast of the Channel and removed the land-buffer of cross-Channel possessions and satellites that had long cushioned England itself against direct attack. The Tudors had answered by building up English naval power. But in these waters, where the prevailing winds blew from between south and west, nature all too often gave the weather-gauge to the French, all the more since their main bases lay at the far western end in Brittany, while those of England must be at the far eastern end around the Thames estuary, close to the great supply center of London and the all-important trade route to Antwerp. For sixteenth-century sailing ships, so subject to the weather and so limited in their ability to sail to windward, these were grave handicaps. The same wind that brought the French (or Spaniards) up the Channel might prevent the main English fleet from the Thames and Medway joining its Channel advanced guard, as in 1545. If the two had already joined, it might pen them in their own harbors, as almost happened in 1588. Or, when they had eaten the west country bare, it might delay their supply ships, as did happen in 1588.

Sea power, therefore, though obviously England's first and

principal defense, could not be regarded as an infallible shield. Henry VIII had felt obliged to build a string of coastal castles, from Sandwich and Walmer in the east to Falmouth and Scilly in the far west. Mary and, rather more effectively, Elizabeth herself were constrained to take in hand the reorganization and reequipment of the antiquated shire levies. More and more those of the southern counties became tied to the defense of England's long southern coastline against invasion from the Continent, as the northern levies had long been tied to defense against Scottish incursions. This reduced accordingly the forces available for cross-Channel offensives and further widened the military disparity between England and her great Continental neighbor.

When Elizabeth came to the throne the situation had looked even more threatening, for the French were taking station on her northern as well as opposite her southern front. The Scottish queen, Mary Stuart, was married to the French dauphin, who in July 1559 became King Francis II of France. Her mother, Mary of Guise, had reduced Scotland almost to the status of a French province. Her Guise uncles, now all-powerful at the French court and fresh from the capture of Calais, were eager to exploit this situation further. For Mary Stuart, great-granddaughter of Henry VII, had the strongest genealogical claim to be regarded as heir presumptive to Elizabeth's throne and, in Roman Catholic eyes, a fair claim to its present possession. Thanks to the national and Protestant resistance to French rule that exploded in Scotland in 1559, to the opposition to the Guises that developed in France, and to the premature death of Francis II, Elizabeth was able to repel these dangers. Even so, at least until Mary Stuart's downfall in 1567 English policy was dominated by the fear that she would seduce the Protestant faction in Scotland, the Guises triumph over their enemies in France, and the two join forces in a Catholic crusade against heretical England. So, for at least the first decade of Elizabeth's reign, France remained the enemy most to be feared, while it was Spanish power and Spanish goodwill (or Spanish self-interest) that restrained the pope from excommunicating Elizabeth and deterred the French from executing his unspoken censures.

However, within a month of Mary's enforced abdication, the Duke of Alva marched into Brussels (August 1567) with a Spanish army that soon grew to 25,000 men. This was a move in Spanish domestic policy rather than in Spanish foreign policy; an expression of Philip II's purpose to be absolute and Catholic master in all the many mansions that were his share of the vast and rambling Hapsburg house. He had sent Alva to crush finally the strong opposition that this policy had provoked in his Netherlands territories and to exact vengeance for the late excesses of the Calvinist minority there. However, so drastic a change in the character of Spanish rule in the Netherlands, so marked a shift in the center of gravity of Spanish military power, could not remain of purely domestic import. The French were alarmed. Elizabeth, who had already manifested anxiety at the absolutist trend of Spanish government in the hitherto harmless and largely self-governing Low Countries, could no more allow those countries to be turned into the main base of Spanish military power than she had been able to let Scotland become a French citadel. To be prepared to defend the Channel against France was burden enough, without having Spanish armies controlling the shipping of Holland and Zeeland, and the resources of Flanders and Brabant, with only the Narrow Seas between them and the nerve centers of English government, sea power, and trade.

Yet this new alarm from Spain did not end anxiety about France. For, as the schemes of Coligny and Louis of Nassau soon manifested and as Anjou's enterprises demonstrated again in the later 1570s and earlier 1580s,[1] the Netherlands rebels were only too ready to call in the French to save them from the Spaniards. And French armies, extending French control of the coast from Calais to Flushing, perhaps to the Ems, would be even more dangerous there than Spanish armies. As Sussex put it: "The case will be hard with the Queen and with England if ever the French possess or the Spaniards tyrannize in the Low Countries."

Elizabeth's answer to this double problem was to try to persuade or force Philip II to recall his armies and restore the Netherlands to their status under his father Charles V, with some more tolerable settlement of their religious differences. Her pressure took many forms—diplomatic expostulation, the seizure of Alva's pay ships (1568), unofficial aid to the rebels, raids by Drake and his fellows upon Spanish America, a defensive alliance with France

---

[1] Admiral Gaspard de Coligny was the Huguenot leader; Louis of Nassau was the younger brother of William of Orange; Francis, Duke of Alençon, succeeded to the dukedom of Anjou after his brother was crowned Henry III.

(1572), even a wary encouragement of the projects of Coligny and Anjou. The forms varied, but the purpose never changed and it was this that eventually brought England and Spain to war. There were, of course, other causes of quarrel. Disputes over English merchants' privileges in their great Netherlands market; Philip's determination not to let Hawkins[2] and his associates trade to Spanish America; the activities of the Inquisition in Spanish ports and of English privateers and pirates on the high seas; the difference of religion, which among other things made English ambassadors intolerable in Spain and turned Spanish ambassadors into Catholic plotters in England; all these played some part. Yet they would hardly in themselves have brought the two governments to war. Even before Alva's arrival English traders were beginning to escape from their difficulties at Antwerp by moving first to Emden and then to Hamburg; what happened on the Spanish Main or in the ports of the peninsula was hardly yet of supreme concern to dominant English interests; piracy, long endemic in west European waters, was as much Huguenot and Dutch as English; and Philip II was a far more reluctant crusader than his ambassadors. It was Elizabeth's determination to frustrate his policy in his Netherlands provinces that eventually provoked him to the enterprise of England.

Even so, as long as France seemed capable of independent action and the Netherlands of prolonged resistance, Philip felt compelled to avoid a war with England and to yield somewhat to English pressure. He repeatedly assured Elizabeth that he desired no more power in the Netherlands than Charles V had possessed. In 1573, despite the collapse of France after the St. Bartholomew Massacre, he recalled Alva and opened negotiations with the rebels. The negotiations broke down on the point of religion; the rebellion went on; and the Spanish army remained. But in 1576 the Spanish Fury drove Catholic and Protestant Netherlanders to join to expel it and the Pacification of Ghent,[3] confirmed in the Perpetual Edict (1577) by the new Spanish viceroy, Don John of Austria, gave virtually all that Elizabeth had required. If the Netherlands could have main

---

[2] John Hawkins first made voyages to Spanish America for trading purposes in the 1560s.

[3] The Estates General of the southern provinces in the Netherlands concluded the Pacification of Ghent, a treaty with Holland and Zeeland, in 1576, following the mutinous massacre by the Spanish troops in Antwerp earlier that year.

tained their newfound unity, England and Spain might have kept the peace.

As things fell out, the growing divisions in the United Netherlands from 1578 onwards opened the way for Parma to reconquer the southern and eastern provinces. By the summer of 1585, with William the Silent assassinated and Antwerp fallen, the returned Spanish army looked within striking distance of final victory over the rebels. Just then, Philip II was also able to eliminate all danger of French intervention. Anjou's death and the childlessness of Henry III left the Huguenot Henry of Navarre heir presumptive to the French throne. This drove the Catholic League and the Guises to take arms and place their cause under the protection of Spain. Their victory would make France the client of Spain. It would unite Catholic Europe under Spanish leadership just when Spain was building up the naval forces acquired by the conquest of Portugal (1580) into an Atlantic fleet that its admiral Santa Cruz believed could be made capable of challenging the sea power of Protestant England. If the League succeeded only in establishing itself in those northern and eastern provinces where its hold was strongest, most of the French shore of the Channel would be at the disposal of this gathering Armada. Thus, even if Philip had not decided to send his Armada against England without waiting for Parma to complete his conquest, Elizabeth could not have stood by and allowed the Dutch to be annihilated, the Huguenots crushed, and the French monarchy made a puppet of the Guises. She could no longer avoid open action against Spain.

Yet this brought no radical change in Elizabeth's aims. She could not allow Spain to destroy England's old enemy, France. Yet, equally, she could not afford to destroy her new enemy, Spain. For England could live, had been living, in a world of two Leviathans; she could not live where there was but one. Besides, a restored France that was not matched by a powerful Spain would be, if possible, a worse danger to England than a triumphant Spain that was not matched by a strong France. For the same reasons, Elizabeth must defend Dutch liberties, but would not fight for their independence. An independent Netherlands would be too weak to withstand a restored France and, if they became French, that would give France too dangerous a preponderance. So, while the whole Netherlands must be freed from

FIGURE 4. Elizabeth Feeding the Cow of the Netherlands, *c.* 1585. Philip II is riding the cow, which is being milked by the Duke of Alva. Francis, Duke of Anjou, is pulling its tail, while William the Silent holds the cow by the horns to enable Elizabeth to feed it. The allegory may refer to Elizabeth's treaty with the Provinces (August 1585), preparatory to Leicester's expedition. (*From a private collection, by kind permission of its owner*)

Spanish armies, restored to their ancient liberties, and given some measure of religious toleration, they must remain under the nominal sovereignty of the king of Spain, who alone had the power to defend them against their mighty neighbor. This was no policy to please Dutch patriots or English Puritans, but what happened a century later, when Spanish power did collapse and the Netherlands had to be saved from Louis XIV, suggests that Elizabeth's purpose was not wholly devoid of prescience.

The queen had, of course, other war aims too. She wanted to secure English merchants and sailors against persecution by the Inquisition in Spanish ports and to obtain recognition of their right to visit the New World and the East "for lawful trade of merchandise." Yet while she insisted upon their right to trade freely to places where neither Spaniards nor Portuguese had "any habitation, residence, or resort," she was prepared to accept in Spanish- or Portuguese-occupied territories any orders that had been in force under the Emperor Charles V or King Sebastian—and incidentally to recognize Philip's conquest of Portugal and deny aid to the defeated claimant, Don Antonio. Moreover, at the Bourbourg negotiations in 1588[4] her commissioners were instructed to deal with "the great matter" of the Netherlands "before any treaty for our own causes." There seems therefore no real doubt that her principal war aim, the principal cause of the conflict with Spain, was her determination to restore all the Netherlands provinces to their ancient liberties and privileges "wherein they lived before the persecutions and oppressions begun by the Duke of Alva"; and to secure the Netherlands Protestants "their liberty of their profession and exercise of the Christian religion." But nominally Spanish they must remain.

To this policy she clung with extraordinary tenacity. It explains her refusal of the Dutch offer of their sovereignty in 1585, though there were financial and military reasons too. It accounts for her fury in 1586 when Leicester allowed, or inspired, the Dutch to thrust upon him the office of governor-general, with its implication that his mistress was their sovereign and he her viceroy. It was, as we saw, "the great matter" at the Bourbourg negotiations two years later. It lay at the root of her extraordinary anxiety in 1590 over reports of the Dutch offering their sovereignty to Henry IV of France. It explains her lack of enthusiasm in 1596 for Henry IV's dream of a great triple attack upon the Spanish Netherlands and her reluctance to admit the Dutch as equal and sovereign partners with herself and Henry in the Triple Alliance. It gathered new hope from the Archduke Albert's appointment as governor of the Spanish Netherlands and from rumors of his coming marriage to the infanta, with the Netherlands as her dowry and the hope of a return to the ways of Charles V. It still formed the basis of English policy during the Vervins negotiations of 1598.[5] The absolute refusal of the Dutch

---

[4] The negotiations themselves, undertaken between the English and the Spanish prior to the coming of the Armada, accomplished nothing, but the English used the opportunity to gather intelligence about Parma's activities.

[5] The Treaty of Vervins (May 1598) established peace between Spain and France, but England and Holland continued in a state of war with Spain.

at that time and again in 1599 to contemplate even the most nominal
return of Spanish overlordship marked its final frustration. In 1585
they might in their weakness have submitted to the queen's policy
if she could have forced it upon the Spaniards. Now, Maurice's
victories[6] had made Elizabeth's solution as intolerable to her ally
as it was unwelcome to her enemy.

When peace was eventually patched up by James I, the French
monarchy had been restored; the Spanish Empire, though somewhat reduced, had certainly not been broken in pieces; the Flemish
coast had been denied to the French and the Dutch coast to the
Spaniard. But the Netherlands had been split in two, into a Spanish
south and an independent north. The Spanish army remained in the
south and the inclination of the new Dutch Republic towards France
looked likely to open the way for new French designs upon Flanders.
The Indies, East and West, remained closed by Spanish law to
English traders. Altogether, the outcome of almost nineteen years
of open hostilities would have disappointed the late queen as well
as her men of war.

How far were these disappointing results due, as Raleigh asserted,
to Elizabeth's own faulty methods and half-hearted strategy? We
may, I think, agree with that experienced man of war, Sir Roger
Williams,[7] that there were three possible ways of bringing the
Spaniard to terms. One was to defeat "his disciplined army," now
based in the Netherlands; a second was to attack him "on the main
of Spain or Portugal"; a third was to intercept or interrupt the flow
of silver from America, upon which he now largely depended to fit
out his armadas, pay his armies, and subsidize the League.

The first course, as almost all the critics agree, was by far
the least promising. Willoughby[8] did advocate something of the
sort in 1589 and Williams thought it could be done in 1591 by aiding
Henry IV. Of them we can only say, with a twentieth-century admiral,
"gallant fellows, these soldiers; they always go for the thickest
place in the fence." If England had had even such Continental allies

[6] Maurice of Nassau and Jan van Oldenbarneveldt gradually provided leadership
for the Dutch in the aftermath of the assassination in 1584 of William the Silent,
Maurice's father.
[7] Williams, a soldier of fortune, was master of the horse at Tilbury in 1588, and
served under the Earl of Leicester and Lord Willoughby in the Low Countries and
the Earl of Essex in France.
[8] Peregrine Bertie, Lord Willoughby, was an English commander in the Low Countries and France.

as she was to have in Marlborough's time, it might have been possible to defeat a commander such as Parma at the head of the finest and most experienced army in Europe. Yet it was to take Marlborough six years to drive the French from the Netherlands and Elizabeth's allies were very different from his. . . .

But what about the money? The 6,000 auxiliary troops sent to the Netherlands in 1585 were expected to cost the queen £126,000 a year, half as much as her whole ordinary revenue apart from parliamentary grants. Yet four-fifths of those troops served in garrisons, where the wastage rate was much lower than in the field. When we remember the shifts used to finance the Portugal expedition of 1589 and the long debates over taxation in the Parliament of 1593, we may well wonder how the money could have been raised to keep in the field an army three or four times as big as the forces in the Netherlands. Something approaching it was indeed done in Ireland during the last years of the reign. But by then both French and Dutch were able to look after themselves. Besides, Ireland was virtually a matter of home defense; and in war all things, even national solvency, yield precedence to home defense.

Finally, large-scale land operations were not only militarily unpromising and financially intolerable, they were also, given the queen's war aims, politically undesirable. She was hardly going to make such efforts to conquer the Netherlands from Spain merely in order to hand them back to Spain. Nor would she bankrupt herself to share her conquests with the French king. Clearly she had reasons not to do more by land in France and the Netherlands.

On the other hand, it is not easy to see how she could well have done less in either country. Imagine the position after the battle off Gravelines in 1588 if the Armada, with many of its 130 ships battered but only seven lost, had been able to find secure refuge and to refit at leisure in Flushing and the Scheldt. In 1585 the Dutch were in such political and military disarray that they could not be relied on to keep Parma out of these vital areas. That was why Elizabeth took them into her protection and sent Leicester over with 6,000 men, and another 1,100 to hold Flushing and Brielle as pledges for the eventual repayment of her expenses. . . .

It is also true that Elizabeth did several times send extra forces —to Sluys in 1587, Bergen-op-Zoom in 1588, Ostend in 1589. Possibly these would have been less necessary if the original body had been kept at full strength by more regular pay. But . . . the blame for this must rest upon the malpractices of Leicester and his captains rather than upon the queen's parsimony. Anyway, the need for these extra troops was created far less by deficiencies in the English auxiliary forces than by weakness in the Dutch. And that weakness grew largely from the disastrous quarrel between Leicester and the States, with the mutinies in the States' garrisons and the virtual civil war that developed out of it. Elizabeth's fury at Leicester's acceptance of the governor-generalship in 1586 helped a little to launch this quarrel and her peace negotiations with Spain in 1587–1588 . . . helped a good deal to fan it. Yet the ultimate blame for it must lie squarely upon Leicester's flagrant disobedience to her instructions in 1586 and his utter inability either to check waste and corruption in his own forces or to cooperate amicably with the prickly Dutch. It was not the queen's policy that was at fault. It was her inability to control its instruments. That being so, the extra forces had to be sent and even then Sluys was lost, although Bergen and Ostend were saved and the English garrisons secured Flushing and Brielle.

*   *   *

In France it was much the same story. Here, again, we have only to imagine a Spanish Armada with a secure advanced base at Brest and with the French Channel ports at its disposal, to see that Elizabeth could not stand indifferent to the fate of northern France. Admittedly, until Henry III's death in 1589 she did avoid any serious commitment. The outcome of the subsidy that she gave to Navarre's German levy in 1586–1587 did not encourage active support of the Huguenots. She therefore fell back upon a waiting policy, trusting that the Huguenots would be able still to defend themselves and that Henry III and the Guises would prove incompatible bedfellows. Meanwhile, by diplomacy she smoothed the way for a royalist-Huguenot understanding when king and League should eventually fall out. Her reward was that royalist influence kept a footing in Brittany, while most of the Channel ports remained in the hands of governors unfriendly to the Guises. . . . Now we may well doubt how far these flimsy barriers would have sufficed in 1588 if the Armada had adhered less rigidly to Philip II's orders that it must not stop or turn aside until it had made its junction with Parma in the Narrow Seas.

But it is hard to see what else Elizabeth could have done without making matters worse. Until Henry III's assassination of the Guises (December 1588) and alliance with Navarre (April 1589), open English intervention could only have been in alliance with the Huguenots and against the French king as well as against the League. It could only, therefore, have plunged the Catholic Henry III more completely under the power of the League and rallied monarchist and patriotic sentiment to the League's cause. Nevertheless, in her French policy between 1585 and 1589 Elizabeth had certainly cut things very fine indeed.

After Henry III's assassination in July 1589, she could no longer afford such risks. For the accession of the Huguenot Henry IV inclined the League to desperate courses and soon brought Spanish armies into France. The parts of France that they were most likely to enter in force were just those that were nearest and most dangerous to England. For the main Spanish army was in the Netherlands and the main strength of the League was in northern France, stretching from Lorraine and the Netherlands frontier in the east, through the great central bastions of Paris and Rouen, to Brittany in the west. . . . The terms on which Philip accepted the formal protectorate over the League in January 1590 showed that he hoped to kill two birds with one stone, to secure a dominating position in France and also advanced bases for an invasion of England.

Here, again, as in the Netherlands, Elizabeth could not depend on her ally to avert the threatened calamity. Henry IV was not likely, except perhaps in defeat, to shut himself off in the Breton peninsula and leave to their fate other provinces of equal or greater importance to his cause. To him the Channel ports were no more vital, except for receiving English aid, than many other towns. He could not therefore be trusted to concentrate his whole attention upon these northern coastal areas, so vital to Elizabeth, so peripheral to him. Nor could he be relied upon, in periods of setback, to resist the temptation to withdraw southwards to the more friendly lands beyond the Loire. If the Channel ports and Brittany were to be kept out of Spanish hands, Elizabeth must herself accept a considerable share in the responsibility for their defense.

She accepted the responsibility and, however reluctantly, during the next five years gave the French king considerable military and financial help. . . .

This continual exceeding of estimates was made necessary (as with the Dutch) by the inadequacies of her ally. Whether from genuine weakness or from a feeling that Elizabeth could be safely left to look after parts of France that so deeply concerned her, Henry IV repeatedly failed to do his share and keep his promises. . . .

It is, therefore, difficult to see how Elizabeth could have done substantially less in France during these years. Without her loans and Willoughby's troops, Henry IV could hardly have campaigned through the winter of 1589; he could assuredly not have kept the field north of the Loire; and it is obvious enough what dangers his withdrawal must have brought to the Breton and Channel ports. To have done less in 1589 could only have made far greater help essential in 1590, when in fact Elizabeth had no troops at all in France. In 1591, without her further financial aid towards the levy of forces in Germany, Henry would again have been hard put to it to face the League and its Spanish allies north of the Loire. Without the additional reinforcement of Essex's expedition, it might well have proved impossible to bring him to center his operations so near to the coast as Rouen. . . .

Now, all of this was surely a most necessary work. As Williams wrote in November 1590: "Without [the Spaniards] possessing either those ports or them of the Low Countries, our dangers cannot be very great." The converse was equally true. Whatever might be the best way of winning the war, one of the easiest and most obvious steps towards losing it would have been to let the Spaniards occupy the French Channel coast or the Netherlands coast or—worst of all—both coasts together. To prevent such a peril had to be one of the very foremost concerns of English strategy, a concern to which all else had to take second place except the defense of the queen's own realms against direct invasion. We can hardly blame Elizabeth for giving it that priority. Nor can we fairly accuse her of employing upon these defensive tasks greater force than the tasks required.

Nevertheless, the effort absorbed in necessary home defense and in defending the French and Netherlands coasts was so substantial that it seldom left much to spare for offensive operations. The queen's sources of revenue were limited and inelastic. Even in peacetime there was little margin between ordinary income and ordinary expenditure—in the last ten years of economical peace before 1585 no more than £300,000 could be put by, including the sizeable windfall from Drake's 1577–1580 voyage. Besides this, Parliament's grants in 1585 and 1587 brought in, on average, about £72,000 a year in the three years 1586–1588. In 1589 it voted twice the usual sum, but spread its collection over four years, so that the annual yield was still about £72,000 until 1593. In 1593 it granted half as much again, again spread over four years (though unevenly) and yielding between £150,000 and £160,000 in 1594 and 1595 and £104,000 in 1596, if we may trust Lord Treasurer Burghley's figures. It is, of course, true that by twentieth-century standards this taxation was not crushing. What counted, however, was the steepness of the rise above the average £26,000 a year in the last seven years of peace. Nor must we forget the additional burdens that fell upon the maritime places in ship money and upon all counties in mustering and equipping their trained bands, levying and arming men for foreign service, and watching the beacons. Burghley believed, apparently with reason, that for some places these burdens amounted in 1587–1588 to the equivalent of four parliamentary subsidies, twice the number voted by Parliament in 1589. And the attitude of the House of Commons in 1593, even in 1589, showed that the government must think carefully before stepping up taxation much more drastically.

Yet for long periods the queen's expenditure on home defense, the Netherlands, and France largely exceeded what Parliament voted her. By the time the Armada came, she had already spent £378,000 in three years in the Netherlands and at least £220,000 in two years on preparations at home. Exchequer issues, a mere £149,000 in 1583, rose to £420,000 in 1588. The £300,000 of peacetime savings was almost gone by then, quite gone by 1590. Then from 1589 to 1595, though the Netherlands expenses were brought to or below £100,000 a year, new burdens were shouldered in France. At one point in the autumn of 1591 fully 15,000 English troops were—or were being paid for—on the Continent: the 6,000 auxiliaries and 1,000 garrisoning the cautionary towns in the Netherlands, 4,000 in Normandy, and 4,000 in Brittany. During the next twelve months another 6,000 at least were sent to make good the wastage in France. Indeed, between September 1589 and February 1595 the queen spent approximately £370,000 in aid to Henry IV, substantially more than the entire parliamentary grant of 1589. Finally, from 1598 until the end of the reign greater sums still were swallowed up in Ireland in crushing Tyrone's rebellion.[9]

The queen could, of course, borrow. Yet privy seal loans usually yielded only around £50,000 and they had to be—or at least, with one exception, were—repaid after one year. Moreover, English lenders, like English taxpayers, grew more reluctant as the war dragged on, while the failure of an attempt to borrow £100,000 in Germany in 1589 showed that foreign loans were hardly to be relied upon at all. The drastic expedient of selling crown lands—for example, £126,000 worth between November 1589 and November 1590— added something and there were occasional windfalls from naval expeditions. Yet it is no marvel that Elizabeth normally let those expeditions be financed by a kind of joint-stock partnership with private venturers or that she was always anxious that the war at sea should at least pay for itself. Even by such devices she could not mount offensive operations, costing perhaps £100,000 to fit out (like that of 1589), except in years when her home defense and Continental commitments were relatively light.

Indeed, it looks as if finance, almost by itself, can explain much, not only of the character but also of the course of the offensive war, the war at sea. Certainly it emphasizes the attractiveness of a "silver blockade." For this idea had the same seductive appearance of simplicity and economy that the theory of "independent" air power, of long-range strategic bombing, had before it was tested by experience in the war of 1939–1945. Spain's power to wage war was coming to depend more and more upon the steady flow of silver from the American mines. That silver had to be shipped across the Atlantic. The Atlantic was, of course, a big ocean, but the silver had to pass certain fixed points within fairly well defined intervals. That from Peru came up the Pacific coast to the isthmus of Panama for transshipment to Havana. At Havana the silver from Mexico was added to it and the whole sent to Spain in ships that could hardly avoid touching at the Azores, the nodal point of the Atlantic sailing routes. Here were the hunting grounds where English seadogs might hope

9 "£1,924,000 from 1593, according to Hist. Mss. Com. *Salisbury*, xv, 2."—Wernham.

to deal Spain crippling wounds and to wage war, not just economically, but at a fabulous profit.

*   *   *

The question was, just how could this "silver blockade" be made effective? Hawkins believed that it could be done by naval forces alone, by stationing the queen's ships, in relays of half a dozen, off the Azores. This might perhaps have worked before the Armada's concentration at Lisbon in the later part of 1587 or again in 1589–1590 before Spain had recovered from the 1588 disaster. But in 1585 Elizabeth preferred to loose Drake against Spanish America. In 1586 she did send Hawkins to sea with five of her ships, but the Babington plot and the uncertainty about French and Scottish reactions to the impending proceedings against Mary Stuart caused her to divert him to patrolling the Channel, unluckily just when the silver ships were coming home to Spain. In 1587 it was Drake who went out and by then his first task had to be to delay and disrupt the Armada's concentration. In 1589 the queen again put her money on Drake. In 1590, however, Hawkins and Frobisher did cruise off Spain and off the Azores with half the royal ships (not the six which he had asked for, but thirteen) and did force Philip to order the year's silver shipment to be held in America. But in 1591 the Spaniards, with twenty good fighting ships and thirty or more other vessels, swept down upon the Azores, captured the *Revenge,* and forced Lord Thomas Howard and his five remaining queen's ships off their station. 1590 had shown that Philip could manage without his silver for a year; 1591, that he could again provide an escort for it too powerful to be faced by such squadrons as Hawkins envisaged. In 1592 the lesson of 1591 was repeated, though this time a smaller English squadron got away without loss and was lucky enough to capture the rich carrack *Madre de Dios* before the enemy came down. After this, in 1593 and 1594, the queen virtually gave up the attempt. And in 1595–1596 Drake's and Hawkins's last expedition learned that what was true at the Azores was true also in the Indies. For on its journey homeward, after the deaths of the two commanders, it had to claw its way out of the Caribbean past a force sent from Spain against it and it owed its escape as much to its ships' superior sailing qualities as to their fire power. So long as

Spain had a powerful fleet in being, an effective silver blockade was not possible unless forces comparable to Spain's could be sent to maintain it.

Such forces could hardly be spared. For the Spanish fleet, based on Lisbon, Cadiz, or Ferrol, could at its own time just as well strike northwards to the Channel to cover an invasion of England as westwards to the Azores to cover the silver ships. Elizabeth therefore felt compelled to keep comparable forces in home waters, ready to go quickly to stations where they could intercept such a northward move; and as Spain's naval power grew, "comparable forces" came to mean the bulk of her navy. Her insistence upon keeping the Channel adequately guarded has often been ridiculed as feminine timidity. Yet even Hawkins's plan would have made half the royal navy, the essential fighting force of the nation, unavailable for home defense. Could any responsible English statesman before 1588 have staked his country's security upon the assumption that one English warship could deal decisively with two Spaniards? Or, indeed, after 1588? For, after all, the Armada of 1588, by its strict adherence to Philip's orders, considerably eased the English navy's task of shepherding it past the danger points. It did not attempt to land in the far west. It averted its eyes from the chance to fall upon Howard's ships as they edged painfully out of Plymouth against the wind. It made no move towards Torbay or Le Havre. Nevertheless, though harried by the full might of English sea power and "shuffled" past the Isle of Wight, it plodded stolidly up the Channel in unbroken formation until the fireships off Calais threw it into panic and allowed the English to get under its guard off Gravelines. Even after that, it had still lost only seven fighting ships and the English had used such unprecedented quantities of powder and shot that they were unable to finish it off, there upon their own doorstep. The victory was notable, but the manner of it must have confirmed Elizabeth's reluctance to dispatch large naval forces to the distant Azores or Caribbean so long as Spain had a fighting navy comparable in size to her own.

*   *   *

Nor was it much less risky or more practicable to station the fleet off the Spanish coast to blockade the Spanish ports. Drake did this for nearly three months and with a comparatively small squadron in 1587, but the Armada was then in the midst of its preparations for the enterprise of England and too dispersed to challenge him. When it was both concentrated and ready, as later in 1587 and in the 1590s, the bulk of England's naval forces would have been required to deal with it. At some point they, or a considerable portion of them, must have gone home to revictual and refit. The Spaniards could then have caught England at a serious disadvantage, like a 1939–1945 aircraft carrier with her fighters down refueling. Indeed, the Armada of 1588 could thus have caught Howard's ships in Plymouth, replenishing their stores after being blown back from the Spanish coast by the winds that brought the Spaniards on. . . .

Moreover, such a blockade of the Spanish ports or of the Azores would probably be ineffective as well as risky. For, to be effective, it must be continuous, lasting all the year round, perhaps for several years. It must stop the flow of silver from the New World, and the hardly less important flow of masts, naval stores, and corn from the Baltic, for long enough to force the Spaniards in desperation to come out and fight. Now, it is very doubtful indeed if Elizabeth's navy was capable of this. Drake in 1587 only kept it up for three months in summer and the latest that any of the queen's ships ever stayed on the Spanish coast was October 21, [1602], whereas the silver ships several times stole home during the winter. . . .

This meant attacking "in the main of Spain or Portugal." It required not only a fleet strong enough to deal with the Spanish ships but also, as Drake soon realized, land forces strong enough to storm the Spanish ports and to hold a base from which the fleet could operate continuously and effectively. But where was the money to be found for this, while home defense, the Netherlands, France, and finally Ireland, swallowed up so much? Most of the time it clearly could not be found. From 1586 to 1588 home defense and the Netherlands claimed too much; from the autumn of 1589 until the end of 1594 France and the Netherlands left little to spare; from 1598 Ireland took all. During these periods the queen had perforce to be content with operations at sea on a more or less limited scale, operations that might harry the enemy but could not hope to cripple him.

We are left with three brief periods of opportunity—right at the start of the war, before Spain's navy was fully developed or the queen's funds exhausted; in 1588–1589, between the Armada's defeat and Henry III's assassination; and from 1595 to 1597, when the heavy expenses in France had ceased and those in Ireland barely begun. Therefore, if the foregoing arguments are accepted, it is upon these three periods of opportunity that we must chiefly focus our criticism of Elizabeth's conduct of the war at sea.

In 1585 she did allow Drake's attempt to strike at the root of the problem. His expedition cost her only £10,000 and two of her ships, but all told it cost its backers £60,000. With the Netherlands commitment just beginning and the possibility still remaining that Spain might again yield to pressure as she had done in 1573, it is understandable if the queen regarded this as enough for the time. Moreover, Drake apparently believed that, with his two queen's ships and 27 others of various sizes and his 2,300 men, he could sack San Domingo and Cartagena, take Panama, and occupy Havana as a base for intercepting the treasure from both Mexico and Peru. And, in fact, it was not the smallness of the force that he set out with, but the unexpected wastage that it suffered during the campaign, which frustrated his design. In that graveyard of so many later expeditions, disease reduced his numbers so swiftly that he had strength only to sack San Domingo and Cartagena before he had to turn homewards. To blame the queen for not foreseeing this would be even more unjust than to blame Drake, who knew the Spanish Main so well. After his return in 1586 the queen, with the Netherlands and Mary Stuart on her hands, was back again upon the defensive.

In 1589 England was offered what was beyond all doubt the greatest opportunity presented to either side during the entire war. Half the Armada had perished on the long voyage home. The fifty or sixty ships that had struggled back lay for months in Santander and San Sebastian unrigged, ungunned, unmanned, despite the efforts of the Spanish dockyards and recruiting officers. For a year the remnant of Spain's naval power lay there, not merely immobilized but helplessly inviting final destruction. Elizabeth was quick to see and seize her opportunity. While the Armada was still straggling home, she called together her men of war and her scribes to advise upon "the intercepting of the King of Spain's treasure from the Indies." Out of these conferences there came a counterstroke fully comparable to the Armada of 1588. The difficulties of finding money, and ships serviceable after the recent campaign, were overcome by the formation of something rather like a joint-stock company with the queen as a partner. There were, of course, the deficiencies, disputes, and delays inseparable from a sixteenth-century enterprise. Nevertheless in April 1589 Drake and Norris sailed with six of the queen's ships, seventy-seven armed merchantmen of various shapes and sizes, sixty Dutch flyboats as transports, and 19,000 soldiers on their muster rolls.

The first, essential, task of this expedition obviously should have been to complete the work of 1588. One stroke would do it, for all but a dozen of the Armada survivors were huddled in the single port of Santander. Their destruction would ruin Spanish naval power past hope of recovery. If the English did that, then Hawkins's silver blockade, Drake's Lisbon dreams, all these things might soon be added unto them. The queen saw this clearly and enjoined it emphatically in her instructions, but unfortunately Drake and Norris were so bent on taking the second step that they were reluctant to take the first. To Drake Lisbon was the key to the situation—as indeed it was when Spain had an effective fleet in being and not tucked away unrigged in Santander. Impressed in 1587 by Lisbon's strength, and perhaps growing more doubtful of Don Antonio's promised Portuguese revolt, he and Norris collected so large an army that the expedition became very unwieldy for operations against Santander, so far to leeward along the rough Biscayan coast. Elizabeth continued to insist upon that; but, being only a partner in the enterprise, her control was limited and the commanders compromised by going first to Coruña. It is just possible, though not very likely, that they planned to hold the place as a convenient base for operations eastward as well as southwards. But without the small siege train that Elizabeth had promised and not provided, they failed to take the upper town and after a fortnight's siege sailed off to Lisbon. They had given the Spaniards time to make their task there much more difficult. They now themselves made it impossible by dividing their land and sea forces for separate and uncoordinated advances upon the city. There was no Portuguese rising and, with their forces wasting away from disease and desertion, they had to abandon the attempt. Contrary gales frustrated a move towards the Azores and, after sacking Vigo, the expedition straggled home at the end of June. By the end of July Henry III of France was dead; the Santander galleons, though by no means battleworthy, were able to work their way round to Coruña; and during the winter the year's silver shipment came safely in from America. The great opportunity had been missed. Some of the blame was clearly the queen's; but it was not she alone, or most signally, who had done all by halves, and she had seen the essential objective more clearly than her men of war.

In 1595 the Queen was slower to seize her opportunity. Her anxiety about France and Ireland helped to delay Drake and Hawkins until most of the year's silver shipment was in Spain. Their expedition, too, though it started with 2,500 soldiers and aimed to seize Panama, was in scale more akin to the purely naval forces of 1590–1591 than to the great expedition of 1589. A force of this size, the ravages of disease apart, was no longer enough to overcome the greatly strengthened and better forewarned defenses of Spanish America; and so far as the queen was responsible for the limitation of its strength, she was guilty here of doing things by halves. The next year it was not so. The treaty of Greenwich (May 1596) assured her that Henry IV would not immediately back out of the war, and its secret articles relieved her of any serious obligation to assist him on land or to conquests on his Netherlands frontier. Thereupon she loosed the Lord Admiral and Essex with eighteen of her ships, eighteen Dutchmen, eleven fighting Londoners, sixty or seventy transports, and rather less than 10,000 troops. The military contingent again looks overlarge, as in 1589, but the expedition began well. It sacked Cadiz and destroyed there six galleons, three of the new *fregatas,* and thirty or forty merchantmen. Then, however, sated with booty, and pleading (not altogether convincingly) a shortage of victuals, its enthusiasm died. Despite Essex's entreaties, "every man cried to set sail homewards," apparently without a thought for the main Spanish forces still unscathed in the Tagus. The damage done to Spanish commerce and to Philip's credit was considerable, but very far from fatal. . . .

Essex at least had learned the lesson. He had begun to see before he sailed to Cadiz, and on his return he recorded in a paper recently discovered, that what was needed was not a large army of invasion but an efficient landing force of, say, four or five thousand good soldiers, enough to seize and hold a base for the fleet and not too many to be kept supplied. The 1596 invasion alarm gave him the chance to start preparing such a force and in 1597 Elizabeth gave him a heartier and more ungrudging support than she had given to any of her men of war—probably because she saw eye to eye with him rather than because Henry IV taunted her with keeping her favorite tied to her petticoats. After all, Essex's plan put the destruction of Spanish naval power first and foremost. It envisaged powerful and sustained operations to accomplish that purpose. It would station her forces where their pressure must compel the Spaniards to risk either wholesale destruction in battle or piecemeal destruction in port. In addition, it would station them in the one place where they could simultaneously blockade both the American silver route and the Baltic trade in corn and naval stores—at the receiving end.

. . . Essex's plan was never tried. Discouraged by administrative deficiencies, adverse weather, and disease among his troops, he dismissed his land forces. Then, assuming too easily that the Spanish fleet was immobilized at Ferrol for the season, he sailed off to the Azores. He was unlucky to miss the silver ships there, but lucky on his way home to miss the Ferrol fleet in the Bay of Biscay. By his rashness he had left England open to attack and by his lack of perseverance he had thrown away the last chance of dealing Spain a truly crippling blow. Henceforward Ireland claimed all attention.

All three opportunities were thus missed and for this the queen must bear some of the blame. In 1589 she had allowed Drake and Norris to make their expedition too unwieldy for the essential operations against Santander and had left them without their promised siege train. In 1595 she had been slow to seize her chance. In 1596, if Essex is to be believed, it was her instructions that forbade an attack upon Lisbon, though the military contingent looks overlarge for any lesser objective and the main Spanish naval forces were there. Yet in 1589 only success in Portugal could excuse failure to go to Santander at all; and it seems quite clear that the failure in Portugal was due chiefly to the commanders' own errors. In 1595 there was still the possibility of heavy commitments in France to keep Henry in the war. In 1596 Cadiz could have provided a base, second only to Lisbon itself, for sustained operations against Spanish shipping. The decision to abandon it was that of the commanders on the spot, Raleigh prominent among them. In 1597 it was Essex (with Raleigh as his rear-admiral) who dismissed his troops, ignored the Ferrol fleet, abandoned his own carefully thought-out plan, and went off on a cruise to the Azores. It was the queen who on these occasions kept her eye steadily upon the first, essential, objective—the destruction of the enemy fleet. It was her men of war who let their gaze be distracted or their purpose falter. Her lack of control over them is, indeed, surprising. Of course, being a woman, she could hardly command in person, and in those days respect for the royal authority diminished rapidly with distance from the royal presence. In 1589 even Lisbon was a good deal more remote than Northumberland, which only twenty years before could be said to know no prince but a Percy. Further the wedding of purposes of state to enterprises for private profit, made necessary by the inadequacy of the royal revenues, also weakened the queen's control over her commanders. Yet can we imagine Henry VIII not demanding heads for such disobedience as that of Drake and Norris in 1589 or of Essex in 1597?

We need not, however, blame the men of war too severely for their errors of judgment. They were experimenting with a novel theory, and a very novel instrument, of war. Sea power had never before been used as an independent arm operating over vast distances of ocean. Because it was so novel, its potentialities were too optimistically estimated and the difficulties of its employment very inadequately foreseen. . . . Nevertheless, when we compare their achievements with their hopes, it is perhaps a little remarkable that a queen so renowned for her hesitations should have listened to her men of war as readily as she did, learned from them as quickly, and given them as many chances. For, when the chances came, we cannot fairly say that she "did all by halves." 1589, 1596, and 1597 at least in size and purpose, were no "petty invasions." On these occasions the queen gave her men of war the tools: it was they who did not finish the job.

We could hardly expect Raleigh to admit this, but it has been recognized by most modern critics of Elizabeth's strategy. Where their picture looks more out of focus is in its overemphasis on the offensive side of the war, on the war at sea. Now, it may be that the sea war launched England decisively out upon the oceans and on the pathway to empire. Yet because great oaks from little acorns grow, we should not forget that this particular acorn was comparatively little. For the Elizabethan war with Spain was not primarily a struggle for dominion over the ocean or for empire overseas. The peculiar vulnerability of Spain's sea communications made the ocean the obvious theater for offensive operations. But Spain's strength

FIGURE 5. Elizabeth as Europa, 1598. Dutch engraving. Elizabeth's left arm is comprised of England and Scotland; the right, of Italy. Her feet are planted between Poland and Russia. France and Germany are located above and below her breasts, respectively. To the left of her head, the defeated Spanish Armada flees; Spain is precariously located below her sword. Beyond Elizabeth's sword the Papacy, with a triple head, flees, escorted by a fleet with code numbers alluding to papal allies. (*Sutherland Collection, Ashmolean Museum, Oxford*)

on land made Europe the theater where the danger of total disaster was gravest and most immediate. Thus the war was first and foremost a European war and its vitally important theaters were the Channel and the Channel ports, the Low Countries and Brittany and Ireland. Elizabeth, who saw the war whole, grasped this and allocated her strength accordingly, first to home defense, then to the defense of those vital areas. Yet she saw clearly enough that she could not win the war there and she kept these defensive efforts to the bare minimum in the hope of having something to spare for winning strokes by sea. It was her misfortune that the weakness of her allies and the power of her enemy left her with so little to spare and so few opportunities to use it. When the rare opportunities came, she tried to seize them in no half-hearted fashion, but neither she nor her men of war learned quickly enough how their new weapon of sea power could be most effectively employed. Her strategy was dictated by cautious common sense, with all the merits and limitations that this implies. Two things in particular she lacked. One was that genius for war which not only sees the goal but also knows instinctively and at once the surest and simplest way to it. The other was the control over her commanders that would have kept their eyes upon the true objectives and might have helped them to find the true way for her. She was not one of England's great war leaders and she only half achieved her aims. Yet to have helped the French monarchy to its feet, to have saved half the Netherlands from Spanish "tyranny," to have kept the other half out of French possession, and England itself out of bankruptcy, was a fair achievement against the Spain of Philip II.

V EPILOGUE

Joel Hurstfield
SOME HISTORICAL PROBLEMS

Joel Hurstfield, born in 1911, was awarded the D.Lit. degree by the University of London. He served as official historian of the Offices of War Cabinet from 1942 to 1946. From 1959 to 1962 he was professor of modern history at University College, London, before being appointed Astor Professor of English History (1962) and a Fellow of University College (1963). His principal works include The Queen's Wards *(1958) and* Elizabeth I and the Unity of England *(1960).*

It is impossible to study the Elizabethan nation without studying the queen who reigned over them. "Both in her life and her death," said her contemporary, Thomas Dekker, "she was appointed to be the mirror of her time." The trouble is that she not only mirrored her own time but all time. From her day onwards she has reflected back to historians many of the notions they brought with them to their task. For example, James Anthony Froude, one of the great nineteenth-century historians, had begun work on the Tudor period with an admiration for Elizabeth. By the end, all that was over. "The private letters which passed between him (Burghley) and Walsingham about Elizabeth," he wrote to a correspondent, "have destroyed finally the prejudice that still clung to me that, notwithstanding her many faults, she was a woman of ability. Evidently in their opinion she had no ability at all worth calling by the name." In his *History of England* the same thing is said, in a famous passage:

> *Vain as she was of her own sagacity, she never modified a course recommended to her by Burghley without injury both to the realm and to herself. She never chose an opposite course without plunging into embarrassments from which his skill and Walsingham's were barely able to extricate her. The good results of her reign were the fruits of a policy which was not her own, and which she starved and mutilated when energy and completeness were most needed.*

Of Lord Burghley, he said elsewhere, in a private letter, "He, it is more and more clear to me, was the solitary author of Elizabeth's and England's greatness."

From *The Elizabethan Nation,* by Joel Hurstfield (New York and London, 1964), pp. 94–102. Reprinted by permission of Professor Joel Hurstfield.

183

Froude is, of course, an extreme example. Deeply involved as he was in the events of his own day, including the Catholic revival —to which he was bitterly opposed—he saw Elizabeth as betraying the just cause by her relative moderation to the Catholics. But the very fact that Froude is such an extreme case reminds us that biography is a subjective thing.

All biography is distortion. However historically well founded his work may be, the biographer takes a man out of his context, and in so doing is forced to alter the focus of the age. It reminds one of the use made by some newspapers of the photograph of a group of young men, when one of them has since become famous. His photograph is cut out from the rest and enlarged. The result is either a flat portrait deprived of the vitality of the group as a whole, or else he emerges as larger than life, his features gross and exaggerated, out of all proportion. In any case, this is not the man he was.

This will seem strange doctrine, coming from one who has written one biography and is engaged in writing another. But because an art form is imperfect, that is no reason for not practicing it. The biographer, conscious of the hazards of his methods, may yet contribute to historical understanding. For he looks at the past from within the life and mind of a single person. If he can, however briefly, establish an intimate contact with a man or woman of a past generation, then he adds something living to his analysis of society, which is his principal function as a historian.

By contemporaries, Elizabeth was vilified and adored, cursed and blessed; and the process has ever continued. It is a difficult task to isolate her from her admirers no less than from her detractors. She was not all wise, all patient, all virtuous. She did not accurately assess all future political developments and take appropriate steps. Who could? She blundered, she grew impatient, she saddled her ministers with the blame for her own failings. She was unsparing— and sometimes cruelly unfunny—in her wit. She could arouse warm emotions on her progresses among her people; but to those who knew her well she must have been a difficult person to love.

Yet when all is said, she tried hard to heal the wounds and divisions of the England she inherited, and she met with a large measure of success. She was a divided person, torn between the individual, private interests of a highly intelligent, vigorous woman and the public tasks which denied her the full enjoyment and expression of her private being. In her public tasks she succeeded admirably during the first thirty years of her reign in healing the wounds and binding the nation to her own purposes; but she failed significantly during the last fifteen. Delay, ambiguity, the elevation of monarchy to raise the aims and unify the purpose of the Elizabethan people were no longer enough. In one sense her reign was both too long and too short. If she had lived ten years less she might have gone down to history as the most successful monarch to sit on the English throne. If she could possibly have lived ten years longer we should perhaps have known the answer to some of the problems of her reign which still elude us; for their issue could not have been long delayed. In many respects the year 1603 does not end an epoch. The Tudor system survived for another forty years; but even before she died it had already started to break down.

How far, then, were the problems of the early Stuarts theirs or Elizabeth's. For example, we know that the Puritan opposition which had been a thorn in her flesh almost from the beginning of the reign, grew in the 1570s more intense, in and out of Parliament, and flared up in an extreme form at the time of the Martin Marprelate tracts in 1588–1589. Yet it seems to have died down, at least in Parliament, in the last decade of her reign. Had it, in fact, died down, and, if so, why did it revive so speedily under James I? We shall know more about this when we have one day plotted our map showing the extent of Puritanism—and Catholicism—in England. How Catholic was Lancashire, how Protestant was Essex? We can only guess. We know too that in the early seventeenth century the political opposition was most powerfully directed against the extension of crown revenue, and against the prerogative courts. Could Elizabeth have contained the opposition must longer? These questions, a few among many, are not mere speculative ones for they raise the whole issue of Elizabeth's authority and power. In short, what power did she enjoy and what was its relation to the social structure of the nation?

This is the most absorbing of all the Tudor problems. Yet here we labor under the gravest handicaps. When Froude said that Burghley was "the solitary author of Elizabeth's and England's greatness," he was exceeding his brief. He did not have the material on which to base this judgment. Nor have we. The process by which the government will is formulated and transmitted is one of the toughest historical questions to answer. It is still openly debated as to how it is done even in our own day. It is incomparably more obscure in a time of personal monarchy. The important decisions are given by word of mouth and may be the result, sometimes, of protracted discussions between monarch and ministers. All the preparatory work is done by the minister and the papers show his hand. But who initiated the inquiry and who was responsible for the final decision? Did the minister persuade and press the monarch or did the monarch direct the minister? We are in a world of shadows. Yet these problems do exercise the historian, although contemporaries rarely see the questions so precisely—and perhaps misleadingly—defined.

In the Elizabethan period we are faced with two additional difficulties. There is evidence that Burghley, who was the queen's closest adviser for forty years, engaged in some deliberate destruction of his papers—and that was not in order to save space! Secondly, he went out of his way to imply that he was a mere servant of the queen, with the minimum of powers, and that these powers consisted mostly of taking the unpopular responsibility for refusing suitors for royal favors. What in fact went on behind this smoke screen of Burghley's it is hard to say. Contemporaries believed with Spenser that this whole picture was false, that Burghley monopolized power and barred other men from sharing it, that he was

> . . . *like an aged tree*
> *Lets none shoot up that nigh him planted be.*

No one can ever again wholly accept Froude's theory—which is very much the same as Spenser's but expressed in favorable terms to Burghley—since the appearance of Sir John Neale's masterly investigation of the Elizabethan parliaments. In two spheres in particular, in the queen's resolution to stand fast to prevent the establishment of a Puritan church, and in her defense of Mary Queen of Scots, it is now clear that she stood out against many of her advisers and parliamentarians, in the one case successfully, in the other failing only after a long struggle. If now we can by some process discover more about the formulation of *economic* policy, the handling of revenue, and the contemporary concepts of law and the constitution, then an answer to our question will be in sight.

Meanwhile, other questions press for an answer. We know that, less than forty years after the death of the queen, England was divided in civil war. Did the divisions have their origins in the Elizabethan period, in some inherent tension between the government and society, or perhaps within society itself? This is no occasion to reopen the dead controversy over the gentry. It is indeed hard to recall that there was a time when the streets of Oxford ran with blood (or printer's ink: it is sometimes hard to tell the difference) on this burning issue. For men were prepared to lay down their (academic) lives in defense of their exposed positions.

But if the argument no longer stirs us, the whole debate was entirely beneficial for Tudor studies. Professor R. H. Tawney, who started it, saw in land the roots of power. He therefore analyzed the rise of a new class of middling landowners, between aristocracy and yeomanry, who extended their territories and modernized their use. Rising to economic power, they sought to express it politically —in other words, to control policy and government—and ran headlong into the entrenched resistance of the Stuart monarchy, a monarchy allied with that section of the aristocracy which had not marched with the times. Such a situation finally deteriorated into civil war. We cannot, of course, summarize in a few lines a brilliant piece of historical analysis, nor the brilliance of the counteroffensive launched by Professor Hugh Trevor-Roper. Challenging Tawney in both his methods and his conclusions, Mr. Trevor-Roper rejected the concept of the gentry class as an entity. To him the division of England came, not over land, but over office, that is office of profit and patronage under the crown. The government had thousands of appointments at its disposal; and the sweets of office tempted all men. Access to office could mean both wealth and power, for the government service was vast, influential, and ever-growing; exclusion could mean exclusion from both wealth and power, whether one belonged to the gentry or not. To him this division separated the "ins" from the "outs," the holders of government office from the opposition.

Here then was a confrontation between two of the most distinguished historians of the time, historians whose methods had much more in common than either might have been prepared to acknowledge. There is no question that the gentry as a class, or more likely a congeries of groups, formed an important element of the English social structure of the time and for long afterwards. There can be no question also that in the use and abuse of office lies the explanation of major aspects of Tudor society and its inner conflicts. But this is not to say that the resolution of the gentry controversy is some vague compromise; rather, that starting from the questions raised we are beginning—but only just beginning—to go forward to a detailed analysis of the social order. This has forced historians and their students to look searchingly at the monarch and Parliament, at administration and patronage. It has made them go out into the shires because the answers to these questions lie only partly in London; the remainder will be found in provincial England. London represented probably no more than one-twentieth of the population as a whole.

But the population of London was still growing. In the reign of Elizabeth it had doubled, reaching about 200,000 by the end. The Thames, on which it stood, was the main artery of southern England. It was the Thames of Spenser's *Prothalamion*—

> . . . the shore of silver streaming Thames,
> *Whose rutty bank the which his river hems,*
> *Was painted all with variable flowers,*
> *And all the meads adorned with dainty gems,*
> *Fit to deck maidens' bowers . . .*

But it was also the Thames which De Maisse, ambassador of France, saw and described in 1597. "From Greenwich to London," he wrote, "it is a magnificent sight to see the number of ships and boats which lie in anchor, insomuch that for two leagues you see nothing but ships that serve as well for war as for traffic." William Camden, historian of Elizabethan England, declared that London was "the epitome of all Britain, the seat of the British Empire." In James I, it aroused other emotions. Alarmed at the size and growth of his capital he urged parliamentarians and others, as soon as their business was over, to pack up and go home—and to take their wives and daughters with them. His capital continued to grow.

London was the center of politics, of administration, of religion, of law, of commerce. It was the social center for the leading men of the age, with their great houses along the Thames. It was a great cultural center with its Inns of Court, its theaters, its Chapel Royal. It was a pioneer in social welfare with its Christ's Hospital, dealing with the care and education for poor children, St. Bartholomew's for the sick, St. Mary Bethlehem (Bedlam) for the mentally sick; it had its Bridewell workhouse, and its system of local taxation to pay for this and much else. All this was consolidated on a national scale in the great statutes of 1598. But London remained a great slum, over-crowded, poverty stricken, diseased, which like a giant mantis spider killed off many thousands of those who were drawn in fascination towards her.

Where did they all come from? This is a large question of social geography which cries aloud for investigation, and with it the whole problem of the continued rise in population during the early decades of the seventeenth century.

And beyond these lie the massive problems of price revolutions, standards of living, social values, political aims. To these great and fascinating issues historians and their students are increasingly directing their minds.

The history of the Elizabethan nation is not just the history of a queen, of her government, of her politics, of the economic system, but of a whole society of diverse people, responding to the pressures of new experiences in all aspects of their lives. It is the history of their developing culture and their intercourse with the civilization of Europe. It is the history of their religious faiths and affiliations. It is the history of their social assumptions, their system of patronage, their attitudes to war and peace, to this world and the next. History is extending its frontiers. Many of us now regard these aspects of the past—which earlier historians would have banished to other disciplines—as inherent to our studies. We hold that *"nihil humani alienum"*—nothing involving man is outside our range.

One of the most stimulating things about the Elizabethan period is therefore the enormous prospects it offers for the exploration of new lines of development by means of entirely new historical methods. For we are only at the beginning of knowledge. "Histories," says Francis Bacon, "make men wise." Faced with so many questions about the Elizabethan period which remain unanswered, one adds that history makes men humble. Or at least, it should do.

Suggestions for Additional Reading

The best bibliographical guides to the Elizabethan period are the *Bibliography of British History, Tudor Period, 1485–1603,* 2d ed. (Oxford, 1959), edited by Conyers Read, and *Tudor England, 1485–1603* (Cambridge, 1968), edited by Mortimer Levine for the Conference on British Studies.

In addition to the biographies of Elizabeth by Creighton, Jenkins, Neale (perhaps the best), and Williams, selections of which have been included, there are several others worthy of mention. Of these the best are by B. W. Beckingsale, *Elizabeth I* (London, 1963), and the shorter *Elizabeth I and the Unity of England* (London, 1960) by Joel Hurstfield, which convincingly portrays English unity as Elizabeth's ideal. For Elizabeth's medical history there is A. S. MacNalty, *Elizabeth Tudor: the Lonely Queen* (London, 1954). Narrower in scope are Elizabeth Jenkins, *Elizabeth and Leicester: A Biography* (New York, 1962), and Lytton Strachey, *Elizabeth and Essex* (London, 1928). An incomplete but well-written introduction to the historiography of Elizabeth is C. H. Williams, "In Search of the Queen," in *Elizabethan Government and Society,* ed. S. T. Bindoff, J. Hurstfield, and C. H. Williams (London, 1961). An introduction to Elizabeth using short selections for the most part by the queen and her contemporaries is edited by J. M. Levine, *Elizabeth I* (Englewood Cliffs, N.J., 1969). Among the numerous volumes containing writings by Elizabeth, the more useful are *The Letters of Queen Elizabeth,* ed. G. B. Harrison (London, 1935); *Queen Elizabeth and Some Foreigners,* ed. Victor von Klarwill (London, 1928); and *Queen Elizabeth and Her Times,* 2 vols., ed. Thomas Wright (London, 1838).

The best short survey of the Tudor period is S. T. Bindoff's *Tudor England* (Harmondsworth, 1950). More substantial is G. R. Elton's *England under the Tudors* (London, 1955, 1962), which is better on Henry VIII than Elizabeth. J. B. Black's *The Reign of Elizabeth, 1558–1603,* 2d ed. (Oxford, 1959), is sound and deserves more credit than it sometimes receives. For provocative but dated and very biased historical writing, there is James Froude's multivolume *History of England,* a selection from which is included in this book.

For constitutional history a good introduction is *The Tudor Constitution: Documents and Commentary* (Cambridge, 1960), ed. G. R. Elton. A short, well-written account of *The Government of*

Elizabethan England has been provided by A. G. R. Smith (New York, 1967). In addition to the two volumes by Neale on Elizabeth and her parliaments, there is Neale's fine study of *The Elizabethan House of Commons* (London, 1949). Of a more specialized nature, but representative of the best recent work on constitutional history, is Hurstfield's *The Queen's Wards: Wardship and Marriage under Elizabeth I* (London, 1958). For constitutional ideas in the Elizabethan era a good beginning may be had in G. L. Mosse, *The Struggle for Sovereignty in England: From the Reign of Queen Elizabeth to the Petition of Right* (East Lansing, Mich., 1950). The possible impact of the English constitution under Elizabeth on the Civil War is examined by Elton, "A High Road to Civil War?" *From the Renaissance to the Counter-Reformation,* ed. C. H. Carter (New York, 1965).

There are two good studies of the succession question: Mortimer Levine, *The Early Elizabethan Succession Question, 1558–1568* (Stanford, 1966); and Hurstfield, "The Succession Struggle in Late Elizabethan England," *Elizabethan Government and Society.* The same collection of essays includes a good analysis by MacCaffrey of "Place and Patronage in Elizabethan Politics." MacCaffrey has also written a fine article on "Elizabethan Politics: the First Decade, 1558–1568," *Past & Present,* no. 24 (April 1963): 25–42. Neale provides a broader perspective in "The Elizabethan Political Scene," *Proceedings of the British Academy* 34 (1948): 97–117. In "The Inflation of Honours, 1558–1641," *Past & Present,* no. 14 (November 1958): 45–70, Lawrence Stone discusses the effects of Elizabeth's reluctance to give substantial rewards to her servants.

For a fuller understanding of the enigma of Mary Stewart, the biographies of T. F. Henderson, *Mary Queen of Scots,* 2 vols. (London, 1905), and Lady Antonia Fraser, *Mary Queen of Scots* (London, 1969), are useful. For "The Execution of Mary, Queen of Scots," see G. R. Batho's article in the *Scottish Historical Review* 34 (April 1960): 35–42, and the related articles by B. M. Ward, "Queen Elizabeth and William Davison," *English Historical Review* 44 (January 1929): 104–106, and Wernham, "The Disgrace of William Davison," *English Historical Review* 46 (October 1931): 632–636. Elizabeth's problems were also compounded by John Knox, the subject of a now standard biography by Jasper Ridley, *John Knox* (New York and Oxford, 1968), which is strong on contemporary political history, if not on Knox's thought. Elizabeth played an instrumental role in helping the Scottish

Protestants, but she failed to intervene effectively to aid Morton, as explained by Maurice Lee, Jr., "The Fall of the Regent Morton: A Problem in Satellite Diplomacy," *Journal of Modern History* 28 (June 1956): 111–29.

The broader sweep of Elizabeth's foreign policy is superbly handled in the relevant portion of Wernham's *Before the Armada: The Growth of English Foreign Policy, 1485–1588* (London, 1966), and the monumental study by Conyers Read of *Mr. Secretary Walsingham and the Policy of Queen Elizabeth,* 3 vols. (Oxford, 1925). There is a classic portrayal of *The Defeat of the Spanish Armada* (London, 1959) by Garrett Mattingly, and a broader, equally superb volume on *Renaissance Diplomacy* (London, 1955) by the same author. Among the best articles on Elizabeth's foreign policy are Neale, "Elizabeth and the Netherlands, 1586–1587," *English Historical Review* 45 (July 1930): 373–396, and Wernham, "English Policy and the Revolt of the Netherlands," in *Britain and the Netherlands,* ed. J. S. Bromley and E. H. Kossmann, vol. 1 (London, 1960).

Elizabeth's military involvements are the subject of several useful studies, among the best being A. L. Rowse's *The Expansion of Elizabethan England* (London, 1955); C. G. Cruickshank, *Elizabeth's Army,* 2d ed. (Oxford, 1966); and Cyril Falls, *Elizabeth's Irish Wars* (London, 1950). One of the most dramatic moments in Elizabeth's life is discussed by Christy Miller, "Queen Elizabeth's Visit to Tilbury in 1588," *English Historical Review* 34 (January 1919): 43–61. Also very helpful to understand Elizabeth are articles by Wernham on "Queen Elizabeth and the Portugal Expedition of 1589," *English Historical Review* 66 (January–April 1951): 1–26, 194–218; and "Queen Elizabeth and the Siege of Rouen in 1591," *Transactions of the Royal Historical Society,* 4th ser. 15 (1932): 163–179.

Religious developments, which were often related to foreign policy, have been well analyzed for Elizabeth's reign. W. H. Frere, *The English Church in the Reigns of Elizabeth and James I* (London, 1904) is a useful older survey. Works specifically valuable for Elizabeth's religious position are J. V. P. Thompson, *Supreme Governor: A Study of Elizabethan Ecclesiastical Policy and Circumstance* (London, 1940); E. T. Davies, *Episcopacy and the Royal Supremacy in the Church of England in the XVI Century* (Oxford, 1950); Claire Cross's dull *The Royal Supremacy in the Elizabethan Church* (London, 1969); J. P. Hodges, *The Nature of the Lion: Elizabeth I and*

Our Anglican Heritage (London, 1962); and C. S. Meyer, *Elizabeth I and the Religious Settlement of 1559* (St. Louis, 1960). William Haugaard gives special attention to Convocation in *Elizabeth and the English Reformation* (Cambridge, 1968). Two articles by Neale explore the relations between Elizabeth and Parliament on religious matters: "The Elizabethan Acts of Supremacy and Uniformity," *English Historical Review* 65 (July 1950): 304–332; and "Parliament and the Articles of Religion, 1571," *English Historical Review* 67 (October 1952): 510–521. There is a related article by T. M. Parker, "The Problem of Uniformity, 1559–1604," in *The English Prayer Book, 1549–1662* (London, 1963). Looking at the problem of uniformity from a different perspective, W. K. Jordan has written a scholarly analysis of *The Development of Religious Toleration in England from the Beginning of the English Reformation to the Death of Queen Elizabeth* (Cambridge, Mass., 1932). To understand Elizabeth's religious policy it is essential to understand something of the position of Lord Burghley and his son Robert; for this see Hurstfield, "Church and State, 1558–1612: The Task of the Cecils," in *Studies in Church History,* ed. C. W. Dugmore, Charles Duggan, and G. J. Cuming, vol. 2 (London, 1965).

For the treatment of the Catholics by Elizabeth, the older work by A. O. Meyer, *England and the Catholic Church under Queen Elizabeth,* trans. J. R. McKee (London, 1916), is still worth reading, but Patrick McGrath's *Papists and Puritans under Elizabeth I* (London, 1967) is better. W. R. Trimble's *The Catholic Laity in Elizabethan England, 1558–1603* (Cambridge, Mass., 1964) has not been well received. For the Catholic writers there are useful works by J. B. Code, *Queen Elizabeth and the English Catholic Historians* (London, 1935), and A. C. Southern, *Elizabethan Recusant Prose, 1559–1582* (London, 1950). J. H. Pollen writes from a distinctly Catholic viewpoint: *The English Catholics in the Reign of Elizabeth* (London, 1920). Among the best articles on Elizabeth and the Catholics are R. B. Merriman, "Some Notes on the Treatment of English Catholics in the Reign of Queen Elizabeth," *American Historical Review* 13 (April 1908): 480–500; R. B. Manning, "Catholics and Local Office Holding in Elizabethan Sussex," *Bulletin of the Institute of Historical Research* 35 (May 1962): 47–61 (where it is shown that many Catholics did not lose their positions under Elizabeth); John Bossy, "The Character of Elizabethan Catholicism," *Past & Present,* no. 21 (April 1962): 39–59;

Leo Hicks, "The Catholic Exiles and the Elizabethan Religious Settlement," *Catholic Historical Review* 22 (July 1936): 128–148; and the series of articles by Pollen, "The Politics of English Catholics during the Reign of Queen Elizabeth," *Month* 99 (January–June 1902): 43–60, 131–148, 290–305, 394–411, 600–618; and 100 (July–August 1902): 71–87, 176–188. Cardinal William Allen is the subject of three good articles by Mattingly, "William Allen and Catholic Propaganda in England," in *Aspects de la propagande religieuse* (Geneva, 1957); T. O. Hanley, "A Note on Cardinal Allen's Political Thought," *Catholic Historical Review* 45 (October 1959): 327–334; and R. M. Kingdon, "William Allen's Use of Protestant Political Argument," in *From the Renaissance to the Counter-Reformation,* ed. Carter.

For the Elizabethan Puritans, the best history is Patrick Collinson's superb *The Elizabethan Puritan Movement* (London, 1967). It supercedes M. M. Knappen's *Tudor Puritanism* (Chicago, 1939), which is still a good account. Leonard Trinterud provides a selection of Puritan documents with sound introductions of high caliber in *Elizabethan Puritanism* (New York, 1971). For *The Worship of the English Puritans* there is a general survey by Horton Davies (Westminster, 1948). The Marxist scholar Christopher Hill—always worth reading —has two books of marked usefulness for Elizabethan Puritanism: *Society and Puritanism in Pre-Revolutionary England* (London, 1964), and *Economic Problems of the Church, from Archbishop Whitgift to the Long Parliament* (Oxford, 1956). The latter deals with the Church of England as a whole, but is necessary reading to understand the socioeconomic status of the church the Puritans were trying to reform. Narrower in scope but interesting is S. S. Babbage, *Puritanism and Richard Bancroft* (London, 1962). The best introduction to Puritan writings is William Haller's classic, *The Rise of Puritanism* (New York, 1938). Haller also analyzes the impact of John Foxe on the idea of Elizabethan England as the "elect nation": *Foxe's "Book of Martyrs" and the Elect Nation* (London, 1963). There is a pro-Puritan study of *The Godly Preachers of the Elizabethan Church* (London, 1965) by Irvonwy Morgan; the "godly preachers" are of course Puritans. If the Catholics were not thoroughly persecuted under Elizabeth, neither were the Puritans, as shown by R. A. Marchant, *The Puritans and the Church Courts in the Diocese of York, 1560–1642* (London, 1960). Marchant has followed this with *The Church under the Law* (Cambridge, 1969), again focusing on the province of York. Of the various controversies in which the Puritans were involved, the best specialized studies are those of H. C. Porter, *Reformation and Reaction in Tudor Cambridge* (Cambridge, 1958); D. J. McGinn, *The Admonition Controversy* (New Brunswick, N.J., 1949); J. H. Primus, *The Vestments Controversy* (Kampen, 1960); and McGinn, *John Penry and the Marprelate Controversy* (New Brunswick, N.J., 1966). For the early Presbyterian leader Thomas Cartwright, the best study is still A. F. S. Pearson's *Thomas Cartwright and Eliza-bethan Puritanism* (Cambridge, 1925). Of the host of excellent articles on Elizabeth and the Puritans, one of the best is Patrick Collinson's "John Field and Elizabethan Puritanism," in *Elizabethan Government and Society,* where it is argued that the failure of Puritanism to make more progress is attributable to Elizabeth herself.

The interrelationship of society and religion in Elizabethan England can be initially approached in the broader study of *Social and Political Forces in the English Reformation* by Conyers Read (Houston, 1953). The best study of Elizabethan social history, including major sections on government and religion, is A. L. Rowse, *The England of Elizabeth: The Structure of Society* (London, 1951). The relevant portions of G. M. Trevelyan's classic, *English Social History* (New York and Toronto, 1942), is well worth reading. Also excellent is A. H. Dodd, *Life in Elizabethan England* (London, 1961), which is to be preferred over the popular account of M. St.C. Byrne, *Elizabethan Life in Town and Country,* 7th ed. (London, 1954). For the daily life of Elizabeth's subjects see L. E. Pearson, *Elizabethans at Home* (Stanford, 1957). For the opposite end of the social scale see Ralph Dutton, *English Court Life from Henry VII to George II* (London, 1963). Much is often made of Elizabeth's progresses and the resulting contact with the people; a good beginning here is Ian Dunlop, *Palaces and Progresses of Elizabeth I* (London, 1962). The literature on the controversy over the gentry is too extensive to list here, but it may be sampled in *Social Change and Revolution in England, 1540–1640* (London, 1965), edited by Lawrence Stone, who arranges the documents in such a manner as to suggest the triumph of his own view. The final word may be had by reading J. H. Hexter's superb essay, "Storm over the Gentry," in Hexter's *Reappraisals in History* (New York and Evanston, Ill., 1963).

Much insight about Elizabeth can also be gleaned from the better biographies of the leading personages of her reign. Selections from

Read's two-volume study of William Cecil and Elizabeth have been provided. There is a good biography of Cecil by Beckingsale, *Burghley: Tudor Statesman* (London, 1967). For Cecil's son Robert there is P. M. Handover, *The Second Cecil: The Rise to Power, 1563–1604, of Sir Robert Cecil* (London, 1959), which is not a highly regarded work. There are two good articles on Robert Cecil that should be noted: Hurstfield, "Robert Cecil, Earl of Salisbury: Minister of Elizabeth and James I," *History Today* 7 (May 1957): 279–289; and Lawrence Stone, "The Fruits of Office: The Case of Robert Cecil, First Earl of Salisbury, 1596–1612," in *Essays in the Economic and Social History of Tudor and Stuart England,* ed. F. J. Fisher (Cambridge, 1961). There is a fine new study of *Robert Earl of Essex* (New York, 1971) by Robert Lacey. For Sir Philip Sidney the older standard *Sir P. Sidney* by M. W. Wallace (Cambridge, 1915) can be enhanced by J. M. Oxborn's *Young Philip Sidney, 1572–1577* (New Haven and London, 1972). For the Earl of Leicester, there is an acceptable but incomplete study by Eleanor Rosenberg, *Leicester, Patron of Letters* (New York, 1955). E. St.J. Brooks has written a biography of *Sir Christopher Hatton: Queen Elizabeth's Favourite* (London, 1946). There is a very good life of *Thomas Howard, Fourth Duke of Norfolk* (London, 1964) by Neville Williams, which is especially helpful for the enigma of Mary Stewart and the Northern Rebellion. The best life of Raleigh is W. M. Wallace, *Sir Walter Raleigh* (Princeton, 1959), but Rowse's *Raleigh and the Throckmortons* (London, 1962) is also good. V. J. K. Brook has written biographies of two leading religious personages: *A Life of Archbishop Parker* (Oxford, 1962), and *Whitgift and the English Church* (London, 1957). Amy Robsart's death was of special importance to Elizabeth: James Gardiner pronounced it accidental in "The Death of Amy Robsart," *English Historical Review* 1 (April 1885): 235–259; and 13 (January 1897): 83–90; whereas Ian Aird argued that it was due to cancer of the breast, "The Death of Amy Robsart," *English Historical Review* 71 (January 1956): 69–79.

The biographical approach can be profitably used to explore military and naval affairs in Elizabeth's reign. J. A. Williamson has well-written and scholarly lives of Drake: *Sir Francis Drake* (London, 1953), and *The Age of Drake,* 5th ed. (London, 1965); and of Hawkins: *Sir John Hawkins, the Times and the Man* (Oxford, 1927), and *Hawkins of Plymouth* (London, 1949). For Grenville there is Rowse's

Sir Richard Grenville of the Revenge, an Elizabethan Hero (London, 1949). There are two good studies of Mountjoy: Cyril Falls, *Mountjoy: Elizabethan General* (London, 1955), and F. M. Jones, *Mountjoy, 1563–1606: The Last Elizabethan Deputy* (Dublin, 1958).

Finally, several works of a miscellaneous character are worthy of mention. For the *Portraits of Queen Elizabeth I* there is a masterful study by R. C. Strong (Oxford, 1963), including plates. Poetic reflections of Elizabeth may be studied in E. C. Wilson's *England's Eliza* (Cambridge, Mass., 1939). L. B. Campbell has provided a study of *Shakespeare's Histories—Mirrors of Elizabethan Policy* (San Marino, Cal., 1947). For aesthetic enjoyment and a deeper insight into the age of Elizabeth, one should examine the splendid plates found in Neville Williams, *The Life and Times of Elizabeth I* (New York, 1972), and L. B. Smith, *The Horizon Book of the Elizabethan World,* ed. N. Kotker (New York and Toronto, 1967).

1 2 3 4 5 6 7 8 9 10

THE PROBLEMS IN EUROPEAN CIVILIZATION SERIES
(Arranged in approximate chronological order)

(continued from inside front cover)

distinguished series of topical readers
centered upon important and controversial events, movements, theories,
and personalities in European history
from ancient times to the present.
Each volume brings together, under
eminent editorship, numerous views o
its theme, inspiring the reader to chec
sift, interpret, and draw conclusions
from a variety of authoritative sources
Suggestions for additional reading are
included. For further details write to
Faculty Correspondent, D.C. Heath an
Company, 125 Spring Street, Lexingto
Massachusetts 02173.